Camping around Washington

Designed, drawn and written
by **JIM CRAIN** and **TERRY MILNE**

Mountain goats are fascinating animals
to watch if you're lucky enough to spot
them. They hang out on the high,
treeless slopes of the mountain peaks,
picking their way along rocky crags and
ledges.

RANDOM HOUSE/BOOKWORKS

copyright © 1974 by Jim Crain and Terry Milne
all rights reserved
under International and Pan-American Copyright Conventions

this first edition of WASHINGTON
has a first printing, in March 1974, of 7,500

coldset in Univers by VERA ALLEN COMPOSITION SERVICE, Hayward, California
camera work by CIRCUS LITHOGRAPH CO, San Francisco
printed and bound under the supervision of
Dean Ragland, Random House

co-published by RANDOM HOUSE INC.
201 East Fiftieth Street
New York 10022

and THE BOOKWORKS
1409 Fifth Street
Berkeley 94710

distributed in the United States by Random House
and simultaneously published in Canada
by Random House of Canada Limited, Toronto

JENNIFER DEWEY, from Tiburon, made the cover drawing for us.
She has a great respect for animals
and does the most fascinating wildlife drawings.

Our friend CHUCK VAN HORN did the sketches inside the book.
He's as good with a pen as he is with a hammer.

Thanks to Pacific First Federal Savings and Loan Assn for
letting us use their sketch-map of Washington, page 68.

A portion of the Hood Canal Map on page 70 was printed with
permission of Pastor Esko Rentola, the artist.

Library of Congress Cataloging in Publication Data

Crain, Jim
    Camping around Washington.

        "A Random House/Bookworks book."
            1. Campsites, facilities, etc. — Washington (State)
    I. Milne, Terry, joint author.
    II. Title.
SK601.5.W3C7   917.97   73-20590
ISBN 0-394-70683-8

To our vanishing friends and relations

the sharp-shinned hawk,
Olympic mudminnow,
Cascade boreal chickadee,
southern sea otter,
the Columbian whitetailed deer,
Arctic grayling,
humpback and Pacific right whales,
the old grizzly bear,
the bald eagle,
American peregrine falcon,
mountain caribou,
Roosevelt elk,
trumpeter swans,
green turtle,
the elephant seal,

using the book

key map

Our KEY MAP on page 8 is your guide to the larger scale maps in this book. It shows how we have divided the state into 23 sections. *EACH MAP SHOWS EXACTLY WHERE THE CAMPGROUNDS ARE IN THAT SECTION AND ALL THE ROADS NEEDED TO GET TO THEM.* Find the section you live in — the map for that section and the maps adjacent will show where the campgrounds nearest your area are located.

- For instructions on how to turn a highway road map into a highly detailed ALTERNATE KEY MAP, see page 70. This is an easy way of orienting yourself to the various parts of the state and to our maps at the same time.

camping index

Our CAMPING INDEX can be a handy means for finding a camping place where you can pursue a favorite activity, such as mushroom gathering, clamming, exploring ghost towns or whatever. Look through the different categories for an appealing "Activity" or "Feature" as a focus for your camping trip. See page 85 for using this INDEX.

- Maps, such as USGS and Forest Service maps, can provide more specific information relating to these activities and features, such as which trail to take to a nearby cave or the precise locations of waterfalls in the area. (See THE MAP TRIP, page 69.)

browsing

There are probably several ways that a campground guide can help you decide where to go camping. One way is to pick up the book and browse — to search each page for some item of information that causes you to say "Yeah, that's where I want to go." Browsing through the campground descriptions and maps can lead to appealing tidbits of information to use for choosing a camping area.

- The introductory heading to each map section points out some of the outstanding things to see and do in that section.

map relationships

Any wilderness-addict knows the value of having good maps along on a camping trip. Therefore, the maps in this book are keyed to the USGS 15-minute quadrangle maps. The "Quadrangle Key," adjacent to each map, will tell you which 15-minute USGS map you need for exploring the area around a particular campground. (See USING THE QUADRANGLE KEY, page 9).

- Refer to THE MAP TRIP, page 69, for an explanation of the kinds of maps available and how to order them.

trip planning

Unless you have definite ideas for planning your own camping trips or tours in Washington, you will be open to suggestions. Keep in mind that National Forests, National Parks and State Parks offer the most appealing and economical camping places. Find out all you can about these areas by writing to the various headquarters for brochures and descriptive leaflets. (See page 79 for ADDRESSES.)

- Chambers of Commerce are good sources of vacation and recreation information. Stop by or write to the county seat of towns in the area of your destination.
- For brochures and general information about places of interest in the state, write to the office of Tourism. (See VACATION INFORMATION, page 79.)

year-round camping

If you have the idea that camping is something that you do only in the summertime, then you're missing out on a variety of adventures and events. Camping is just as good any time of the year, provided you know where to go and the sort of experience you're in for. Washington's changing seasons have much to offer, and we'll provide you with some alternatives.

- The CAMPING CALENDAR, on page 74, is your guide to year-round camping. It's a collection of accessible camping areas for any time of the year, with interesting reasons to help you decide where to go.

on your own

If campgrounds are becoming too populated to suit your spirit, and you are seeking quieter and more adventuresome paths, you're in luck. There are several ways to escape the crowds. Backpacking is one, provided you pick the right area. With the rush to the wilderness, the most scenic and ideal trails are rapidly becoming freeways for hikers. On the other hand, our rivers are still somewhat secluded and not so over-used. Latch on to a canoe and paddle your way through the backcountry. If you want to stick to the main roads, try bicycling along the scenic routes through National Forests. It's a sensible pace for enjoying the scenery, and any sideroad can offer a suitable camping area.

- See the section ON YOUR OWN for more suggestions.

the maps

the map trip

stuff everyone should know

camping calendar

table of contents

the first time camper

info directory

several interesting tours

on your own

camping index

north to alaska

visiting canada

how to beat the gas shortage

notes

key map

The number in each rectangle refers to the corresponding Map number on the following pages. The 23 maps cover the entire state and can be used as road maps. A full-page map covers an area about 48 by 70 miles.

See page 70 for a way of creating a highly detailed ALTERNATE KEY MAP.

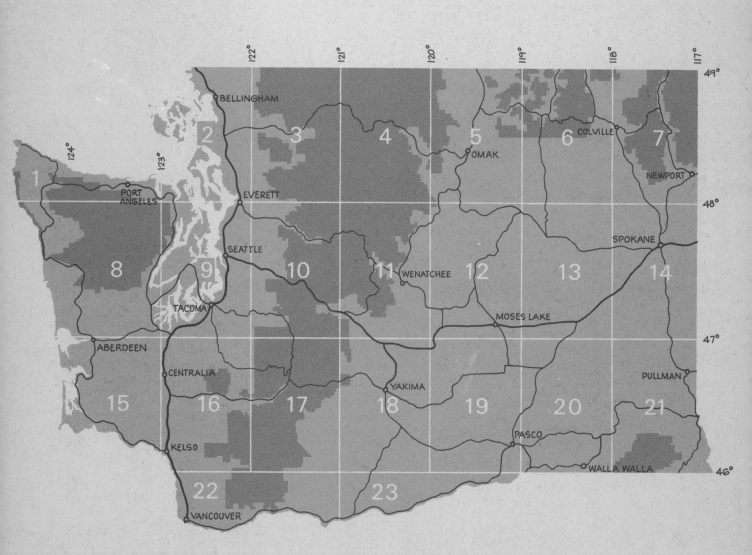

abbrev.

BC	Boat Camp
Co PK	County Park
FH	Forest Highway
FR	Forest Road
GC	Group Camp
KOA	Kampground of America
NF	National Forest
NP	National Park
NRA	Natl Recreation Area
RS	Ranger Station
SF	State Forest
SP	State Park
TC	Trail Camp
USFS	US Forest Service
VC	Vistor Center

We want you to have a pleasant camping trip. As you search through this book for a place to go, keep in mind that we have listed only the most enjoyable campgrounds that Washington has to offer. We chose to be selective to prevent you from driving miles out of the way to reach a campground that turns out to be nothing more than a parking place for trailers. All the camps have at least some tent sites, and hopefully they will offer a rewarding camping experience. If you disagree, let us know.

legend

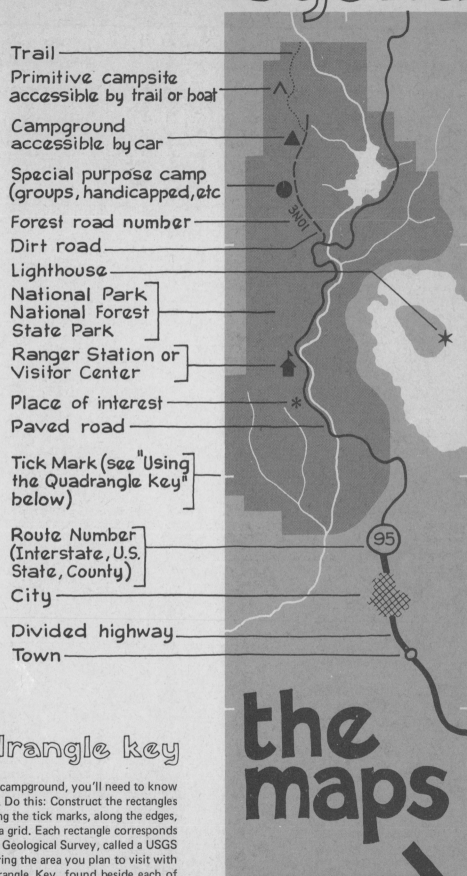

Trail

Primitive campsite accessible by trail or boat

Campground accessible by car

Special purpose camp (groups, handicapped, etc

Forest road number

Dirt road

Lighthouse

National Park
National Forest
State Park

Ranger Station or
Visitor Center

Place of interest

Paved road

Tick Mark (see "Using the Quadrangle key" below)

Route Number (Interstate, U.S. State, County)

City

Divided highway

Town

the maps

using the quadrangle key

If you plan to explore the area around a campground, you'll need to know the name of the USGS map for that area. Do this: Construct the rectangles on any of the following maps by connecting the tick marks, along the edges, with horizontal and vertical lines to form a grid. Each rectangle corresponds to a topographic map published by the US Geological Survey, called a USGS 15-minute map. Match the rectangle covering the area you plan to visit with the corresponding rectangle in the Quadrangle Key, found beside each of our Maps, to determine the name of the USGS map for that area. If a name doesn't show up in the Quadrangle Key, consult the USGS "Index to Topographic Maps of Washington" for a map in another series. Instructions for ordering the maps and the USGS "Index" are found on page 69.

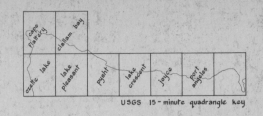

USGS 15-minute quadrangle key

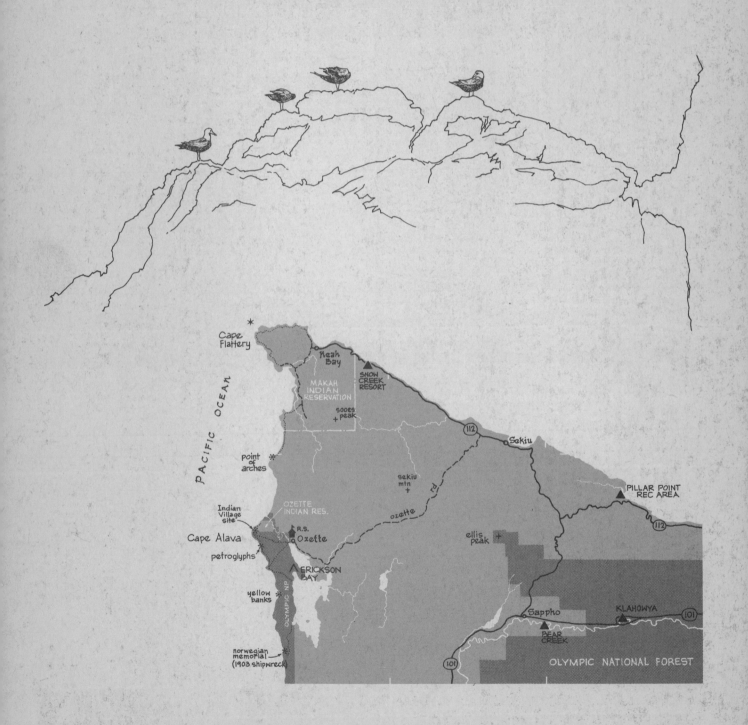

Cape
Flattery

Keah
Bay

SNOW
CREEK
RESORT

MAKAH
INDIAN
RESERVATION

sooes
+ peak

PACIFIC OCEAN

point
of
arches

112

Sekiu

sekiu
mtn
+

rd

ozette

PILLAR POINT
REC AREA

112

Indian
Village
site

OZETTE
INDIAN RES.

R.S.
Ozette

Cape Alava

ellis
peak +

petroglyphs

ERICKSON
BAY

OLYMPIC NP

yellow
banks

Sappho

KLAHOWYA

101

BEAR
CREEK

norwegian
memorial
(1903 shipwreck)

101

OLYMPIC NATIONAL FOREST

CAPE ALAVA is a rare stretch of wilderness beach, accessible by a 9-mile loop trail from Lake Ozette. Along the way, you'll see the early Indian Village site, Cannonball Island, seastacks, and petroglyphs at Wedding Rock. • **DUNGENESS SPIT**, a narrow sand formation, extends about 5 miles out into the Strait, NW of Sequim. A trail winds down to the beach — good beachcombing, agate hunting, piles of driftwood and a lighthouse at the end of the spit. • **POINT OF ARCHES** can be reached by a rough dirt road to Portage Head then along the beach for a couple of miles. Giant seastacks stand offshore with a variety of arches formed by the pounding waves. • **CAPE FLATTERY** is an explorer's dream. Trails and dirt roads lead to wilderness beaches, surf battered coves, old World War II bunkers, waterfalls and an abandoned Indian village.

AGATE AND CRESCENT BEACH PARK (sea level) 15 mi west of Port Angeles off State 112 at Crescent Bay. 300 campsites, 250 with all hookups, fee, open all year, no limit of stay, reservations accepted for hookup sites only, grocery, hot showers, laundry. Charter boat fishing, tackle shop, boat rentals, trails along beautiful beaches, rockhounding, beachcombing, skindiving, wildflowers, storm and bird watching, outstanding sunrises and sunsets. This is the site of historic Port Crescent, pioneer cemetery nearby. Rt 1, Box 294, Port Angeles 98362. Privately owned.

ALTAIRE (450') 8 mi west on US 101 from Port Angeles to the Elwha River then 4 mi south. 29 campsites in dense woods for tents or trailers — 18' max, May to Oct, 14 day limit, community kitchen. Fishing in swift flowing Elwha River, trails near the entrance. Olympic NP.

BEAR CREEK (600') 2 mi east of Sappho on US 101. Several campsites for tents and RVs, fishing in the Soleduck River. Dept of Natural Resources.

DUNGENESS RECREATION AREA (200') 9 mi NW of Sequim. 65 campsites for tents or trailers, fee, group facilities, all year, 9 day limit, disposal station, hot showers, bicycle and horse trails, hiking along 7 mi of beach, hunting for ducks and pheasants, views of Vancouver Island and Olympic Mtns, agates and driftwood, 200-foot sand cliff, clamming, wildlife refuge. Rt 3, Box 438, Sequim 98382. Clallam County.

ELWHA (390') 8 mi west on US 101 from Port Angeles to the Elwha River then 3 mi south. 23 campsites for tents or trailers — 18' max, all year, 14 day limit, community kitchen. Campfire circle across the road, naturalist program, dense woods. Near the camp exit a trail leads to Lookout Point. Olympic NP.

ELWHA RESORT (156') 8 mi west of Port Angeles on US 101. 50 campsites for tents or trailers, fee, all year, no limit of stay, reservations accepted, country store, disposal station, all hookups, hot showers, laundry. Excellent fishing area, boat rentals, launch, square dancing on weekends, scenic Lake Aldwell. Rt 3, Box 464, Port Angeles 98362. Privately owned.

ERICKSON BAY TRAIL CAMP (30') 2 mi west on State 112 from Sekiu then 21 mi SW to Ozette then 5 mi south by boat. 15 tent sites, open all year. Boating, fishing, swimming, access to the wilderness beaches around Cape Alava. Olympic NP.

FAIRHOLM (580') 26 mi west of Port Angeles on US 101 at the west end of Lake Crescent. 90 campsites for tents and trailers — 21' max, May to Oct, 14 day limit, supplies and restaurant nearby. Boat launch, campfire circle, fishing, swimming, water skiing, good canoeing. Olympic NP.

HEART OF THE HILLS (1957') 5½ mi south of Port Angeles on State 111 (Race St). 100 campsites for tents or trailers — 21' max, May to Oct, 14 day limit, campfire circle. Olympic NP.

KLAHOWYA (800') 8 mi east of Sappho off US 101. 37 tent sites, 5 trailer spaces — 22' max, Apr 1 to Nov 15, 14 day limit, boat launch, hunting, fishing in Soleduck River, Pioneer's Path Nature Trail. Olympic NF.

LOG CABIN RESORT (578') At Piedmont on Lake Crescent. 20 tent sites, 65 trailer spaces — 35' max, fee, Apr 15 to Oct 15, no limit of stay, no reservations, supplies, laundry, snack bar, hot showers. Fishing, motor and rowboat rentals, swimming. Rt 1, Box 416, Port Angeles 98362. Privately owned.

LYRE RIVER PARK (30') 5 mi west of Joyce off State 112. 58 campsites, trailers — 40' max, fee, open all year, no limit of stay, reservations accepted, all hookups, laundry, hot showers. Fishing, bicycle and hiking trails. Agates, jasper and driftwood on the beach. Rt 1, Box 385, Port Angeles 98362. Privately owned.

MAPLE GROVE RESORT (500') 15 mi west of Port Angeles on US 101 at Lake Sutherland. 20 tent sites, 25 trailer spaces — 32' max, fee, Apr to Oct, no limit of stay, no reservations, supplies, laundry, hot showers. Fishing, swimming, sailing, canoeing, motorboating, rentals, ramp, hiking. Rt 1, Box 426, Port Angeles 98362. Privately owned.

PILLAR POINT RECREATION AREA (sea level) 30 mi west of Port Angeles on State 112 at Butler Cove. 45 campsites for tents or trailers — 24' max, fee, May 1 to Sep 30, 9 day limit, supplies 15 mi, no fireplaces or firewood. Excellent salmon fishing, canoeing and motorboating, launch, skindiving, swimming, clamming. Clallam County.

SALT CREEK RECREATION AREA (30') 12 mi west on State 112 from Port Angeles to Ramapo then north on Hayden Rd. 50 campsites for tents or trailers, fee, group facilities, open all year, no limit of stay, supplies 3 mi, disposal station, no tables or fireplaces. Fishing, views of Vancouver Island, trailhead for 5 mi hike over Striped Peak to Freshwater Bay. Rt 1, Box 289, Port Angeles 98362. Clallam County.

SEQUIM BAY STATE PARK (sea level) 4 mi south of Sequim on US 101. 81 wooded tent sites on a hillside, 26 trailer spaces with hookups, fee, laundry, hot showers. Saltwater fishing and swimming, boat launch, clamming, beachcombing, hiking thru the forest.

SNOW CREEK RESORT (10') 59 mi west of Port Angeles on State 112. 32 campsites for tents and trailers — 30' max, fee, May 15 to Sep 15, no limit of stay, reservations accepted, all hookups, supplies 4 mi, fishing tackle. Boat rentals, charter trips, swimming, clamming, berrypicking, mushroom gathering, interesting rock formations and small ocean caves. Whales, sea lions and gulls. PO Box 141, Neah Bay 98357. Privately owned.

WHISKEY CREEK BEACH (sea level) 3 mi west of Joyce off State 112. 40 campsites for tents or trailers — 20' max, fee, Feb 15 to Dec 1, no limit of stay, water hookups. Stream and surf fishing, boat ramp, bicycle and hiking trails, hunting, rockhounding, fossils, beachcombing on 5 mi of beach, rock clams. Joyce 98343. Privately owned.

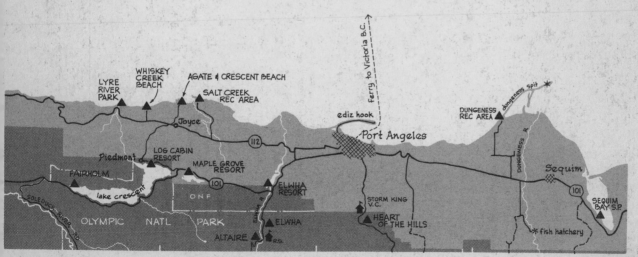

1

2

STEAM TRAIN EXCURSIONS on the Lake Whatcom Railway provide a 9 mile, 1½ hour round trip from Park to Wickersham. The train operates only on Saturdays, Sundays and holidays between Memorial Day and Labor Day. • SKAGIT STATE GAME RANGE, SW of Mt Vernon, is one of the most popular places to watch migratory water birds. • A variety of NATURAL ENVIRONMENTS exist in the Cornet Bay area at Deception Pass State Park. Explore the fascinating plant and animal life in saltwater marshes, tidal flats, freshwater ponds and pine forests. • For information about FERRY SERVICE, see the heading to Map 9.

USGS 15-minute quadrangle key

BAY VIEW STATE PARK (sea level) 7 mi NW of Mt Vernon. 100 tent sites, 10 trailer spaces, fee, supplies, hot showers. Swimming, saltwater beach, good views of the San Juan Islands.

BIRCH BAY STATE PARK (sea level) 10 mi south of Blaine. 179 tent sites, 52 trailer spaces, fee, store, cafe, RV hookups, disposal station, hot showers. Golf course, swimming, fishing, clamming, hiking along the beach.

CAMANO ISLAND STATE PARK (200') 16 mi SW of Stanwood on State 532. 129 wooded tent sites, fee. Swimming, saltwater fishing, clamming, boat launch, hiking trails.

CEDAR GROVE RESORT (400') 6 mi north on Int 5 from Marysville then 6 mi west. 80 campsites for tents and trailers — 30' max, fee, open all year, no limit of stay, reservations accepted, RV hookups, hot showers, supplies 1 mi. Fishing, boating, boat rentals, swimming, water skiing. 16529 52nd Ave NW, Stanwood 98292. Privately owned.

DECEPTION PASS STATE PARK (200') 8 mi north of Oak Harbor on State 525. 267 tent sites, fee, store, cafe, hot showers, golf course, boat launch, mooring facilities, boat rentals. Swimming, fishing, clamming, Nature Trails, interesting shoreline. One of the most popular parks in the state.

FORT CASEY STATE PARK (6') On Whidbey Island 3½ mi south of Coupeville. 35 campsites for tents or trailers — 28' max, fee, all year, cafe, hot showers. Fishing, boat ramp, hiking on the beach, Interpretive Center. The park is the site of historic Ft Casey, established during the 1890's for the defense of Puget Sound. 1280 So Ft Casey Rd, Coupeville 98239.

FORT FLAGLER STATE PARK (100') 10 mi NE of Chimacum. 82 campsites for tents and RVs, fee, boat launch, mooring facilities. Swimming, fishing, clamming, hiking trails, remains of an old coastal defense fort.

JONES ISLAND STATE PARK Boat-in (100') Located between San Juan and Orcas Islands, accessible by private boat only. 19 tent sites on a small heavily forested island, good boat mooring and launching facilities, swimming, fishing, clamming, hiking trails.

LARRABEE STATE PARK (100') 7 mi south of Bellingham on State 11. 75 tent sites, 26 trailer spaces, group camping, fee, all year, hookups, kitchens, showers, amphitheater. Fishing, boat ramp, swimming, water skiing, trails to Fragrance and Lost Lakes, lookout points, clamming, beach walking. 245 Chuckanut Dr, Bellingham 98225.

MATIA ISLAND STATE PARK Boat-in (10') 3 mi NE of Orcas Island, accessible by private boat only. 6 tent sites on a remote forested island, good boat mooring and launch facilities. Swimming, fishing, clamming, hiking trails.

MORAN STATE PARK (1000') On the east side of Orcas Island, accessible by ferry from Anacortes. Several campgrounds with 175 campsites, group camp, fee, kitchen shelters, hot showers, boat launch and mooring, boat rentals. Swimming, fishing, hiking, waterfalls, stone lookout tower on Mt Constitution.

OAKS (100') 2½ mi south of Friday Harbor on San Juan Island, accessible by ferry from Anacortes. Secluded camping area with 50 tent sites, 16 trailer spaces — 65' max, fee, all year, no limit of stay, reservations accepted, disposal station, RV hookups. Good lake fishing for trout and bass, ocean fishing, clamming and beachcombing 3 mi. Rt 1, Box 58-A, Friday Harbor 98250. Privately owned.

OLD FORT TOWNSEND STATE PARK (74') 4 mi south of Port Townsend off State 113. 27 campsites for tents or trailers — 22' max, fee, groups up to 60, open all year, 7 day limit, supplies 2 mi, hot showers. Water sports, sailing, good clamming and oystering in the area. Riding, hiking and bicycle trails. This is the site of a pioneer military fort with an interpretive history display. Rt 1, Box 50, Port Townsend 98368.

OLSON'S LAKE GOODWIN RESORT (400') 6 mi north on Int 5 from Marysville to Lakewood exit then 5 mi west. 25 tent sites, 70 trailer spaces — 32' max, open all year, reservations accepted, supplies, disposal station, laundry, hot showers, snack bar. Fishing, boating, swimming, water skiing, bicycling, hiking, waterfowl refugee. 4726 — 176th NW, Stanwood 98292. Privately owned.

PREVOST HARBOR STATE PARK Boat-in (10') On Stuart Island, accessible by private boat only. 6 tent sites, boat dock and mooring facilities, swimming, fishing, clamming, crabbing, hiking trails.

REID HARBOR STATE PARK Boat-in (10') On Stuart Island, accessible by private boat only. 7 tent sites, mooring and docking facilities, swimming, fishing, clamming, crabbing, hiking.

SILVERLAKE PARK (750') 4 mi north of Maple Falls on Silver Lake Rd. 56 campsites for tents and trailers — 25' max, group sites, fee, open all year, 14 day limit, reservations accepted from Whatcom County residents only, RV hookups, disposal station, snack bar, showers. Fishing, water sports, rowboat rentals, riding and hiking trails. Rt 1, Maple Falls 98266. Whatcom County.

SOUTH WHIDBEY STATE PARK (200') 15 mi south of Coupeville off State 525. 55 wooded tent sites on a bluff overlooking Puget Sound, fee, hot showers. Swimming, fishing, boating, clamming, hiking trails.

SUCIA ISLAND STATE PARK Boat-in (10') 3 mi north of Orcas Island, accessible by private boat only. 33 informal tent sites, good boat mooring and launch facilities. Swimming, fishing, clamming, hiking.

WASHINGTON PARK (20') 4 mi west of Anacortes. 48 campsites for tents or trailers — 22' max, fee, Apr 1 to Nov 1, 14 day limit, supplies ½ mi, hot showers. Saltwater fishing, boating, swimming, water skiing, bicycling, hiking on 220 acres, glacial polish on rocks. Rt 1, Box 139, Anacortes 98221. City of Anacortes.

WENBERG STATE PARK (400') 6 mi north on Int 5 from Marysville to Lakewood exit then 8 mi west. 65 tent sites, 10 trailer spaces, fee, RV hookups, hot showers, boat launch. Swimming beach, fishing, hiking.

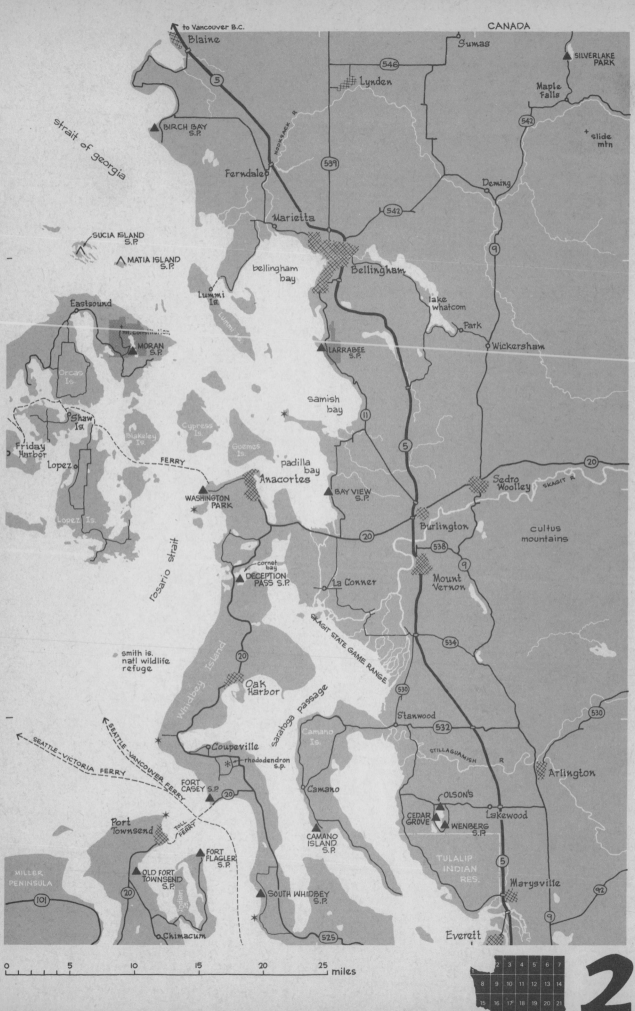

to Vancouver B.C.
Blaine
CANADA
Sumas
SILVERLAKE PARK
Lynden
546
Maple Falls
542
slide mtn
Strait of georgia
BIRCH BAY S.P.
Ferndale
NOOKSACK R
539
Deming
Marietta
542
9
SUCIA ISLAND S.P.
bellingham bay
Bellingham
MATIA ISLAND S.P.
Lummi Is.
Lummi
lake whatcom
Park
Eastsound
Wickersham
Mt. Constitution
MORAN S.P.
LARRABEE S.P.
Orcas Is.
samish bay
Shaw Is.
11
Cypress Is.
FERRY
Friday Harbor
Blakeley Is.
Guemes Is.
5
20
Lopez
padilla bay
Anacortes
Sedro Woolley
SKAGIT R
WASHINGTON PARK
BAY VIEW S.P.
Lopez Is.
Burlington
cultus mountains
cornet bay
538
DECEPTION PASS S.P.
La Conner
9
Mount Vernon
rosario strait
smith is. nat'l wildlife refuge
SKAGIT STATE GAME RANGE
534
20
Oak Harbor
Saratoga Passage
530
Stanwood
532
Whidbey Island
Camano Is.
STILLAGUAMISH R
SEATTLE-VANCOUVER FERRY
Coupeville
Arlington
SEATTLE-VICTORIA FERRY
rhododendron s.p.
OLSON'S
Lakewood
FORT CASEY S.P.
Camano
20
CEDAR GROVE
WENBERG S.P.
Port Townsend
TOLL FERRY
CAMANO ISLAND S.P.
TULALIP INDIAN RES.
FORT FLAGLER S.P.
MILLER PENINSULA
5
OLD FORT TOWNSEND S.P.
SOUTH WHIDBEY S.P.
Marysville
92
101
20
Indian Spit
9
Chimacum
525
Everett

0   5   10   15   20   25 miles

2

3

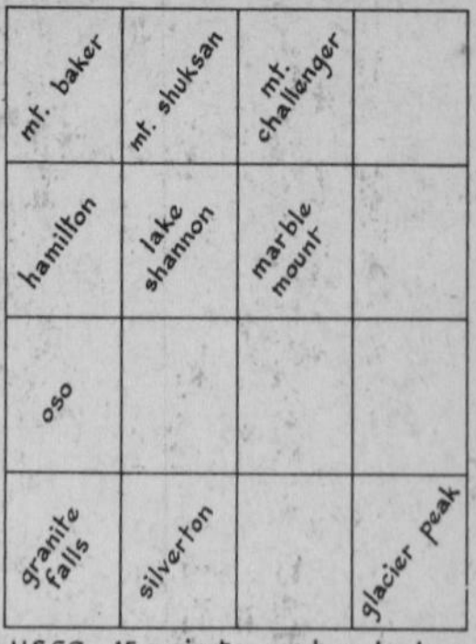

USGS 15-minute quadrangle key

The old **MONTE CRISTO GHOST TOWN** is 30 miles SE of Darrington, off the Mountain Loop Highway. The townsite and mines are privately owned, but tours are available. You'll still find a few old buildings and ruins, rusted mining equipment and a museum, all located in a highly scenic area. • **MAIDEN OF THE WOODS** is a 15-foot tall figure of an Indian maiden carved on a living cedar tree. Dudley Carter used only a double-bit axe to create the figure in 1948. The carving is accessible by a ¼-mile trail at the end of Benson Creek Rd (FR 3013), east of the Verlot Ranger Station. • **NORTH CASCADES HIGHWAY GUIDE** will help you fully explore the scenic highway and its attractions. See page 80.

BACON CREEK (400') 5 mi north of Marblemount on State 20. 2 tent sites, 4 trailer spaces, Apr 15 to Nov 15, 10 day limit, stream water. Fishing, hunting, hiking, river running on Skagit R. Mt Baker NF.

BAKER LAKE (730') 16 mi north of Concrete on Baker River Rd (FH 25). 12 campsites, trailers – 22' max, Apr 20 to Oct 20, 14 day limit, boat launch. Swimming, water skiing, fishing, hunting, hiking. Mt Baker NF.

BEAR LAKE TRAIL CAMP (2800') 4½ mi east from Verlot on FH 7, then 3 mi south on FR 3015, then 3 mi west on FR 3015B, then ¼ mi SW on Trail 703. 6 campsites, June 15 to Oct 1, lake water. Fishing. Mt Baker NF.

BEDAL (1300') 19 mi SE of Darrington on Mtn Loop Hwy (FR 322). 8 tent sites, 4 trailer spaces – 22' max, May 30 to Oct 31, 10 day limit, river water, shelter. Fishing, hunting. Mt Baker NF.

BIG BEAVER TRAIL CAMP (1600') 4 mi north from Ross Dam on Ross Lake, accessible by boat or trail only. 7 campsites, June 1 to Nov 1, 14 day limit, lake water. Fishing, swimming, boating, hiking. Ross Lake NRA.

BIG FOUR (1700') 14 mi east of Verlot on Mtn Loop Hwy (FH7). 6 tent sites, May 1 to Nov 15, 10 day limit, stream water. Beaver dams, fishing, hunting, hiking, mtn climbing, old Big Four Dam site, ruins of an old resort. Mt Baker NF.

BLUE LAKE TRAIL CAMP (4000') 10 mi north from Concrete on FH 25, then 7 mi west on FR 3725, then 4 mi east on FR 3770, then ¾ mi SW on Trail 604. 2 campsites, June 15 to Oct 1, lake water, 300-foot deep lake. Fishing, trail to Dock Butte. Mt Baker NF.

BOULDER CREEK (1100') 14 mi north of Concrete on Baker River Rd (FH 25). 6 campsites, trailers – 16' max, Apr 20 to Oct 20, 14 day limit. Hunting, hiking, fishing and water sports 2 mi. Mt Baker NF.

BOULDER RIVER SHELTER (100') Accessible by trail only. 8 mi west from Darrington on State 530, then 4 mi SW on FR 320, then 1½ mi SE on Trail 641. 1 campsite, Apr 30 to Nov 15, 10 day limit, river water, shelter. Fishing, trail to Three Fingers. Mt Baker NF.

BRIDGE (1300') 5½ mi east of Glacier on State 542. 4 tent sites, 3 trailer spaces – 16' max, May 1 to Oct 1. 10 day limit, river water, cafe, horse rentals. Fishing, hunting, nature trail. Mt Baker NF.

BUCK CREEK (1200') 7½ mi north on the Rockport Hwy from Darrington then 15½ mi east on FR 345. 43 tent sites, 6 trailer spaces – 22' max, May 30 to Oct 31, 10 day limit, stream water. Fishing, hunting, hiking. Mt Baker NF.

CANYON LAKE (2700') 7 mi east on FH 7 from Granite Falls, then 2 mi north on FR 320, then 2 mi east on FR 318, then 6½ mi east on FR 3032. 3 tent sites, June 15 to Oct 1, no limit of stay, lake water, fishing. Mt Baker NF.

CAT ISLAND BOAT CAMP (1600') 12½ mi north of Ross Dam on Ross Lake, accessible by boat only. 7 campsites, June 1 to Nov 1, 14 day limit, lake water. Fishing, swimming, boating, hunting. Ross Lake NRA.

CHOKWICH (1500') 21 mi SE of Darrington on Mtn Loop Hwy (FR 322). 6 tent sites, 5 trailer spaces – 22' max, May 30 to Oct 31, 10 day limit. Fishing, hunting, hiking. Mt Baker NF.

CLEAR CREEK (600') 3 mi SE of Darrington on FR 3211. 1 tent site, 8 trailer spaces – 22' max, May 30 to Oct 31, 10 day limit, river water, community kitchen. Fishing, hunting, Clear Creek Trail. Mt Baker NF.

COAL CREEK (1615') 12½ mi east of Verlot on Mtn Loop Hwy. 3 tent sites, 3 trailer spaces – 32' max, May 1 to Nov 15, 10 day limit, river water. Fishing, hunting, hiking. Mt Baker NF.

COLONIAL CREEK (1200') On the south shore of Diablo Lake on North Cascade Hwy (State 20). 160 campsites, several walk-in sites, mid-Apr to Nov, 14 day limit, disposal station, supplies 5 mi. Campfire programs, nature walks, boating, launch, water sports, fishing for rainbow and Dolly Varden trout, Thunder Cr Trail, boat excursions on Diablo Lake. North Cascades NP.

COUGAR ISLAND BOAT CAMP (1600') 2 mi north of Ross Dam on Ross Lake, accessible by boat only. 3 campsites, June 1 to Nov 1, 14 day limit, lake water. Fishing, swimming, boating, hunting. Ross Lake NRA.

CRYSTAL CREEK (1700') 11 mi SE from Darrington on FR 322 then 5½ mi east on FR 314. 1 tent site, May 30 to Oct 31, 10 day limit, river water. Fishing in White Chuck R, hunting, hiking. Mt Baker NF.

DEVILS DOME BOAT CAMP (1600') 9 mi north of Ross Dam on Ross Lake, accessible by boat or trail only. 1 campsite, June 1 to Nov 1, 14 day limit, lake water. Boating, swimming, fishing, hunting, hiking. Ross Lake NRA.

DOUGLAS FIR (1000') 2 mi NE of Glacier on State 542. 26 tent sites, 10 trailer spaces – 32' max, Apr 15 to Oct 30, 10 day limit, supplies, cafe, community kitchen, horse rental. Fishing, hunting, nature trail. Mt Baker NF.

DOWNEY CREEK (1420') 7½ mi north on Rockport Hwy from Darrington then 21 mi east on FR 345. 3 tent sites, May 30 to Oct 31, 10 day limit, stream water. Fishing, hunting, trail northward to Glacier Peak Wilderness. Mt Baker NF.

DRY CREEK BOAT CAMP (1600') 10 mi north of Ross Dam on Ross Lake, accessible by boat only. 3 campsites, June 1 to Nov 1, 14 day limit, lake water. Boating, swimming, fishing, hunting, hiking. Ross Lake NRA.

EXCELSIOR (1300') 6½ mi east of Glacier on State 542 (rough, narrow access rd not recommended for trailers). 10 tent sites, May 1 to Oct 1, 10 day limit, river water. Fishing, hunting, hiking, riding, Ft Nooksack Natural Area 2½ mi east. Mt Baker NF.

FINNEY CREEK SHELTER (800') 11 mi SE from Concrete on county rd then 5 mi SW on FR 353. 2 tent sites, May 15 to Oct 30, 10 day limit, stream water, fishing. Mt Baker NF.

FRENCH CREEK (700') 8 mi west on State 530 from Darrington then 1 mi south on FR 320. 10 tent sites, 10 trailer spaces – 22' max, May 30 to Oct 31, 10 day limit, stream water, community kitchen. Hunting, hiking. Mt Baker NF.

GOAT LAKE TRAIL CAMP (2200') 21½ mi SE from Darrington on FR 322, then 4 mi SE on FR 309, then 2½ mi south by trail. 6 campsites, June 15 to Oct 1, lake water. Swimming, fishing, hiking, mtn climbing. Mt Baker NF.

GOLD BASIN (1000') 2 mi east of Verlot on Mtn Loop Hwy. 10 tent sites, 45 trailer spaces – 32' max, Apr 1 to Nov 30, 10 day limit, goldpanning in the area, fishing, hunting, hiking. Mt Baker NF.

GOODELL CREEK (500') ½ mi west of Newhalem on State 20. 25 campsites beside the river, open all year although snow covers the ground between Dec and Apr, 14 day limit, 2 group campsites across the road are available by reservation, stream water. Fishing in Skagit R, hunting. North Cascades NP.

GREEN POINT BOAT CAMP (1600') 1 mi north of Ross Dam on Ross Lake, accessible by boat or trail only. 10 campsites, June 1 to Nov 1, 14 day limit, lake water. Fishing, swimming, boating, hunting, hiking. Ross Lake NRA.

GRINERS (800') 23 mi north from Concrete on FH 25, then ½ mi north on FR 382. 1 campsite, May 20 to Sep 15, 14 day limit, stream water. Boat launch and water sports 3 mi, fishing, mtn climbing, trailhead to North Cascades NP. Mt Baker NF.

HANNEGAN HORSE CAMP (3110') 12½ mi east from Glacier on State 542 then 5½ mi east on FR 402 (Ruth Cr Rd). 3 tent sites, 3 trailer spaces – 16' max, June 1 to Oct 15, 10 day limit, stream water, shelter. Hunting, hiking, riding, trail to North Cascades NP. Primarily a back-packer's base camp. Mt Baker NF.

HANNEGAN PASS TRAIL CAMP (5100') 8 mi east from Glacier on State 542 then 8 mi east on FR 402 then 4 mi east on Trail 674. 3 campsites, June 15 to Oct 1, no water supply, mtn climbing. Mt Baker NF.

HEMPLE CREEK (1000') 1½ mi east of Verlot on Mtn Loop Hwy. 3 campsites, trailers – 32' max, Apr 1 to Nov 30, 10 day limit. Fishing, hunting, hiking. Mt Baker NF.

HORSESHOE COVE (750') 12 mi north from Concrete on FH 25 then 2 mi east on FR 373. 28 campsites for tents or trailers – 22' max, Apr 20 to Oct 20, 14 day limit. Boat launch, swimming, water skiing, fishing, hunting. Mt Baker NF.

HOZOMEEN BOAT CAMP (1600') 19 mi north of Ross Dam on Ross Lake, accessible by boat or trail only. 60 campsites, group camping area, May 30 to Nov 1, 14 day limit. Fishing, swimming, hunting, hiking, boat launch. The water level in the lake is sometimes too low to launch boats prior to mid-June. Ross Lake NRA.

HYAKCHUCK (600') 5 mi SE of Darrington on FR 322. 2 tent sites, May 30 to Oct 31, 10 day limit, stream water. Fishing in Sauk River, hunting, hiking. Mt Baker NF.

INDEPENDENCE LAKE TRAIL CAMP (3800') 14½ mi east from Verlot on FH 7, then 4½ mi north on FR 3006, then 1 mi NW on Trail 712. 3 campsites, June 15 to Oct 1, lake water. Fishing, trail to North Lake. Mt Baker NF.

KULSHAN CABIN TRAIL CAMP (4800') 1 mi east from Glacier on State 542, then 7½ mi south on FR 3904, then 2 mi east on Trail 677. 4 campsites, June 15 to Oct 1, stream water. This is a primary starting point for climbing Mt Baker. Mt Baker NF.

LAKE ANN TRAIL CAMP (4700') 22 mi east from Glacier on State 542 then 4 mi SE on Trail 600. 2 campsites, June 15 to Oct 1, lake water. Mtn climbing on Mt Shuksan. Mt Baker NF.

LIGHTNING CREEK BOAT CAMP (1600') 12 mi north of Ross Dam on Ross Lake, accessible by boat or trail only. 6 campsites, June 1 to Nov 1, 14 day limit, lake water. Fishing, swimming, boating, trail to Pasayten Wilderness. Ross Lake NRA.

LITTLE BEAVER BOAT CAMP (1600') 16 mi north of Ross Dam on Ross Lake, accessible by boat only. 7 campsites, June 1 to Nov 1, 14 day limit. Fishing, swimming, boating, trail to Perry Cr Shelter. Ross Lake NRA.

LOWER SANDY CREEK (700') 14½ mi north on FH 25, then 1 mi east on FR 3719, then 1 mi SE on FR 3719A. 4 campsites, trailers – 32' max, May 20 to Sep 15, 10 day limit, lake water. Boating, water skiing, fishing. Mt Baker NF.

MAPLE GROVE BOAT CAMP (760') 1½ mi NW from Horseshoe Cove Campground, accessible by boat only. 6 tent sites, June 15 to Sep 30, 14 day limit, stream water. Boating, rentals 3 mi, water sports, fishing, East Bank Trail, views of Mt Baker. Mt Baker NF.

(Continued on following page)

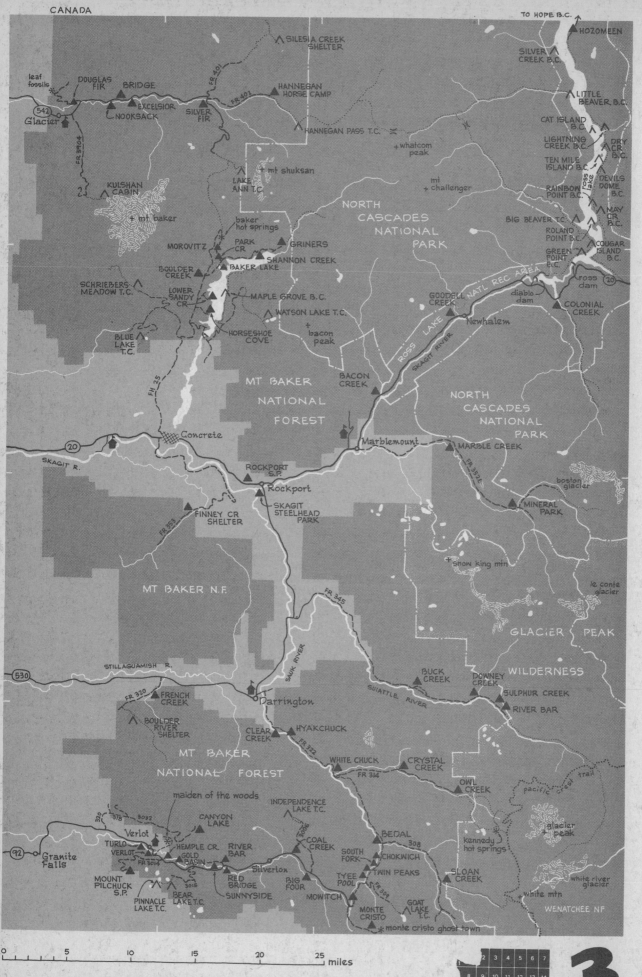

CANADA

TO HOPE B.C.

HOZOMEEN

SILESIA CREEK SHELTER

SILVER CREEK B.C.

leaf fossils

DOUGLAS FIR BRIDGE
FR 401

HANNEGAN HORSE CAMP

LITTLE BEAVER B.C.

542 EXCELSIOR
Glacier NOOKSACK SILVER FIR

FR 3904

HANNEGAN PASS T.C.

+ whatcom peak

CAT ISLAND B.C.

LIGHTNING CREEK B.C.

DRY CR. B.C.

KULSHAN CABIN

+ mt shuksan
LAKE ANN T.C.

mt + challenger

TEN MILE ISLAND B.C.

ross lake

DEVILS DOME

+ mt baker

baker hot springs

MOROVITZ PARK CR.

GRINERS

NORTH CASCADES NATIONAL PARK

RAINBOW POINT B.C.

MAY CR. B.C.

BIG BEAVER T.C.

ROLAND POINT B.C.

SHANNON CREEK

BOULDER CREEK

BAKER LAKE

COUGAR ISLAND B.C.

GREEN POINT B.C.

SCHRIEBERS MEADOW T.C.
LOWER SANDY CR.

MAPLE GROVE B.C.

WATSON LAKE T.C.

GOODELL CREEK

NATL REC AREA

diablo dam

ross dam

20

COLONIAL CREEK

BLUE LAKE T.C.

HORSESHOE COVE

+ bacon peak

ROSS LAKE

SKAGIT RIVER

Newhalem

FH 25

MT BAKER NATIONAL FOREST

BACON CREEK

NORTH CASCADES NATIONAL PARK

boston glacier

SKAGIT R.

20

Concrete

Marblemount

MARBLE CREEK

FR 3528

MINERAL PARK

ROCKPORT S.P.

Rockport

le conte glacier

FINNEY CR SHELTER

FR 353

SKAGIT STEELHEAD PARK

+ snow king mtn

MT BAKER N.F.

FR 345

GLACIER PEAK

STILLAGUAMISH R.

SAUK RIVER

530

FR 320 FRENCH CREEK

BOULDER RIVER SHELTER

Darrington

SUIATTLE RIVER

BUCK CREEK

DOWNEY CREEK

WILDERNESS

SULPHUR CREEK

RIVER BAR

MT BAKER NATIONAL FOREST

CLEAR CREEK

HYAKCHUCK

FR 322

WHITE CHUCK

FR 314

CRYSTAL CREEK

OWL CREEK

pacific crest trail

maiden of the woods

330 378 3022

CANYON LAKE

INDEPENDENCE LAKE T.C.

Verlot

92 Granite Falls

TURLO VERLOT

HEMPLE CR.

GOLD BASIN

RIVER BAR

3015 301

COAL CREEK

SOUTH FORK

BEDAL

308

CHOKWICH

kennedy hot springs

glacier peak

FR 3014

Silverton

RED BRIDGE

MOUNT PILCHUCK S.P.

SUNNYSIDE

BIG FOUR

TYEE POOL

MOWITCH

TWIN PEAKS

FR 308

SLOAN CREEK

white river glacier

PINNACLE LAKE T.C.

BEAR LAKE T.C.

3015

MONTE CRISTO

GOAT LAKE T.C.

white mtn

monte cristo ghost town

WENATCHEE NF

0   5   10   15   20   25 ⎯ miles

3

MARBLE CREEK (900') 8 mi east of Marblemount on FR 3528. 27 campsites, trailers — 16' max, Apr 15 to Nov 15, 10 day limit, river water. Fishing, hunting, hiking, mtn climbing. Mt Baker NF.

MAY CREEK BOAT CAMP (1600') 5 mi north of Ross Dam on Ross Lake, accessible by boat only. 1 campsite, June 1 to Nov 1, 14 day limit, lake water. Boating, swimming, fishing. Ross Lake NRA.

MINERAL PARK (1400') 15 mi SE on Marblemount on FR 3528. 2 tent sites, 17 trailer spaces — 16' max, Apr 15 to Nov 15, 10 day limit, river water. Fishing in Cascade R, hunting, hiking, mtn climbing. Mt. Baker NF.

MONTE CRISTO (1800') 19½ mi east of Verlot on FH 7 then 4 mi SE on FR 2963. 3 tent sites, June 15 to Nov 15, 10 day limit, stream water, cafe 1 mi. Fishing, hiking, mtn climbing, Monte Cristo ghost town. Mt. Baker NF.

MOROVITZ (900') 17 mi north on FH 25 from Concrete then 1 mi NW on FR 3816. 2 tent sites, May 20 to Sep 30, 14 day limit, stream water. Meadows, hunting, hiking, water sports and fishing 1 mi, bathing in wooden tubs at Baker Hot Springs 2 mi north. Mt Baker NF.

MOUNT PILCHUCK STATE PARK (3000') 20 mi east of Granite Falls, follow signs at Verlot. 5 tent sites, snack bar, excellent skiing facilities, ski lifts and rope tows, ski shop, good forest trails, alpine environment.

MOWITCH (2100') 19½ mi east from Verlot on FH 7 then 1½ mi NE on FR 322. 1 tent site, May 1 to Nov 15, 10 day limit, river water, shelter. Mushroom gathering in the fall, fishing, hunting, hiking, mtn climbing. Mt Baker NF.

NOOKSACK (1200') 4½ mi east of Glacier on State 542. 4 tent sites, 12 trailer spaces — 32' max, Apr 15 to Oct 30, 10 day limit, supplies, cafe, horse rental. Fishing. Hunting, nature trail. Mt Baker NF.

OWL CREEK (1800') 11½ mi SE from Darrington on FR 322 then 10 mi east on FR 314. 4 campsites, trailers — 22' max, May 30 to Oct 31, 10 day limit, stream water, unloading dock for horses. Trailhead to Glacier Peak Wilderness. Mt Baker NF.

PARK CREEK (800') 17 mi north of Concrete on FH 25. 12 campsites, trailers — 16' max, May 15 to Oct 20, 14 day limit, stream water. Hunting, hiking, fishing and water sports 1 mi. Mt Baker NF.

PINNACLE LAKE TRAIL CAMP (3700') 4½ mi east from Verlot on FH 7, then 3 mi south on FR 3015, then 3 mi west on FR 3015B, then 1½ mi SW on Trail 703. 3 campsites, June 15 to Oct 1, lake water. Fishing. Mt Baker NF.

RAINBOW POINT BOAT CAMP (1600') 6 mi north of Ross Dam on Ross Lake, accessible by boat or trail only. 4 campsites, June 1 to Nov 1, 14 day limit, lake water. Fishing, swimming, boating, hiking. Ross Lake NRA.

RED BRIDGE (1300') 7 mi east of Verlot on Mtn Loop Hwy. 10 campsites, trailers — 32' max, Apr 1 to Nov 30, 10 day limit, river water. Fishing, goldpanning, hunting, Black Chief Mine across the road. Mt Baker NF.

RIVER BAR (1600') 7 mi east of Verlot on Mtn Loop Hwy. 7 tent sites, trailers — 32' max, Apr 1 to Nov 30, 10 day limit, river water. Fishing, hunting. Mt Baker NF.

RIVER BAR (1600') 7½ mi north from Darrington on the Rockport Hwy then 23 mi SE on FR 345. 1 campsite for horsemen, May 30 to Oct 31, 10 day limit. Trailhead to Glacier Peak Wilderness. Mt Baker NF.

ROCKPORT STATE PARK (300') 1 mi west of Rockport on State 20. 50 campsites for tents or trailers, fee, disposal station, hot showers. Good hiking trails, dense woods with ferns and mossy growth. Across the hwy from the park entrance is a memorial marker to David Douglas, a botanist for whom the Douglas fir was named.

ROLAND POINT BOAT CAMP (1600') 4 mi north from Ross Dam on Ross Lake, accessible by boat only. 2 campsites, June 1 to Nov 1, 14 day limit, lake water. Fishing, swimming, boating, hiking. Ross Lake NRA.

SCHRIEBERS MEADOW TRAIL CAMP (3400') 9 mi north from Concrete on FH 25, then 4 mi NW on FR 3725, then 6 mi NW on FR 372, then ½ mi west on Trail 603. 2 campsites, June 15 to Oct 1, stream water, trail shelter. Huckleberries, trail to Cathedral Crag. Mt Baker NF.

SHANNON CREEK (730') 9½ mi north from Concrete on FH 25, then 12 mi north on FR 394, then 1 mi SE on FR 3830. 2 tent sites, 18 trailer spaces — 32' max, Apr 20 to Oct 30, 10 day limit, lake water. Boating, launch, swimming, water skiing, fishing, hiking. Mt Baker NF.

SILESIA CREEK TRAIL SHELTER (2600') 11½ mi east from Glacier on State 542, then 7 mi north on FR 401, then 4½ mi NE on Trail 672. 2 campsites, June 15 to Oct 1, stream water. Fishing, hiking along Silesia Cr. Mt Baker NF.

SILVER CREEK BOAT CAMP (1600') 20 mi north of Ross Dam on Ross Lake, accessible by boat only. 1 campsite, June 1 to Nov 1, 14 day limit, lake water. Boating, swimming, fishing, hiking. Ross Lake NRA.

SILVER FIR (2000') 12½ mi east of Glacier on State 542. 19 tent sites along the river, 12 trailer spaces — 32' max, May 1 to Oct 1, 10 day limit, community kitchen, shelter. Fishing, riding, nature trail. Mt Baker NF.

SKAGIT COUNTY STEELHEAD PARK (230') At Rockport on State 20. 60 campsites for tents and trailers — 28' max, fee, all year, no limit of stay, supplies ½ mi, disposal station, RV hookups, hot showers, no firewood, restaurant. Fishing, boating, ramp. Porter Cabin, first in the area, is in the park. Indian canoes on display. PO Box 36, Rockport 98283. Skagit County.

SLOAN CREEK (2000') 18½ mi SE from Darrington on FR 322 then 6½ mi SE on FR 308. 7 walk-in sites, May 30 to Oct 31, 10 day limit, river water, shelter. Fishing, hunting, riding, trailhead to Glacier Peak Wilderness, mtn climbing, mineral spring on the north side of the trail not far from camp. Mt Baker NF.

SOUTH FORK (1500') 21 mi SE of Darrington on Mtn Loop Hwy (FR 322). 5 tent sites, 3 trailer spaces — 22' max, May 30 to Oct 31, 10 day limit, river water. Fishing, hunting, hiking, riding. Mt Baker NF.

SULPHUR CREEK (1500') 7½ mi north on the Rockport Hwy from Darrington then 22½ mi east on FR 345. 14 tent sites, May 30 to Oct 31, 10 day limit, stream water. Fishing, hunting, hiking along Sulphur Cr — mineral spring 1 mi. Mt Baker NF.

SUNNYSIDE (1300') 6 mi east of Verlot on Mtn Loop Hwy. 7 tent sites, trailers — 32' max, Apr 1 to Nov 30, 10 day limit, river water. Fishing, goldpanning, hunting, hiking, earthslide nearby. Mt Baker NF.

TEN MILE ISLAND BOAT CAMP (1600') 10 mi north of Ross Dam on Ross Lake, accessible by boat only. 1 campsite, June 1 to Nov 1, 14 day limit, lake water. Fishing, swimming, boating. Ross Lake NRA.

TURLO (900') 11 mi east of Granite Falls on FH 7 at Verlot, just south of the Ranger Sta and across the rd. 19 campsites, trailers — 32' max, Mar 15 to Dec 15, 10 day limit, supplies. Fishing, hunting. Mt Baker NF.

TWIN PEAKS (1600') 21½ mi SE of Darrington on Mtn Loop Hwy (FR 322). 4 tent sites, May 30 to Oct 31, 10 day limit, river water. Fishing, hunting. Mt Baker NF.

TYEE POOL (1700') 21½ mi SE of Darrington on Mtn Loop Hwy (FR 322). 2 tent sites, May 30 to Oct 31, 10 day limit, river water, fishing, hunting. Mt Baker NF.

VERLOT (900') 11 mi NE of Granite Falls in Verlot. 7 tent sites, 15 trailer spaces — 32' max, May 15 to Dec 10, heavily-used camp, 10 day limit, supplies. Fishing, swimming, hunting, river running on Sauk R. Mt Baker NF.

WATSON LAKE TRAIL CAMP (4400') 11½ mi north from Concrete on FH 25, then 2 mi SE on FR 3720, then 9 mi north on FR 3721, then 3 mi SE on Trail 611. 2 campsites, June 15 to Oct 1, lake water. Fishing, hiking. Mt Baker NF.

WHITE CHUCK (970') 11 mi SE of Darrington on FR 322. 9 tent sites, May 30 to Oct 31, 10 day limit, river water. Fishing, hunting, hiking and riding, river running on Sauk R. Mt. Baker NF.

Maiden of the Woods

If you're traveling the new **NORTH CASCADES HIGHWAY**, stop off at the **WASHINGTON PASS OVERLOOK**. There is a spectacular view of Liberty Bell Mountain, and you may even spot some mountain goats on the far slopes. • **GOAT WALL**, near Mazama, is a 2000-foot high, nearly vertical cliff created by the shearing action of glaciers when they flowed through the area. • **CHANCELLOR MINING DISTRICT**, about 40 miles NW of Winthrop, offers a chance to explore the remains of heavy mining activity that took place during the 1800's. Some old shacks and machinery are still around. • **STEHEKIN**, at the upper end of Lake Chelan, is an isolated mountain resort area; accessible only by boat service, seaplane or on foot. A bus serves as transportation on the 20-mile road NW to Cottonwood Camp. There are 8 campgrounds along the route and numerous trails leading to the backcountry. **LAKE CHELAN BOAT COMPANY** operates a taxi-boat and tour service from Chelan to Stehekin. • **SLATE PEAK LOOKOUT**, NW of Mazama, is the highest point in the state that you can drive to (open July-Oct). **FOSSILS** can be found on the backslopes.

ALPINE MEADOW (2700') 16 mi NW on US 2 from Leavenworth (see Map 11), then 4 mi north on State 207, then 1 mi east on County 22, then 19½ mi NW on FR 311. 4 tent sites, June 15 to Oct 15, 14 day limit, river water. Fishing in Chiwawa R, hunting, riding, hiking, scenic meadow. Wenatchee NF.

ANDREWS CREEK (3000') 23½ mi north of Winthrop on Chewack Rd (FR 392). 1 tent site, June 1 to Oct 1, no limit of stay, stream water. Fishing, hunting, riding, horse corral and truck dock, trailhead to Pasayten Wilderness. Okanogan NF.

BALLARD (2600') 13½ mi NW on State 20 from Winthrop to Mazama then 9 mi NW on FR 374. 6 tent sites, 1 trailer space — 22' max, June 1 to Oct 15, no limit of stay. Stream fishing, hunting. Okanogan NF.

BIG CREEK BOAT CAMP (1100') 27 mi NW of Chelan (see Map 11) on Lake Chelan, accessible by boat or seaplane only. 3 camp sites, May 1 to Oct 31, 14 day limit, lake water, boat dock. Water sports, fishing, hunting, small waterfall nearby. Wenatchee NF.

BIG TWIN LAKE (2000') 3 mi south on State 20 from Winthrop then 2½ mi west on county rd. 50 tent sites, 70 trailer spaces — 32' max, fee, group facilities, Apr to Oct, no limit of stay, reservations accepted, RV hookups, supplies 3 mi, concession. Fishing, row boat rentals, hiking 1 mi, hunting, no rattlesnakes, scenic mtns. Winthrop 98862. Privately owned.

BLACK PINE LAKE (4200') 11 mi south from Twisp on State 153 then 12 mi NW on FR 3202. 29 tent sites, 6 trailer spaces — 22' max, June to Nov 15, no limit of stay. Hunting, fishing, boat launch. Okanogan NF.

BRIDGE CREEK (2100') 16 mi NW of Stehekin via shuttle bus; Stehekin is accessible only by boat or seaplane. 8 campsites, May 15 to Nov 1, 14 day limit, no pets, stream water. Fishing, Pacific Crest Trail passes thru the camp. North Cascades NP.

BUCK LAKE (3200') 9½ mi north from Winthrop on Chewack Rd (FR 392), then ½ mi NW on FR 383, then 2½ mi NW on FR 3626. 4 tent sites, May 15 to Oct 15, no limit of stay. Boating, fishing, hunting. Okanogan NF.

CAMP 4 (2400') 18 mi north of Winthrop on Chewack Rd (FR 392). 4 tent sites, no limit of stay, river water, fishing in Chewack River, hunting, spawning salmon in Aug. Okanogan NF.

CHANCELLOR (4800') 13½ mi NW from Winthrop on State 20 then 28½ mi NW on FR 374. 6 tent sites, July 1 to Oct 1, no limit of stay, stream water, shelter. Fishing, hunting, riding, huckleberries, old mining town sites, trailhead to Pasayten Wilderness. Okanogan NF.

CHEWACK (2200') 15 mi north of Winthrop on Chewack Rd (FR 392). 4 tent sites, June 1 to Oct 15, no limit of stay, river water. Fishing, hunting. Salmon spawn in pools during Aug. Okanogan NF.

COMPANY CREEK (1300') 4 mi NW of Stehekin via shuttle bus or trail; Stehekin is accessible only by boat or seaplane. 7 campsites, May 1 to Nov 15, 14 day limit, supplies at Stehekin. Fishing, trailhead to Glacier Peak Wilderness. Lake Chelan NRA.

COTTONWOOD (2740') 23 mi NW of Stehekin via shuttle bus; Stehekin is accessible only by boat or seaplane. 5 campsites, May 15 to Oct 15, 14 day limit, no pets, stream water. Fishing in Stehekin R, trail to Cascade Pass. North Cascades NP.

COTTONWOOD (3100') 38 mi NW of Entiat (see Map 11) on Entiat Rd (FR 317). 26 campsites for tents and RVs, June 15 to Oct 15, 14 day limit. Fishing in Entiat R, hunting, riding, horse corral, trailhead to Glacier Peak Wilderness. Wenatchee NF.

CORRAL CREEK BOAT CAMP (1100') 28 mi NW of Chelan (see Map 11) on Lake Chelan, accessible by boat or seaplane only. 1 campsite, May 1 to Nov 1, 14 day limit, lake water, boat dock. Water sports, sailing, fishing. Wenatchee NF.

CUTTHROAT CREEK (4000') 26½ mi NW from Winthrop on State 20 then 1 mi west on FR 3511. 3 tent sites for trail users only, July 1 to Oct 15, one night stay. Horse facilities include hitching rails, truck dock and water troughs. Mtn climbing, riding, fishing. Cutthroat Trail leads westward and connects with the Pacific Crest Trail. Okanogan NF.

DEER PARK (6000') 13½ mi NW from Winthrop on State 20, then 20½ mi NW on Harts Pass Rd (FR 374). 1 tent site, July 1 to Oct 1, no limit of stay, stream water, hunting. Okanogan NF.

DEER POINT BOAT CAMP (1100') 22 mi NW of Chelan (see Map 11) on Lake Chelan; accessible by boat or seaplane only. 2 campsites, May 1 to Nov 1, 14 day limit, lake water, boat dock. Fishing, water sports, sailing. Wenatchee NF.

DOLLY VARDEN (1850') 14 mi NW of Stehekin via shuttle bus; Stehekin is accessible only by boat or seaplane. 1 campsite, May 15 to Nov 1, 14 day limit, stream water, supplies at Stehekin, no pets. Fishing in Stehekin R. North Cascades NP.

DOMKE FALLS BOAT CAMP (1100') 37 mi NW of Chelan (see Map 11) on Lake Chelan, accessible by boat or seaplane only. 1 campsite, May 1 to Nov 1, 14 day limit, boat dock. Water sports, sailing, fishing, spectacular waterfall nearby. Wenatchee NF.

DOMKE LAKE TRAIL CAMP (2200') 2½ mi south of Lucerne on the north shore of Domke Lake; accessible by trail or seaplane only. 2 campsites, May 1 to Nov 1, 14 day limit, lake water, supplies at Lucerne. Boating, swimming, fishing, hiking and riding trails. Wenatchee NF.

EARLY WINTERS (2400') 16 mi NW of Winthrop on State 20. 6 tent sites, June 1 to Oct 15, no limit of stay, sparse shade. View of Goat Wall, info station, fishing, hunting, hiking, riding, pack trips at Early Winters Resort. Okanogan NF.

ELEPHANT ROCK BOAT CAMP (1100') 43 mi NW of Chelan (see Map 11) on Lake Chelan, accessible by boat or seaplane only. 1 campsite, May 1 to Nov 1, 14 day limit, lake water, boat dock. Water sports, sailing, fishing. Wenatchee NF.

FALLS CREEK (2300') 12 mi north of Winthrop on Chewack Rd (FR 392). 6 tent sites, 1 trailer space — 16' max, June 1 to Oct 15, no limit of stay. Fishing, hunting. A trail across the road leads to Fall Cr Falls — watch for snakes while hiking. Okanogan NF.

FISH CREEK TRAIL SHELTER (1200') 5 mi SE of Stehekin by trail. 1 campsite and covered shelter, July 1 to Sep 30, no water supply. Horse rental, fishing, hiking. Wenatchee NF.

FLAT (2600') 9½ mi north from Winthrop on Chewack Rd (FR 392) then 2 mi NW on FR 383. 10 tent sites, June 1 to Oct 15, no limit of stay, river water. Fishing, hunting. Okanogan NF.

FLICK CREEK BOAT CAMP (1100') 4 mi south of Stehekin on Lake Chelan, accessible by boat or trail only. 1 campsite, Apr 15 to Nov 1, 14 day limit, lake water. Boating, swimming, fishing, hiking along the shore of Lk Chelan. Lake Chelan NRA.

FOGGY DEW (2400') 14½ mi south from Twisp on State 153 then 5 mi west on Gold Cr Rd (FR 3109). 15 tent sites, May 15 to Nov 15, no limit of stay. Fishing in Gold Cr, hunting. Okanogan NF.

GATE CREEK (1800') 13½ mi NW from Winthrop on State 20 then 4½ mi NW on County 1163. 3 tent sites, 1 trailer space — 22' max, June 1 to Oct 15, no limit of stay. Fishing, hunting, riding. The sheer cliffs of Goat Wall provide a scenic backdrop for the camp. Okanogan NF.

GRAHAM HARBOR BOAT CAMP (1100') 31 mi NW of Chelan (see Map 11) on Lake Chelan, accessible by boat or seaplane only. 4 campsites, May 1 to Nov 1, 14 day limit, stream water, trail shelter, boat dock. Water sports, sailing, fishing. Wenatchee NF.

HARTS PASS (6200') 13½ mi NW from Winthrop on State 20 then 19½ mi NW on Harts Pass Rd (FR 374). 6 tent sites, July 1 to Oct 1, no limit of stay, no water supply. Hunting, riding, hiking, fossil area below Slate Peak, mtn climbing. The Pacific Crest Trail passes by the camp, access to Pasayten Wilderness. Okanogan NF.

HATCHERY BOAT CAMP (2200') 3½ mi south of Lucerne on the south shore of Domke Lake, accessible by boat or seaplane only. 2 campsites, June 1 to Nov 1, 14 day limit, lake water. Boating, fishing, swimming. Wenatchee NF.

HIGH BRIDGE (1550') 11 mi NW of Stehekin via shuttle bus; Stehekin is accessible only by boat or seaplane. 2 campsites, May 1 to Nov 1, 14 day limit, stream water, supplies at Stehekin. Fishing, hunting, trailhead to Glacier Peak Wilderness, Pacific Crest Trail passes by the camp. Lake Chelan NRA.

HOLDEN (3200') 11 mi west of Lucerne on FR 3100; Lucerne is accessible only by boat or seaplane. 2 campsites, June 15 to Sep 30, 14 day limit, stream water, cafe and showers 1 mi. Swimming, fishing, hunting, riding, mtn climbing, access to Glacier Peak Wilderness. Wenatchee NF.

HONEYMOON (3300') 9½ mi north of Winthrop on Chewack Rd (FR 392) then 9 mi NW on FR 383. 5 tent sites, June 1 to Oct 15, no limit of stay, stream water. Fishing, hunting. Okanogan NF.

KLIPCHUCK (3100') 17½ mi NW from Winthrop on State 20 then 1 mi north on FR 3610. 26 tent sites, 20 trailer spaces — 32' max, June 1 to Oct 15, 5 day limit. Fishing, hunting, hiking trail. Okanogan NF.

LAKE CREEK (2800') 21 mi north of Winthrop on Chewack Rd (FR 392). 3 tent sites, June 1 to Oct 15, no limit of stay, river water. Fishing, hunting, horse corrals and truck dock. Okanogan NF.

LAKE CREEK CORRAL (3200') 21 mi north from Winthrop on Chewack Rd (FR 392) then 2½ mi NW on FR 3801. 1 tent site, June 1 to Oct 1, no limit of stay, stream water. Fishing, riding, horse corral, trailhead to Pasayten Wilderness. Okanogan NF.

LEN'S PEARRYGIN LAKE RESORT (2000') 3 mi north of Winthrop. 30 tent sites, 64 trailer spaces — 35' max, fee, Apr 15 to Nov 5, no limit of stay, reservations accepted, store, RV hookups, disposal station, laundry, hot showers, no firewood. Fishing, canoeing, motorboat rentals, swimming, water skiing, hunting. PO Box 38A, Winthrop 98862. Privately owned.

(Continued on following page)

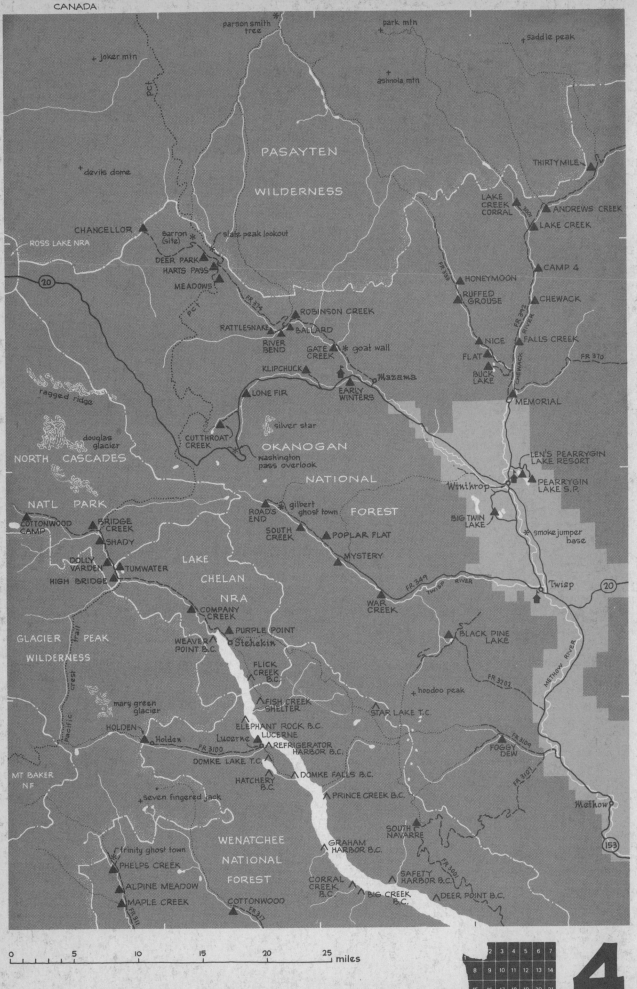

CANADA

+ joker mtn

PASAYTEN

WILDERNESS

parson smith
tree

park mtn
+

+ saddle peak

+ devils dome

+ ashnola mtn

THIRTYMILE

CHANCELLOR

ROSS LAKE NRA

Barron
(site)

slate peak lookout

DEER PARK

HARTS PASS

MEADOWS

FR 374

PCT

ROBINSON CREEK

RATTLESNAKE   BALLARD

RIVER
BEND

GATE   * goat wall
CREEK

KLIPCHUCK

Mazama

LONE FIR

EARLY
WINTERS

ragged ridge

silver star

CUTTHROAT
CREEK

washington
pass overlook

douglas
glacier

OKANOGAN

LAKE
CREEK
CORRAL

ANDREWS CREEK

LAKE CREEK

CAMP 4

HONEYMOON

RUFFED
GROUSE

CHEWACK

FR 372

FR 388

FR 370

NICE   FALLS CREEK

FLAT

BUCK
LAKE

MEMORIAL

LEN'S PEARRYGIN
LAKE RESORT

NORTH   CASCADES

NATIONAL

NATL   PARK

COTTONWOOD
CAMP

BRIDGE
CREEK

SHADY

DOLLY
VARDEN

HIGH BRIDGE

TUMWATER

GLACIER   PEAK

WILDERNESS

LAKE

CHELAN

NRA

COMPANY
CREEK

PURPLE POINT

WEAVER
POINT B.C.

Stehekin

mary green
glacier

HOLDEN

Holden

FR 3100

FOREST

ROAD'S
END

SOUTH
CREEK

gilbert
ghost town

POPLAR FLAT

MYSTERY

WAR
CREEK

FR 349

Twisp River

Winthrop

BIG TWIN
LAKE

* smoke jumper
base

Twisp

20

BLACK PINE
LAKE

PEARRYGIN
LAKE S.P.

METHOW RIVER

FLICK
CREEK
B.C.

FISH CREEK
SHELTER

ELEPHANT ROCK B.C.
LUCERNE

Lucerne   REFRIGERATOR
HARBOR B.C.

DOMKE LAKE T.C.

HATCHERY
B.C.

DOMKE FALLS B.C.

PRINCE CREEK B.C.

STAR LAKE T.C.

+ hoodoo peak

FR 3201

FOGGY
DEW

FR 3109

FR 3107

MT BAKER
NF

+ seven fingered jack

Pacific   Crest   Trail

trinity ghost town

PHELPS CREEK

ALPINE MEADOW

MAPLE CREEK

FR 311

WENATCHEE

NATIONAL

FOREST

COTTONWOOD

FR 317

GRAHAM
HARBOR B.C.

CORRAL
CREEK
B.C.

BIG CREEK
B.C.

SOUTH
NAVARRE

SAFETY
HARBOR B.C.

DEER POINT B.C.

FR 300

Methow

153

0   5   10   15   20   25   miles

4

LONE FIR (3700') 26½ mi NW of Winthrop on State 20. 14 tent sites, 6 trailer spaces — 22' max, June 15 to Oct 15, 10 day limit. Fishing, hunting, hiking, mtn climbing, access to Silver Star Glacier. The camp is named for a lone fir that was the sole survivor of a snow slide 150 years ago. In spite of the name, there is adequate shade at most of the campsites. There is also an old trapper's cabin that was used by men setting winter trap lines for sleek marten. Okanogan NF.

LUCERNE (1100') 41 mi NW of Chelan (see Map 11) on Lake Chelan at Lucerne; accessible only by boat, seaplane or trail. 2 campsites, May 1 to Nov 1, 14 day limit, boat dock. Water sports, sailing, fishing, hunting, hiking. Wenatchee NF.

MAPLE CREEK (2600') 16 mi NW on US 2 from Leavenworth (see Map 11), then 4 mi north on State 207, then 1 mi east on County 22, then 19 mi NW on FR 311. 3 tent sites, 4 trailer spaces — 22' max, June 15 to Oct 15, 14 day limit, stream water. Fishing, berrypicking, hunting, riding. Little Giant Trail leads to Glacier Peak Wilderness. Wenatchee NF.

MEADOWS (6300') 13½ mi NW from Winthrop on State 20 then 19½ mi north on Harts Pass Rd (FR 374) then 1 mi south on FR 3739. 14 tent sites, July 1 to Oct 1, no limit of stay, stream water. Rockhounding, riding, hunting, access to the Pacific Crest Trail. Okanogan NF.

MEMORIAL (2000') 7½ mi north of Winthrop on Chewack Rd (FR 392). 2 tent sites, June 1 to Oct 15, 10 day limit, hot and dry during the summer. Fishing in rushing Chewack R, rocky stream bed, hunting, hiking. Okanogan NF.

MYSTERY (2800') 18 mi west of Twisp on Twisp River Rd (FR 349). 3 tent sites, May 15 to Nov 15, no limit of stay, river water. Fishing. Okanogan NF.

NICE (2700') 9½ mi north from Winthrop on Chewack Rd then 4 mi NW on FR 383. 3 tent sites, June 1 to Oct 15, no limit of stay. Fishing, hunting. Okanogan NF.

PEARRYGIN LAKE STATE PARK (2000') 5 mi NE of Winthrop. 60 tent sites, 50 trailer spaces, fee, store, cafe, snack bar, hot showers, boat launch. Swimming, fishing, hiking.

PHELPS CREEK (2800') 16 mi NW on US 2 from Leavenworth (see Map 11), then 4 mi south on State 207, then 1 mi east on County 22, then 21 mi NW on FR 311. 7 tent sites, June 15 to Oct 15, 14 day limit, river water. Fishing in Chiwawa R, hunting, horse corral and unloading dock, trail to Glacier Peak Wilderness, ghost town of Trinity. Wenatchee NF.

POPLAR FLAT (2900') 20 mi west of Twisp on Twisp River Rd (FR 349). 14 tent sites, 1 trailer space — 22' max, May 15 to Nov 15, no limit of stay, community kitchen. Fishing, hunting. Okanogan NF.

PRINCE CREEK BOAT CAMP (1100') 35½ mi NW of Chelan (see Map 11) on Lake Chelan; accessible only by boat, seaplane or trail. 5 campsites, May 1 to Nov 15, 14 day limit. Boat dock, water sports, sailing, fishing, hiking along Prince Cr. Wenatchee NF.

PURPLE POINT (1100') At Stehekin on Lake Chelan; Stehekin is accessible only by boat or seaplane. 4 campsites, Apr 15 to Nov 30, 14 day limit, lake water, supplies, boat rentals, water taxi. Swimming, fishing, hiking. Lake Chelan NRA.

RATTLESNAKE (2700') 13½ mi NW from Winthrop on State 20, then 9½ mi NW on FR 374, then 1 mi west on FR 3700. 3 tent sites, June 1 to Oct 15, no limit of stay. Fishing, hunting, riding. A trail leads SW to the Pacific Crest Trail approx 7 mi. Okanogan NF.

REFRIGERATOR HARBOR BOAT CAMP (1100') 41 mi NW of Chelan (see Map 11) on Lake Chelan at Lucerne; accessible only by boat, seaplane or trail. 4 campsites, May 1 to Nov 1, 14 day limit, lake water, supplies, boat dock. Water sports, sailing, fishing, hiking. Wenatchee NF.

RIVER BEND (2700') 13½ mi NW from Winthrop on State 20, then 12½ mi NW on County 1163, then ½ mi west on FR 3700. 4 tent sites, 1 trailer space — 22' max, June 1 to Oct 15, no limit of stay. Stream fishing, hunting. Okanogan NF.

ROADS END (3600') 25 mi NW of Twisp on Twisp River Rd (FR 349). 4 tent sites, June 1 to Nov 1, no limit of stay, river water. Fishing, hunting, trailhead to Lake Chelan NRA, Gilbert historical site 1 mi east. Okanogan NF.

ROBINSON CREEK (2400') 13½ mi NW from Winthrop on State 20 then 8½ mi NW on Harts Pass Rd (FR 374). 4 campsites, June 1 to Oct 15, no limit of stay, stream water, facilities for horses. Fishing, riding, trailhead to Pasayten Wilderness. Okanogan NF.

RUFFED GROUSE (3200') 9½ mi north from Winthrop on Chewack Rd then 8 mi NW on FR 383. 4 tent sites, June 1 to Oct 15, no limit of stay. Fishing, hunting. Okanogan NF.

SAFETY HARBOR BOAT CAMP (1100') 25 mi NW of Chelan (see Map 11) on Lake Chelan, accessible only by boat or seaplane. 2 campsites, May 1 to Nov 1, 14 day limit, lake water. Boat dock, water sports, sailing, fishing. Wenatchee NF.

SHADY (1920') 15 mi NW of Stehekin via shuttle bus; Stehekin is accessible only by boat or seaplane. 1 campsite, May 15 to Nov 1, 14 day limit, stream water, no pets. Fishing in Stehekin R. North Cascades NP.

SOUTH CREEK (3100') 22 mi west of Twisp on Twisp River Rd (FR 349). 4 tent sites, June 1 to Nov 15, no limit of stay, stream water. Fishing, hunting, trailhead to Lake Chelan NRA. Okanogan NF.

SOUTH NAVARRE (6000') 39 mi NW of Chelan (see Map 11) via State 150 and FR 3001 (rough, narrow access road not recommended for trailers). 2 tent sites, July 1 to Oct 31, 14 day limit. Hunting, scenic vistas. Summit Trail leads to Miners Basin and Boiling Lake. Wenatchee NF.

STAR LAKE TRAIL CAMP (6700') 6 mi east on Trail 1246 from Stehekin then 12 mi SE on Trail 1259. 2 campsites, July 15 to Sep 15, lake water. Fishing, riding, hiking. Wenatchee NF.

THIRTYMILE (3600') 30 mi north of Winthrop on Chewack Rd (FR 392). 9 tent sites, June 1 to Oct 1, no limit of stay, stream water. Fishing, hunting, riding. Corrals and hitching rails are available for campers with horses. Chewack Trail leads northward to Chewack Falls, Cabin Camp Trail Shelter and Pasayten Wilderness. Wild berries are found along the trail in Aug. Okanogan NF.

TUMWATER (1750') 12 mi NW of Stehekin via shuttle bus; Stehekin is accessible only by boat or seaplane. 2 campsites, May 15 to Nov 1, 14 day limit, supplies at Stehekin, stream water. Fishing. North Cascades NP.

WAR CREEK (2500') 14 mi west of Twisp on Twisp River Rd (FR 349). 8 tent sites, 3 trailer spaces — 22' max, May 15 to Nov 15, no limit of stay. Hunting, hiking, riding. There is good trout fishing in Twisp River after the spring runoff. Okanogan NF.

WEAVER POINT BOAT CAMP (1100') 1 mi NW of Stehekin by boat, or accessible by trail from Company Creek Campground. 22 campsites, Apr 15 to Nov 1, 14 day limit, supplies at Stehekin. Boating, swimming, fishing, trailhead to Glacier Peak Wilderness. Lake Chelan NRA.

SALMON FALLS, 9 miles west of Conconully, is a series of 4 waterfalls that drop 300 feet in less than a quarter of a mile. A short, steep trail from the parking area leads to good viewpoints. • Old RUBY TOWNSITE once had about 1,000 residents when it sprang up as a mining community. Now you'll find only some foundations and an interpretive marker. The site is a few miles south of Conconully. • At HEHE ROCK, on the Oroville-Chesaw Rd, an historical marker tells about the Indian legend associated with the rock. • MOLSON GHOST TOWN has a museum with a collection of pioneer tools and belongings (open continuously). About 15 miles NE of Oroville via Chesaw Rd and up Mud Lake Valley. • FORT OKANOGAN State Park is the site of the first American settlement in Washington (est. 1811). It's 4 miles east of Brewster on the Okanogan River. Museum and interpretive center.

AENEAS SPRING (3600') 12½ mi east from Tonasket on State 20 then 9½ mi SE on County 164 then 4½ mi SE on FR 3612. 2 tent sites, June to Nov, no limit of stay, no water supply, hunting, hiking. Okanogan NF.

ALDER (3200') 4½ mi north of Conconully on FR 391. 5 tent sites, trailers — 22' max, June 1 to Oct 30, no limit of stay, stream water. Fishing in Salmon Creek, hunting, hiking. Okanogan NF.

ALTA LAKE STATE PARK (1200') 7 mi SW on US 97 from Brewster to Pateros then 2 mi SW off State 153. 247 tent sites, 16 trailer spaces, fee, open all year, store, hot showers. Boat launch, swimming, fishing, several hiking trails, riding, horse rentals, ice skating on the lake in winter.

BEAVER LAKE (3000') 20 mi east from Tonasket on State 20 then 11 mi north on FR 396. 5 tent sites, 1 trailer space — 16' max, May 1 to Oct 10, 14 day limit. Boating, swimming, fishing, hunting, hiking trail along the lake. Okanogan NF.

BONAPARTE LAKE (3600') 20 mi east from Tonasket on State 20 then 6 mi north on FR 396. 22 tent sites, 4 trailer spaces — 32' max, May 1 to Oct 15, 14 day limit, supplies. Boat rentals, water sports, fishing, hunting. Okanogan NF.

BONAPARTE LAKE RESORT (3600') 20 mi east from Tonasket on State 20 then 6 mi north on FR 396. 20 wooded campsites for tents and trailers — 25' max, fee, group facilities, Apr to Nov, no limit of stay, reservations accepted, groceries, RV hookups, laundry, hot showers. Fishing, boating, sail and row boat rentals, swimming, hunting, hiking around the lake. Fir and tamarack trees. Tonasket 98855. Privately owned.

CONCONULLY STATE PARK (2400') 15 mi NW of Okanogan at Conconully. 81 campsites, trailers — 28' max, fee, Apr 1 to Oct 15, 7 day limit, store, hot showers, cafe, golf course nearby, boat launch and rentals. Swimming beach, fishing, hiking around the lake, bicycle rentals.

COTTONWOOD (2700') 2 mi north of Conconully on FR 391. 5 tent sites, June 1 to Oct 30, no limit of stay, artesian well. Fishing in Salmon Creek, hunting. Okanogan NF.

CRAWFISH LAKE (4500') 17½ mi east from Riverside on County 9320, then 1½ mi south on FR 3612, then ½ mi SE on FR 3525. 21 campsites, trailers — 32' max, May 1 to Oct 15, 14 day limit, boat launch. Water sports, fishing, hunting. A small balanced rock sits in a meadow near Balanced Rock Spr. Okanogan NF.

DAISY (4800') 2 mi north from Loomis on County 9425 then 15½ mi west on FR 390. 2 tent sites, July 1 to Oct 30, no limit of stay, stream water. Fishing 2 mi, hunting, hiking. Okanogan NF.

(Continued on following page)

horseshoe basin	loomis	oroville	mt. bonaparte
tiffany mtn	conconully	tonasket	aeneas valley
loup loup	okanogan	omak lake	disautel
brewster	bridgeport	boof mtn	alameda flat

USGS 15-minute quadrangle key

EAST OMAK PARK (820') ¼ mi east of Omak on State 155. 20 tent sites, 24 trailer spaces — 30' max, fee, group facilities, Apr 1 to Oct 1, 5 day limit, RV hookups, disposal station, hot showers, no firewood, cooking shelters, swimming pool, playground. Fishing, canoeing, motorboating, ramp, water skiing, swimming in the Okanogan River, some shade trees and grassy lawns. City of Omak.

FOURTEEN MILE (4700') 2 mi north from Loomis on County 9425 then 8 mi west on FR 390 then 4½ mi NW on T1100. 1 tent site, July 1 to Oct 15, no limit of stay, stream water. Fishing, facilities for horses, trail to Pasayten Wilderness. Okanogan NF.

HIDDEN (3500') 12½ mi east on State 20 from Twisp (see Map 4) then 1½ mi north on FR 3621. 3 tent sites, June 1 to Nov 15, no limit of stay, hunting, hiking. Okanogan NF.

J.R. (3400') 12 mi east of Twisp (see Map 4) on State 20 then ¼ mi north on FR 3325. 5 tent sites, May 15 to Nov 15, no limit of stay, hunting. Okanogan NF.

KERR (3100') 4 mi north of Conconully on FR 391. 5 tent sites, June 1 to Oct 30, no limit of stay, stream water. Fishing in Salmon Creek, hunting. Okanogan NF.

KOOTENAI (2400') 4 mi NE of Conconully on County 4015. 1 tent site, June 1 to Oct 30, no limit of stay, lake water. Boat launch, water skiing, fishing. Okanogan NF.

LAKE BETH (3000') 7½ mi SE from Chesaw on County 9480. 17 campsites for tents or trailers — 32' max, May 1 to Oct 10, no limit of stay. Fishing, hiking, boating, launch, swimming. Okanogan NF.

LAKE OSOYOOS STATE PARK (1000') ½ mi north of Oroville on the south shore of the lake. 100 campsites, fee, Apr 1 to Oct 15, 7 day limit, hot showers. Fishing, boating, ramp, swimming, water skiing, hunting, ice-skating in winter. Rt 1, Box 102-A, Oroville 98844.

LONG SWAMP (5500') 2 mi north from Loomis on County 9425, then 21½ mi west on FR 390. 2 tent sites, July 1 to Oct 30, no limit of stay, stream water. Fishing, hunting, riding, trail to Pasayten Wilderness. Okanogan NF.

LOST LAKE (3800') 2½ mi west from Wauconda on State 20, then 10½ mi NE on FR 396, then 6½ mi NW on FR 3912, then ½ mi south on FR 397. 10 tent sites, 6 trailer spaces — 32' max, May 1 to Oct 15, 14 day limit. Boat launch, water sports, fishing, hunting, Big Tree Botanical Area nearby. Okanogan NF.

LOUP LOUP (3500') 12½ mi east on State 20 from Twisp (see Map 4) then ½ mi north on FR 3621. 6 tent sites, June 1 to Nov 15, no limit of stay, hunting. Okanogan NF.

LYMAN LAKE (2900') 12½ mi east from Tonasket on State 20 then 13 mi SE on County 9455 then 2½ mi south on FR 357. 5 campsites, trailers — 32' max, May 15 to Oct 10, no limit of stay, lake water, supplies 4 mi, fishing, hunting, Okanogan NF.

ORIOLE (2900') 2½ mi NW from Conconully on FR 391 then ½ mi NW on FR 362. 3 tent sites, 3 trailer spaces — 22' max, June 1 to Oct 30, no limit of stay, fishing in Salmon Creek, hunting. Okanogan NF.

ROGER LAKE (6000') 23½ mi west from Conconully on FR 364, then 1½ mi NE on FR 370. 1 tent site, July 1 to Sep 30, no limit of stay, lake water, boating, fishing, hunting, hiking. Okanogan NF.

SALMON MEADOWS (4500') 9 mi NW of Conconully on FR 391. 13 tent sites, trailers — 22' max, June 1 to Oct 30, no limit of stay, community kitchen. Fishing, hunting, nature trail, riding. Okanogan NF.

STATE ROAD CABIN (3400') 34¼ mi SW from Cononully on FR 364, then 3½ mi SW on FR 352. 2 tent sites, July 1 to Oct 30, no limit of stay, stream water, fishing, hunting. Okanogan NF.

SUGAR LOAF (2400') 4½ mi NE of Conconully on Conconully Lake Rd (4051). 5 tent sites, June 1 to Oct 30, no limit of stay, boat launch, swimming, fishing in Conconully Lake, hunting. Okanogan NF.

THIRTYMILE MEADOWS (6200') 2 mi north from Loomis on County 9425, then 23½ mi west on FR 390, then 8½ mi south on FR 391. 1 tent site, July 1 to Sep 30, no limit of stay, stream water, hunting, hiking. Okanogan NF.

TIFFANY MEADOW (6200') 23 mi NW of Conconully on FR 364 then 6½ mi NE on FR 370. 1 tent site, July to Sep 30, no limit of stay, stream water, fishing, hunting. Okanogan NF.

TIFFANY SPRING (6800') 23 mi NW of Conconully on FR 364 then 7½ mi NE on FR 370. 2 tent sites, July 1 to Sep 30, no limit of stay, no water supply, fishing 1 mi, Tiffany Lake Trail. Okanogan NF.

UPPER BEAVER LAKE (3000') 20 mi east from Tonasket on State 20, then 11 mi north on FR 396, then 3½ mi NW on FR 3945. 5 tent sites, 1 trailer space — 16' max, May 1 to Oct 10, no limit of stay. Water sports, fishing, hiking along the lake. Okanogan NF.

WAGON CAMP (3900') 7½ mi west of Conconully on FR 364, then 1½ mi NW on FR 3619. 2 tent sites, July 1 to Sep 30, no limit of stay, stream water, hunting, fishing in Wilder Creek. Okanogan NF.

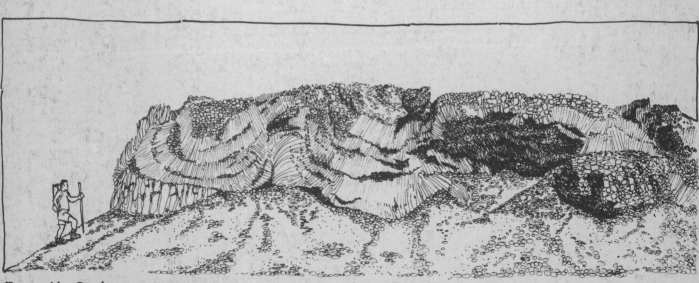

Basalt Outcropping

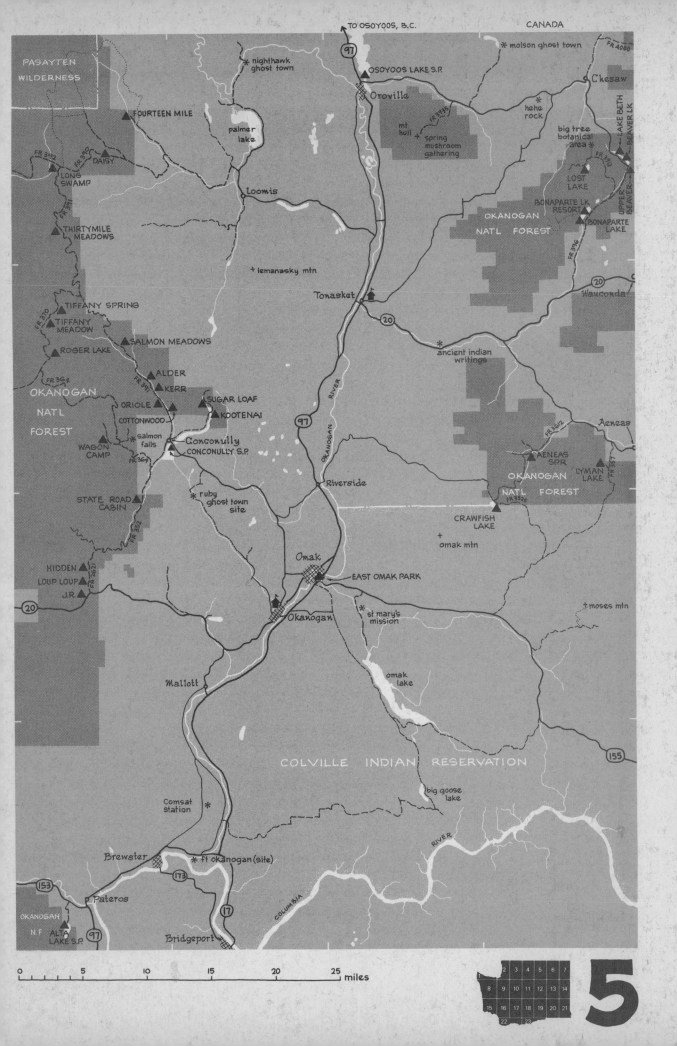

TO OSOYOOS, B.C.   CANADA

PASAYTEN
WILDERNESS

* molson ghost town   FR 4000

* nighthawk ghost town
97   OSOYOOS LAKE S.P.

◣ FOURTEEN MILE   C'hesaw

palmer lake   * heha rock   LAKE BETH — BEAVER LK

mt hull   big tree botanical area *   ◣ BEAVER LK

FR 362   ◣ DAISY
LONG SWAMP   * spring mushroom gathering   LOST LAKE   FR 3212

Loomis   BONAPARTE LK RESORT
◣ THIRTYMILE MEADOWS   OKANOGAN NATL FOREST   ◣ BONAPARTE LAKE

FR 361   UPPER BEAVER —

+ lemanasky mtn   20

Tonasket   Wauconda
◣ TIFFANY SPRING   97
◣ TIFFANY MEADOW   20

◣ ROGER LAKE   * ancient indian writings
FR 370   ◣ SALMON MEADOWS

FR 364   ◣ ALDER
FR 391   ◣ KERR   RIVER   Aeneas
OKANOGAN   ◣ SUGAR LOAF
NATL   ◣ ORIOLE   FR 3612
FOREST   COTTONWOOD   ◣ KOOTENAI   AENEAS SPR
WAGON CAMP   salmon falls   Conconully   OKANOGAN   ◣ LYMAN LAKE
FR 367   CONCONULLY S.P.   NATL FOREST   FR 357

STATE ROAD CABIN   ◣   Riverside   FR 3526
FR 362   * ruby ghost town site   CRAWFISH LAKE

+ omak mtn

HIDDEN ◣
LOUP LOUP ◣   Omak
J.R. ◣   EAST OMAK PARK   + moses mtn
20   Okanogan   * st mary's mission

Mallott   omak lake   155

COLVILLE   INDIAN   RESERVATION

Comsat station *   big goose lake

RIVER

Brewster   * ft okanogan (site)
153   173
Pateros   17
OKANOGAN   COLUMBIA
N F   ALTA LAKE S.P.   97   Bridgeport

0   5   10   15   20   25 ___ miles

5

There is a group of rustic log cabins at **OLD TORODA GHOST TOWN** between Wauconda and Bodie. Take Highway 20 west from Republic to Wauconda then NE on the Bodie Rd. • **COULEE DAM NATL RECREATION AREA** is dominated by 150-mile long Roosevelt Lake, formed by the backwaters of Grand Coulee Dam. By taking a boat trip along the lake, you'll see hoodoos (rocks resting on pillars of soil), landslides, inviting islands, coves and strange geological formations. A booklet, "Boater's Guide to FDR Lake," is available from the park headquarters (see ADDRESSES, page 79). It gives a mile-by-mile description of the features along the way. • **ST PAUL'S MISSION** was originally built in 1845 and constructed with wooden pegs; no nails were used. The restored structure was moved from the flooded reservoir area to higher ground, at Fort Colville, just west of Kettle Falls.

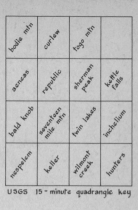

USGS 15-minute quadrangle key

BARNABY ISLAND BOAT CAMP (1300') 16 mi SW of Kettle Falls, accessible by boat only. Docking is best on the west side of the island. 4 campsites in a grove of aspens, open all year, no limit of stay, no drinking water. Sandy beach, boating, swimming, fishing. Coulee Dam NRA.

BRADBURY BEACH (1300') 8 mi south of Kettle Falls on State 25. 5 campsites for tents and RVs, open all year, no limit of stay, no drinking water. Boat ramp and dock, swimming, fishing. Coulee Dam NRA.

CLOVER LEAF (1300') 1 mi south of Gifford on State 25. 8 campsites on a cloverleaf-shaped bay, open all year, no limit of stay. Boating, swimming, fishing. Coulee Dam NRA.

CURLEW LAKE STATE PARK (2400') 8 mi NE of Republic on State 21. 54 tent sites, 18 trailer spaces, fee, hot showers, RV hookups, boat launch. Swimming, fishing, hiking, old ghost towns and mining camps in the area.

DEER CREEK SUMMIT (4600') 11½ mi east of Curlew on County 602. 4 campsites for tents or trailers — 16' max, June 1 to Oct 31, no limit of stay, no water supply. Hunting, berrypicking. Colville NF.

EVANS (1300') 1 mi south of Evans on State 25. 62 campsites for tents and RVs, May 1 to Oct 1, no limit of stay, boat dock, high water launch ramp. Swimming beach with lifeguard, fishing, horseshoe pits. Coulee Dam NRA.

FERRY LAKE (3300') 7 mi south on State 21 from Republic, then 6 mi SW on FR 353, then 1 mi north on 1488. 4 campsites, trailers — 22' max, May 15 to Sep 30, no limit of stay. Boating, launch, fishing. Colville NF.

GIFFORD (1300') 2 mi south of Gifford on State 25. 8 campsites beside the lakeshore, open all year, no limit of stay. Boat ramp and dock, swimming, water skiing, fishing. Ponderosa pines among the campsites are infested with dwarf mistletoe. Coulee Dam NRA.

HAAG COVE (1300') 3 mi west from Kettle Falls on US 395, then 4 mi SW on State 20, then 1½ mi SE on county rd. 12 campsites, open all year, no limit of stay. Boat dock, long sandy beach, swimming, water skiing, fishing. Coulee Dam NRA.

HUNTERS PARK (1300') Just south of Hunters off State 25. 40 campsites, May 1 to Oct 1, no limit of stay, boat ramp and docking facilities. Swimming beach, fishing, sand spit. Coulee Dam NRA.

KAMLOOPS ISLAND (1300') 6 mi NW of Kettle Falls on US 395. 7 campsites, open all year, no limit of stay, no drinking water, small floating dock, fishing. The campsites are located on a hillside overlooking the Kettle R. Coulee Dam NRA.

KETTLE FALLS (1300') 2 mi west of Kettle Falls off US 395. 79 campsites beside the lake in an open stand of ponderosa pine, all year, 14 day limit, disposal station, marina, Park Hdqtrs and info center. Swimming beach with lifeguard, boat dock and ramp, fishing, summer campfire programs. Coulee Dam NRA.

KETTLE RIVER (1300') 9 mi NW of Kettle Falls on US 395. 4 primitive campsites accessible by a path from the hwy, open all year, no limit of stay, no drinking water. Boating, fishing. Coulee Dam NRA.

LAKE ELLEN (2300') 3½ mi west from Kettle Falls on US 395, then 4 mi south on State 20, then 4½ mi south on County 3, then 5½ mi SW. on FR 351. 11 campsites, trailers — 22' max, May 15 to Oct 15, no limit of stay. Fishing, swimming, boat launch. Colville NF.

LONG LAKE (3200') 7 mi south on State 21 from Republic, then 8 mi SW on FR 353, then 1½ mi south on FR 1487. 5 campsites, trailers — 22' max, May 15 to Oct 15, no limit of stay, boat launch 1 mi. Fishing, berrypicking. Colville NF.

MARCUS ISLAND (1300') ½ mi north of Marcus on State 25. 7 campsites for tents and RVs, open all year, no limit of stay, boat ramp and dock. Sandy beach downstream, fishing, chokeberry picking in Aug. Coulee Dam NRA.

NORTH GORGE (1300') 20 mi north of Kettle Falls on State 25. 9 campsites on a rock outcropping overlooking Lk Roosevelt, open all year, no limit of stay, boat ramp, fishing. Watch out for poison ivy. Spawning carp can be seen in the shallow inlet during summer. Coulee Dam NRA.

PIERRE LAKE (2000') 4 mi east on County 818 from Orient, then 3¼ mi north on County 815. 16 campsites, trailers — 32' max, May 1 to Oct 15, 14 day limit, supplies and boat rentals 1 mi, boat launch. Water sports, fishing. Colville NF.

SANPOIL BAY (1300') 2 mi south of Keller on State 21. 15 campsites, open all year, no limit of stay, small beach. Swimming, boating, high water boat ramp and dock, water skiing. Fishing for kokanee, rainbow and brook trout — Indian Reservation license required. Coulee Dam NRA.

SHERMAN CREEK BOAT CAMP (1300') 3 mi west of Kettle Falls, accessible by boat only. 5 primitive campsites, open all year, no drinking water. Boating, good fishing. The remains of an old lumber mill can be seen along the lower end of Sherman Cr. Coulee Dam NRA.

SNAG COVE (1300') 7 mi SE of Barstow on a gravel road. 3 campsites, open all year, no limit of stay. Boat dock, good swimming in the shallow cover, fishing. This is a quiet, peaceful and lightly-used camp. Coulee Dam NRA.

SUMMIT LAKE (3600') 4 mi east on County 818 from Orient then 5 mi north on County 815 then 3 mi north on FR 1206. 5 tent sites, May 15 to Oct 15, no limit of stay. Boat launch, fishing. Colville NF.

SWAN LAKE (3600') 7 mi south from Republic on State 21 then 8 mi west on FR 353. 15 campsites, trailers — 32' max, May 15 to Oct 15, no limit of stay, community kitchen, shelter. Boat ramp, beach, swimming, fishing, berrypicking. Colville NF.

SWEAT CREEK (3500') 9 mi west of Republic on State 20. 6 campsites for tents or trailers — 32' max, June 1 to Sep 30, no limit of stay. Fishing, hunting. Okanogan NF.

TEN MILE (2200') 10 mi south of Republic on State 21. 9 campsites for tents or trailers — 16' max, May 15 to Oct 15, no limit of stay. Fishing in the Sanpoil River. Colville NF.

TROUT LAKE (3000') 3½ mi west from Kettle Falls on US 395, then 5½ mi SW on State 20, then 5 mi NW on FR 360. 5 campsites for tents or trailers — 16' max, June 1 to Oct 15, no limit of stay. Fishing, boat launch. Colville NF.

WEST FORK SANPOIL (2300') 6 mi SE of Aeneas on FR 359. 8 campsites for tents or trailers — 32' max, June 1 to Oct 10, no limit of stay, stream water. Hunting, hiking. Okanogan NF.

WILMONT CREEK BOAT CAMP (1300') 20 mi east of Keller on Roosevelt Lake, accessible by boat only. 4 secluded campsites shaded by pines and firs, open all year, no drinking water. Boating, fishing. Nearby Wilmont Fall spills into a series of pools. Coulee Dam NRA.

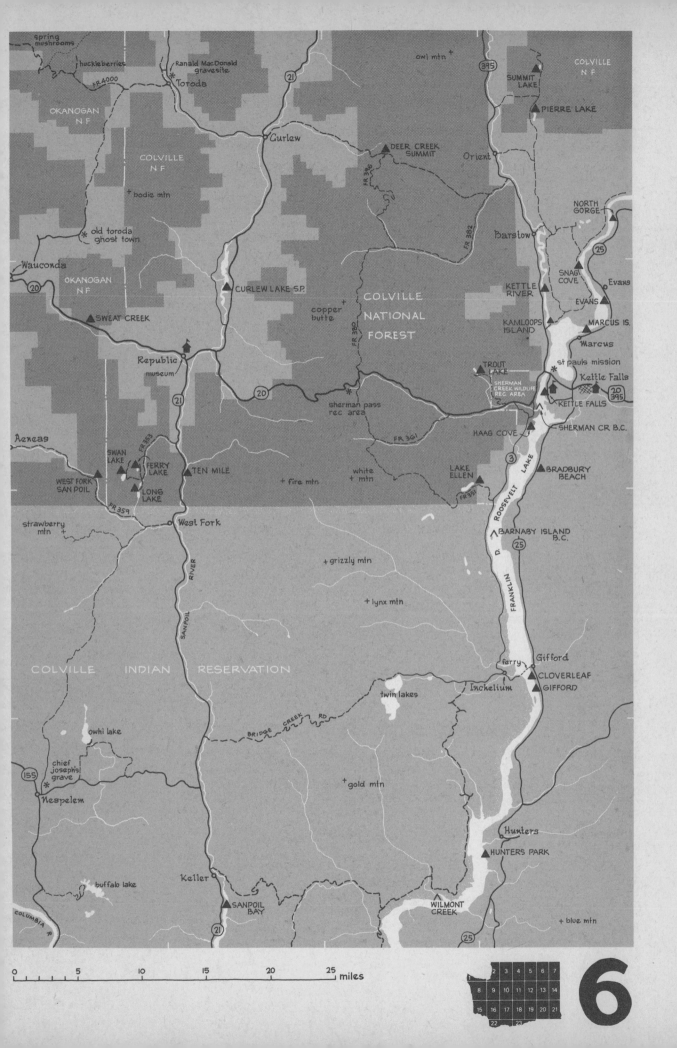

spring
mushrooms
huckleberries
FR 4000
OKANOGAN
N F
COLVILLE
N F
Ranald MacDonald
gravesite
* Toroda
owl mtn +
395
SUMMIT
LAKE
COLVILLE
N F
21
PIERRE LAKE
Curlew
DEER CREEK
SUMMIT
Orient
FR 396
+ bodie mtn
COLVILLE
N F
NORTH
GORGE
* old toroda
ghost town
Barstow
25
FR 382
Wauconda
20
OKANOGAN
N F
SWEAT CREEK
CURLEW LAKE S.P.
copper
butte +
COLVILLE
NATIONAL
FOREST
KETTLE
RIVER
SNAG
COVE
Evans
EVANS
KAMLOOPS
ISLAND
MARCUS IS.
Marcus
Republic
museum
FR 380
TROUT
LAKE
st pauls mission
*
SHERMAN
CREEK
WILDLIFE
REC. AREA
Kettle Falls
KETTLE FALLS
20
395
21
20
sherman pass
rec area
*
FR 361
SHERMAN CR B.C.
Aeneas
FR 353
HAAG COVE
SWAN
LAKE
FERRY
LAKE
TEN MILE
white
+ mtn
LAKE
ELLEN
3
BRADBURY
BEACH
WEST FORK
SAN POIL
+ fire mtn
LONG
LAKE
FR 351
strawberry
mtn +
FR 359
West Fork
BARNABY ISLAND
B.C.
25
SAN POIL
RIVER
+ grizzly mtn
FRANKLIN
D.
ROOSEVELT
LAKE
+ lynx mtn
COLVILLE   INDIAN   RESERVATION
owhi lake
ferry
Gifford
CLOVERLEAF
GIFFORD
chief
joseph's
grave
BRIDGE
CREEK
RD
twin lakes
Inchelium
155
*
Nespelem
+ gold mtn
buffalo lake
Keller
Hunters
HUNTERS PARK
SANPOIL
BAY
21
WILMONT
CREEK
25
+ blue mtn
COLUMBIA R

0   5   10   15   20   25   miles

2	3	4	5	6	7
8	9	10	11	12	13	14
15	16	17	18	19	20	21
22	23

6

7

MANRESA INDIAN ROCK CAVES are about 5 miles north of Usk on the Kalispel Indian Reservation. These caves have been the site of Indian religious meetings since 1844. The priest has a church now, but mass is still said in the caves, occasionally. ("There are seats, made out of stone, in them for the people to sit on. I was raised here and used to go to church in the caves when I was a little girl. They are really quite interesting." — Jane Landry, local resident.) • The largest limestone cavern in the state is GARDNER CAVE at Crawford Caves State Park, 13 miles north of Metaline Falls. Underground erosion has created some excellent stalagmites, stalactites, columns and rimstone pools. The cave is 1,050 feet long, safe, well lighted and quite impressive. • PEEWEE FALLS is not so peewee at all. It spills over limestone cliffs into Boundary Reservoir, just south of the Canadian border off State 31. • ROOSEVELT GROVE OF ANCIENT CEDARS, near the Idaho border, offers a quiet, relaxing place for recreational, inspirational, botanical and scientific uses. It's a 137-acre area of 800-year-old Western redcedar.

USGS 15-minute quadrangle key

BLUESLIDE RESORT (2100') 37 mi north of Newport on State 20 at Blueslide. 40 campsites, fee, all year, no limit of stay, reservations accepted, hot showers, all hookups, supplies, free bikes and games. Fishing, boat rentals, ramp, swimming, water skiing, bicycle trails, hiking, hunting, rockhounding. Located in the Selkirk Mtns overlooking the Pend Oreille R. Rt 2, Box 35, Usk 99180. Privately owned.

BROWNS LAKE (3400') 6½ mi NE on FR 305 from Usk then 3 mi north on FR 309. 16 campsites, trailers — 22' max, June 1 to Sep 15, 14 day limit, lake water, boat launch. Water skiing, fishing, berrypicking. Kaniksu NF.

BUSHBY'S RESORT (2450') 9 mi SW of Newport on US 2 at Diamond Lake. 10 tent sites, 10 trailer spaces — 30' max, fee, Apr 1 to Oct 30, no limit of stay, reservations accepted, store, lunch counter, hookups, hot showers. Fishing, boat rentals, swimming, water skiing. Rt 3, Box 54, Newport 99156. Privately owned.

CARNEY'S BLACK LAKE RESORT (3700') 12½ mi east on State 20 from Colville then 1½ mi north on County 633. 16 campsites, trailers — 28' max, fee, hot showers. Fishing for Eastern brook trout, canoeing, barge and boat rentals, swimming, hiking, hunting, snowmobile trails. Box 37, Tiger Star Rt, Colville 99114. Privately owned.

CIRCLE MOON (2200') 14 mi SW on US 195 from Newport then 4 mi north on State 311. 100 tent sites, 50 trailer spaces — 60' max, fee, groups, all year, no limit of stay, reservations accepted, store, RV hookups, disposal station, restaurant, hot showers. Fishing, water sports, bicycle and hiking trails, riding and horse stabling facilities, ice-skating, winter skiing, snowmobile races and trails. Rt 3, Newport 99156. Privately owned.

CRESCENT LAKE (2600') 11 mi north of Metaline Falls on State 31. 13 campsites, trailers — 32' max, June 1 to Sep 15, 14 day limit, Visitor Center. Boat launch and water sports 1 mi, fishing, trail to Boundary Dam Viewpoint. Colville NF.

GILLETTE RECREATION AREA (3200') 11 mi SW on State 20 from Tiger then ½ mi east on County 647. 40 campsites, trailers — 21' max, June 1 to Sep 15, 14 day limit, supplies and boat rentals 2 mi, boat launch. Swimming, water skiing, fishing, bicycle trails. Colville NF.

IONE (2100') 1 mi south on State 31 from Ione then ½ mi east on County 303. 23 campsites for tents or trailers — 24' max, May 15 to Oct 15, 14 day limit. Box Canyon Reservoir, boat launch, swimming beach, water skiing, fishing, berrypicking. Colville NF.

JUMP-OFF-JOE LAKE RESORT (2000') 10 mi south from Chewelah on US 395 then 1 mi west on Jump-Off Rd. 9 tent sites, 21 trailer spaces, fee, Apr 20 to Oct 31, no limit of stay, reservations accepted, store, snack bar, hot showers, RV hookups. Fishing, boat launch, swimming. Heavily-wooded area. Rt 2, Valley 99181. Privately owned.

LAKE LEO (3200') 7 mi SW of Tiger on State 20. 8 campsites for tents or trailers — 18' max, June 1 to Sep 30, 14 day limit, supplies and boat rentals 2 mi. Boat launch, swimming, water skiing, fishing, hunting, hiking trails. Colville NF.

LAKE THOMAS (3200') 10½ mi SW on State 20 from Tiger then 1 mi NE on County 647. 15 tent sites, June 1 to Sep 15, 14 day limit, supplies and boat rentals 4 mi. Swimming, water skiing, fishing, hiking, hunting. Pine and cedars. Colville NF.

LAKE THOMAS RESORT (3500') 10 mi SW on State 20 from Tiger. 12 campsites for tents or trailers — 25' max, fee, all year, no limit of stay, reservations accepted, supplies 1½ mi, disposal station, RV hookups, hot showers, playground. Boat rentals, fishing, swimming, water skiing, riding and hiking trails, bicycling, hunting. Tiger Star Rt, Colville 99114. Privately owned.

LITTLE TWIN LAKES (3800') 12½ mi east on State 20 from Colville then 1½ mi north on County 633 then 4½ mi north on FR 617. 4 campsites, trailers — 16' max, May 1 to Oct 31, no limit of stay, supplies 2 mi, boat rentals 1 mi, boat launch. Fishing. Colville NF.

MARSHALL LAKE RESORT (2600') Cross the Pend Oreille River at Newport, then 2½ mi NW on County 1019, then 5 mi north on FR 320, then 1¼ mi north on FR 1071. 35 campsites for tents or trailers — 35' max, fee, Apr 15 to Oct 31, no limit of stay, reservations accepted, RV hookups, hot showers. Water sports, canoe rentals, bicycle and hiking trails, stand of virgin cedar, Lucky Joe Mines 1½ mi. Rt 4, Box 55A, Newport 99156. Privately owned.

MILLPOND (2400') 3½ mi east of Metaline Falls on County 302. 11 campsites for tents or trailers — 22' max, June 1 to Sep 15, 14 day limit. Boating, fishing. Colville NF.

NOISY CREEK (2600') 9 mi NE of Ione on County 303. 19 campsites, trailers — 32' max, June 1 to Sep 15, 14 day limit, supplies 5 mi, boat launch. Swimming, water skiing, sailing, fishing, Sullivan Lake Trail along the east shore. Colville NF.

PANHANDLE (2050') ½ mi east on County 91 from Usk then 16¼ mi north on County 7. 11 campsites, trailers — 22' max, June 1 to Sep 15, 14 day limit, boat launch. Beach, water skiing, fishing. Kaniksu NF.

PEND OREILLE STATE PARK (2200') 15 mi SW of Newport off US 195. 36 campsites for tents and trailers, fee, Apr 1 to Sep 30, 7 day limit, supplies 5 mi, hot showers. Fishing and water sports 5 mi, riding and hiking trails, wildlife reserve, deer and bear. Pine, fir and cedar. Rt 3, Box 102, Newport 99156.

PIONEER PARK (2050') ½ mi NE on US 2 from Newport to the east end of Pend Oreille River Bridge, then 2 mi north on County 7. 14 campsites, trailers — 22' max, June 1 to Sep 15, 14 day limit. Boating, water skiing, fishing, Box Canyon Reservoir. Kaniksu NF.

SKOOKUM CHINOOK (4000') 8 mi NE of Usk on FR 305. 25 campsites for tents or trailers — 35' max, fee, May 1 to Oct 31, no limit of stay, reservations accepted, hot showers. Fishing, water sports, boat rentals, hiking and bicycle trails, fire lookout nearby, Indian Caves 8 mi. "Naturealm" used primarily by local people, year round, for fishing, camping and snowmobiling. Rt 4, Box 55A, Newport 99156. Private development.

SOUTH SKOOKUM LAKE (3600') 7½ mi NE of Usk on FR 305. 14 campsites, trailers — 22' max, June 1 to Sep 15, 14 day limit, lake water. Boat launch, water skiing, fishing, berrypicking. Kaniksu NF.

STAGGER INN (3200') 1½ mi east on State 31 from Metaline Falls then east on County 302. 4 tent sites, June 1 to Aug 31, stream water. Fishing, berrypicking, Roosevelt Grove of Ancient Cedars ½ mi north. Kaniksu NF.

STYMANS RESORT (2400') 17 mi south on US 395 from Chewelah then 2 mi east. 10 tent sites, 44 trailer spaces — 40' max, fee, Apr 15 to Nov 1, no limit of stay, reservations accepted, RV hookups, disposal station, supplies, laundry, hot showers. Fishing, water sports, boat rentals, hunting. Rt 1, Box 68, Deer Lake 99148. Privately owned.

SULLIVAN LAKE (2600') 5 mi east of Metaline Falls on County 302. 15 campsites for tents or trailers — 32' max, June 1 to Sep 15, 14 day limit, supplies 2 mi. Boat launch and swimming 1 mi, water skiing, sailing, fishing. Colville NF, Metaline Falls 99153.

SULLIVAN LAKE GROUP CAMP (2600') 5 mi east of Metaline Falls on County 302. 8 group campsites, reservations required in advance, trailers — 32' max, lake water, supplies and boat launch 1 mi. Water sports, sailing, fishing, Sullivan Lake Trail along the east shore. Metaline Falls 99153. Colville NF.

SULLIVAN ROAD 1 (2700') 5½ mi east of Metaline Falls on County 302. 2 campsites, trailers — 22' max, June 1 to Sep 15, 14 day limit, stream water, supplies and boating facilities 2 mi. Fishing. Colville NF.

SULLIVAN ROAD 2 (2700') 7 mi east of Metaline Falls on County 302. 2 campsites, trailers — 22' max, June 1 to Sep 15, 14 day limit, stream water, supplies and water sports 3 mi. Fishing. Colville NF.

TAYLOR'S WAITTS LAKE RESORT (1900') 6 mi south from Chewelah on US 395 then 4 mi west on State 232. 33 campsites for tents and trailers — 40' max, fee, group facilities, Apr to Nov, no limit of stay, reservations accepted, supplies 3 mi, all hookups, cafe. Fishing, boating, boat and motor rentals, launch, swimming, water skiing. Rt 1, Box 50, Valley 99181. Privately owned.

TWIN LAKES (3800') 12½ mi east on State 20 from Colville then 1½ mi north on County 633 then 4½ mi north on FR 617. 8 campsites, trailers — 16' max, May 1 to Oct 31, no limit of stay, supplies and boat rentals 2 mi, water sports, fishing. Colville NF.

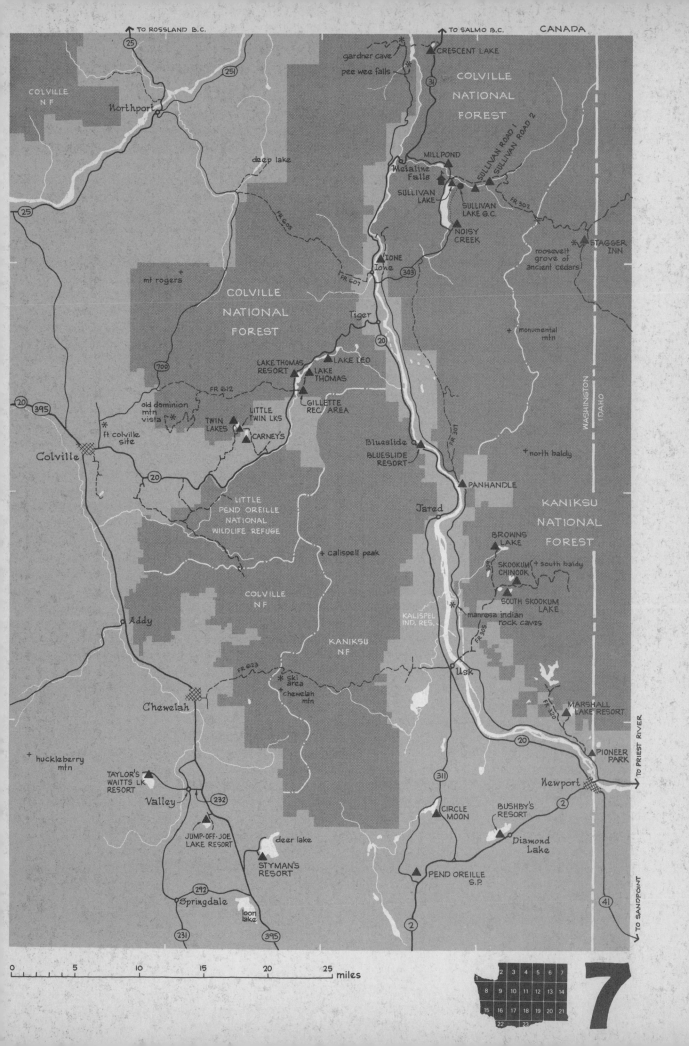

↑ TO ROSSLAND B.C.

25

251

↑ TO SALMO B.C.

* CRESCENT LAKE ▲

gardner cave *
pee wee falls *

31

COLVILLE
NATIONAL
FOREST

COLVILLE
N F

Northport

SULLIVAN ROAD 1
SULLIVAN ROAD 2

MILLPOND ▲

deep lake

Metaline
Falls

SULLIVAN
LAKE

SULLIVAN LAKE G.C.

FR 302

25

FR 605

NOISY
CREEK

* STAGGER
INN

roosevelt
grove of
ancient cedars

20

395

mt rogers +

COLVILLE

NATIONAL

FOREST

FR 607

IONE
Ione

303

Tiger

monumental
mtn +

20

700

LAKE THOMAS
RESORT ▲

LAKE LEO

LAKE
THOMAS

FR 612

old dominion
mtn vista *

* ft colville
site

TWIN
LAKES ▲

LITTLE
TWIN LKS

GILLETTE
REC AREA

CARNEY'S ▲

Blueslide ▲

BLUESLIDE
RESORT

FR 307

north baldy +

WASHINGTON IDAHO

20

Colville

20

LITTLE
PEND OREILLE
NATIONAL
WILDLIFE REFUGE

PANHANDLE ▲

Jared

KANIKSU

NATIONAL

FOREST

calispell peak +

BROWNS
LAKE ▲

SKOOKUM
CHINOOK

south baldy +

COLVILLE
NF

Addy

SOUTH SKOOKUM
LAKE

KALISPEL
IND. RES.

* manresa indian
rock caves

KANIKSU
NF

FR 623

FR 305

Usk

FR 320

MARSHALL
LAKE RESORT ▲

TO PRIEST RIVER →

* ski area
* chewelah
mtn

20

PIONEER
PARK

Chewelah

huckleberry +
mtn

TAYLOR'S
WAITTS LK
RESORT ▲

311

CIRCLE
MOON ▲

BUSHBY'S
RESORT ▲

2

Newport

41

Valley

232

JUMP-OFF-JOE
LAKE RESORT ▲

deer lake

Diamond
Lake

STYMAN'S
RESORT ▲

PEND OREILLE
S.P. ▲

292

Springdale

loon
lake

231

395

2

↓ TO SANDPOINT

0   5   10   15   20   25   miles

7

Peewee Falls

RAIN FORESTS are the most unique natural features of Olympic Natl Park. The most notable is the Hoh Rain Forest, 33 miles SE of Forks. Nature trails, behind the Visitor Center, guide you through the damp valley floor under moss-draped trees, and interpretive signs give an explanation of the lush environment. Other major rain forests are located at Quinault Lake and on the Queets River. • Look through the telescopes at **HURRICANE RIDGE** for close up views of glaciers and mountain goats on Mt Olympus and its neighbors. The lodge sells Indian crafts, and there are several hiking trails to the upper ridges. • At **OLYMPIC HOT SPRINGS**, 21 miles SW of Port Angeles, you'll find the remains of an old resort and mineral springs in a scenic canyon below Boulder Creek Campground. The springs are being returned to their natural state, and a nature trail will be completed soon.

BOGACHIEL STATE PARK (200') 6 mi south of Forks on US 101. 44 campsites, fee, supplies, hot showers, fishing, swimming, hiking trails, rain forest environment.

BOULDER CREEK (2200') 9 mi west on US 101 from Port Angeles (see Map 1) then 12 mi SW along Elwha River. 50 campsites for tents and camp trailers — 15' max, June to Sep, 14 day limit, fishing, trails to Boulder Lake (3½ mi), Appleton Pass (5¼ mi), and Solduc Hot Sprs (14½ mi). The campsites are located high on the mountain above Boulder Creek. Below the camp are the ruins of old Olympic Hot Springs Resort. Olympic NP.

BROWN CREEK (600') 7½ mi north on US 101 from Shelton then 12 mi NW on County 242 and FR 226 then ½ mi east on FR 2286. 10 tent sites, 6 trailer spaces — 22' max, May 25 to Nov 25, 14 day limit. Fishing, hunting, berrypicking, Skykomish River trailhead 1 mi NE. Olympic NF.

CAMPBELL TREE GROVE (1100') 4 mi NE on US 101 from Humptulips then 22 mi NE on FR 2302. 5 tent sites, 15 trailer spaces — 22' max, June 1 to Nov 20, no limit of stay. Fishing in W Fork Humptulips River, hunting, hiking, berrypicking. Olympic NF.

DEER PARK (5400') 3½ mi east on US 101 from Port Angeles (see Map 1) then 18 mi south on winding Deer Park Rd. 10 tent sites in a pleasant alpine environment, no trailers, June to Sep, 14 day limit. Trails lead to the park interior, views of Strait of Juan de Fuca from the top of Blue Mtn, alpine wildflowers, meadows. Olympic NP.

DOSEWALLIPS (1640') 1 mi north on US 101 from Brinnon then 15½ mi NW on FR 261. Steep, narrow road not suitable for trailers. 33 tent sites, May to Sep, 14 day limit, Ranger Sta. Fishing in the Dosewallips River, trailheads to the park interior. Olympic NP.

DRIFTWOOD ACRES (sea level) ¼ mi north of Copalis Beach on State 109. 170 campsites for tents and trailers — 35' max, fee, group camping, Mar 1 to Sep 15, no limit of stay, reservations accepted, RV hookups, hot showers, clam cleaning facilities, community kitchen. Surf fishing ½ mi, swimming, hunting for geese and doves, razor clamming, beachcombing, rockhounding, caves. Box 216, Copalis Beach 98535. Privately owned.

DUNGENESS FORKS (100') 4 mi SE on US 101 from Sequim (see Map 1) then 7½ mi south on Camp Colonel Rd and FR 2958. 9 tent sites, Apr 1 to Nov 1, no limit of stay, community kitchen, fishing, hunting, hiking. Olympic NF.

EAST CROSSING (1200') 3 mi SE on US 101 from Sequim (see Map 1), then 7½ mi south on County 30, then 3 mi south on FR 295. 7 tent sites, Apr 1 to Nov 1, 14 day limit, stream water. Fishing, hunting. Olympic NF.

ELKHORN (600') 1 mi north on US 101 from Brinnon then 10 mi west on FR 261. 18 campsites for tents or trailers — 22' max, May 15 to Nov 20, no limit of stay. Fishing in the Dosewallips R, hunting, mtn climbing, Lake Constance trailhead 2 mi west. Olympic NF.

FALLS CREEK (200') ¼ mi NE of Quinault on the shore of Quinault Lake. 24 campsites for tents and RVs — 16' max, Apr 1 to Nov 15, 14 day limit, community kitchen, boat launch. Fishing, swimming, Big Tree Grove Nature Trail, Quinault Loop Trail, fish ladder, rain forest environment. Olympic NF.

GRAVES CREEK (550') 16½ mi NE of Quinault on narrow Quinault River Valley Rd. 45 campsites for tents and small trailers — 15' max, open all year, 14 day limit, Ranger Sta. Fishing, trailhead 3 mi at the end of the road. Olympic NP.

HAMMA HAMMA (600') 1½ mi north on US 101 from Eldon then 6½ mi west on FR 249. 13 campsites for tents and RVs — 22' max, May 1 to Nov 20. Fishing in Hamma Hamma R, hunting, mtn climbing, Lena Lake trailhead 2½ mi west. Olympic NF.

HARLEY'S RESORT (10') At La Push. 80 tent sites, 90 trailer spaces, fee, group camping, Apr 15 to Sep 30, no limit of stay, no reservations, RV hookups, disposal station, hot showers, laundry, restaurant. Fishing, motor boat rentals, salmon charters, swimming, bicycle and hiking trails, caves, clamming. Box 68, La Push 98350. Privately owned.

HOH (578') 14 mi south on US 101 from Forks then 19 mi east on Hoh River Rd. 95 campsites for tents and RVs — 21' max, all year, 14 day limit, Visitor Center. Hoh Rain Forest, summer campfire programs, guided walks, 2 nature trails, Hoh River Trail leads to Mt Olympus, river running on Hoh R, fishing, wildflowers, Roosevelt elk sometimes seen in the area. Olympic NP.

JULY CREEK (200') 2 mi NW on US 101 from Amanda Park then 4 mi NE on the northern shore of Quinault Lake. 31 walk-in campsites, no trailers, open all year, 14 day limit. Fishing. Olympic NP.

KALALOCH (sea level) ½ mi north of Kalaloch on US 101. 195 campsites for tents and RVs, some sites face the ocean, open all year, 14 day limit, lodge and store ½ mi, disposal station. Campfire circle, guided tidepool and forest walks during the summer, ocean fishing, swimming, razor clamming, whales sometimes seen off-shore. Heavily-used camp due to the coastal environment. Olympic NP.

KLAHANIE (300') 2 mi NW on US 101 from Forks then 5½ mi east on FR 300. 9 tent sites, 1 trailer space — 22' max, Apr 1 to Oct 31, 14 day limit. Fishing, hunting, berrypicking. Olympic NF.

LAKE CUSHMAN STATE PARK (750') 7 mi NW of Hoodsport. 50 tent sites, 30 trailer spaces, RV hookups, hot showers, swimming, boating, launch, boat rentals nearby, lake and stream fishing, Douglas fir forest.

LAKE NAHWATZEL RESORT (600') 12½ mi west of Shelton on Matlock Rd. 20 tent sites, 35 trailer spaces, fee, reservations accepted, RV hookups, cafe, store. Fishing, rowboat rentals, ramp, swimming, water skiing, hunting. Rt 10, Box 275, Shelton 98584. Privately owned.

LENA CREEK (700') 1½ mi north on US 101 from Eldon then 9 mi west on FR 249. 7 tent sites, 7 trailer spaces — 22' max, Mar 1 to Nov 20, no limit of stay. Fishing, hunting, mtn climbing, Lena Lake Trail ½ mi east. Olympic NF.

LILLIWAUP CREEK (1000') 10 mi NW on county rd from Hoodsport then 2 mi east on FR 245 (Cushman-Jorstad Rd). Several campsites for tents and RVs. Lake Cushman 4 mi. Dept of Natural Resources.

MORA (sea level) 2 mi north on US 101 from Forks then 13 mi west. 91 campsites for tents and trailers — 21' max, dense forest, open all year. Campfire circle, guided walks, swimming and ocean fishing at Rialto Beach 2 mi. Olympic NP.

NORTH FORK QUINAULT (520') 2 mi NW on US 101 from Amanda Park then 18 mi NE. 10 tent sites in a secluded area, not suitable for trailers, May to Sep, no limit of stay, Ranger Sta. Fishing, trailhead to Paradise and Queets Rain Forest. A trail ½ mi at the end of the road leads to the interior of the park. Olympic NP.

OCEAN CITY STATE PARK (sea level) 3 mi SE of Ocean City. 151 tent sites and 29 trailer spaces in scrub trees, fee, hot showers, RV hookups. Surf fishing, swimming, beachcombing, surfing, clamming, plenty of rolling sand dunes, wild strawberries.

(Continued on following page)

OLALLIE (200') 1 mi SW of Quinault on the shore of Quinault Lake. 14 tent sites, May 15 to Sep 15, 14 day limit, community kitchen, boat launch ½ mi. Fishing, swimming, Quinault Lake Loop Trail just north of the camp, lush rain forest environment. Olympic NF.

POTLATCH STATE PARK (10') 18 mi north of Shelton on US 101. 15 tent sites, 18 trailer spaces, fee, RV hookups, disposal station, hot showers. Hiking, swimming, salmon fishing, clamming, maple trees.

QUEETS RIVER (290') 8 mi SE on US 101 from Queets then 15 mi NE on Queets River Rd. 12 campsites, not suitable for trailers, all year, 14 day limit, stream water. Fishing, Queets Campground Loop Trail, elk in the area, Queets Rain Forest. You'll have to ford the river to reach the interior of the park by trail. Olympic NP.

RAIN FOREST RESORT (200') At Lake Quinault, 3½ mi NW of US 101. 44 tent sites, 31 trailer spaces, fee, open all year, no limit of stay, reservations accepted for weekly or monthly stay, RV hookups, supplies, laundry, restaurant, hot showers. Fishing, boat rentals, swimming, water skiing, bicycle and hiking trails, waterfalls, Big Trees, rain forest environment. Quinault Lake 98575. Privately owned.

SCHAFER STATE PARK (60') 5 mi west on US 12 from Elma to Satsop then 8 mi north. 44 tent sites, 6 trailer spaces, fee, hot showers. Swimming, fishing, dense woods.

SLAB (2600') 3½ mi west on US 101 from Sequim (see Map 1), then 8 mi south on County 30, then 3½ mi SW on FR 2926. 6 tent sites, Apr 15 to Nov 1, no limit of stay, hunting. Gray Wolf Trail just south of the camp leads to Olympic NP and trail shelters. Olympic NF.

SOLEDUCK (1680') 30 mi west on US 101 from Port Angeles (see Map 1) then 12 mi south on Soleduck River Valley Rd. 84 campsites for tents and RVs, May to Oct, 14 day limit, restaurant and supplies ½ mi. Fishing, swimming, summer naturalist programs, guided walks, campfire circle, Soleduck Falls 2½ mi, several trails lead to the park backcountry, spawning salmon in late summer and early fall. Olympic NP.

STAIRCASE (1000') 12 mi NW on county rd from Hoodsport then 6 mi west on FR 245. 50 campsites for tents and trailers — 15' max, May to Sep, 14 day limit, Ranger Sta. Fishing, trail to Staircase Rapids. Olympic NP.

STEELHEAD (600') 1 mi north on US 101 from Brinnon then 8½ mi west on FR 261. 7 tent sites, Mar 15 to Nov 20, no limit of stay. Fishing in Dosewallips R, hunting, Tunnel Creek Trail. Olympic NF.

WILLABY (200') ½ mi SW of Quinault on the shore of Quinault Lake. 12 tent sites, 7 trailer spaces — 22' max, May 15 to Oct 15, 14 day limit. Fishing, swimming, boat launch, water skiing, Quinault Loop Trail, rain forest environment. Olympic NF.

WYNOOCHEE FALLS (1000') 18½ mi north on Wynoochee River Rd (County 141) from Montesano (see Map 15) then 26½ mi north on FR 220 then 10 mi NE on FR 2312. 9 tent sites, June 1 to Nov 25, 14 day limit. Fishing, hunting, hiking, berrypicking, Wynoochee Falls. Beware to dam construction vehicles and logging trucks. Olympic NF.

WYNOOCHEE RIVERSIDE PARK (50') 8 mi north of Montesano (see Map 15) on Wynoochee River Rd. 30 large, grassy campsites for tents or trailers — 24' max, fee, group camping, May to Oct, no limit of stay, reservations accepted. Fishing, drifting on the river, swimming, hiking trails. Rt 1, Box 1455, Montesano 98563. Privately owned.

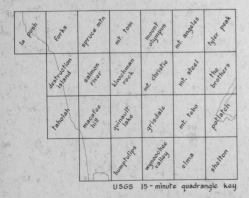

USGS 15-minute quadrangle key

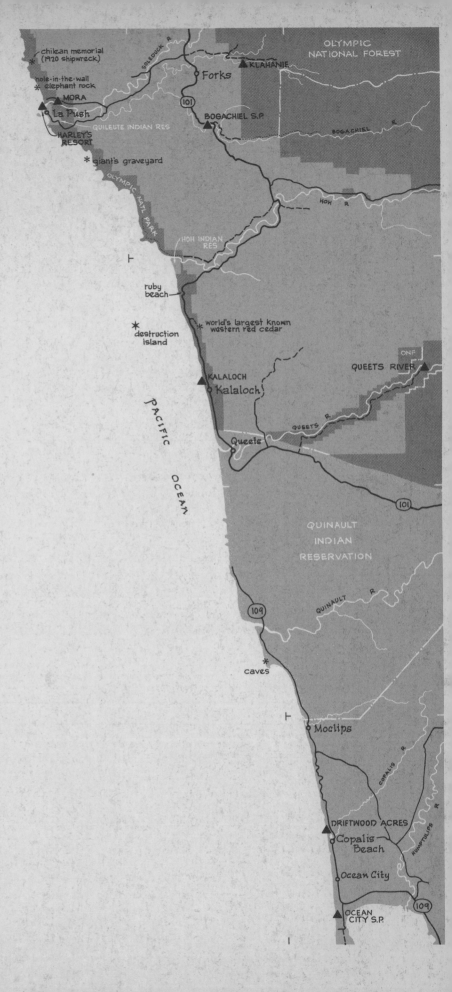

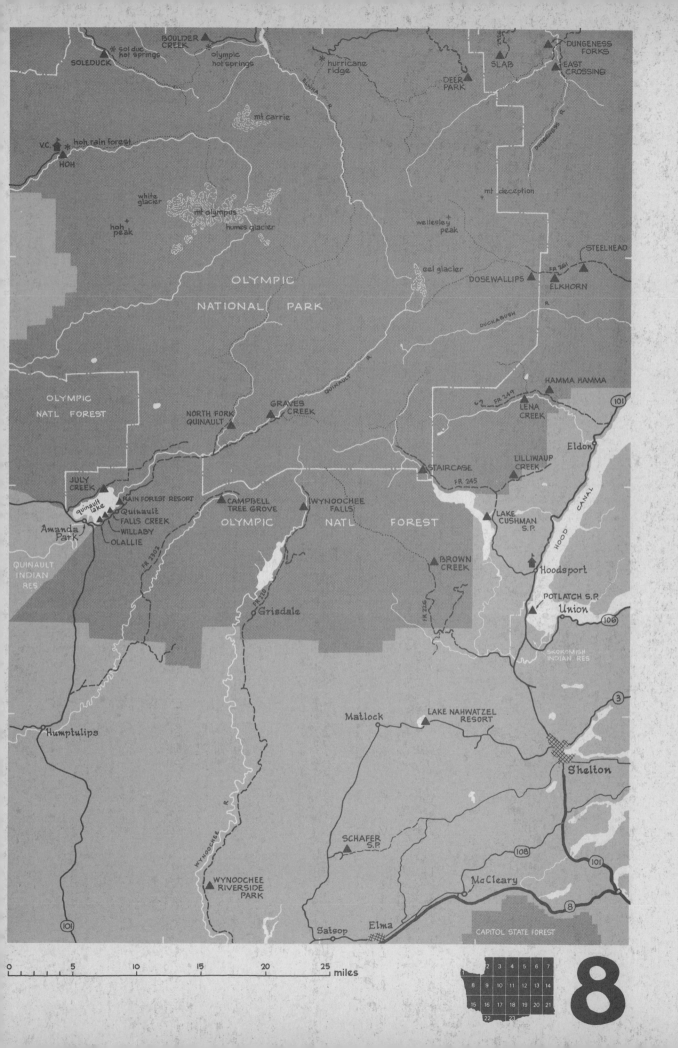

SOLEDUCK

* sol duc
hot springs

BOULDER
CREEK

* olympic
hot springs

* hurricane
ridge

SLAB

DUNGENESS
FORKS

EAST
CROSSING

DEER
PARK

mt carrie

V.C. * hoh rain forest

HOH

mt deception

white glacier

mt olympus

hoh +
peak

humes glacier

wellesley +
peak

STEELHEAD

eel glacier

DOSEWALLIPS

FR 261

ELKHORN

OLYMPIC

NATIONAL PARK

DUCKABUSH R.

R.

QUINAULT R.

HAMMA HAMMA

OLYMPIC

NATL FOREST

NORTH FORK
QUINAULT

GRAVES
CREEK

FR 249

LENA
CREEK

101

Eldon

STAIRCASE

LILLIWAUP
CREEK

JULY
CREEK

quinault lake

RAIN FOREST RESORT

Quinault

FALLS CREEK

WILLABY

OLALLIE

Amanda
Park

QUINAULT
INDIAN
RES.

FR 2207

CAMPBELL
TREE GROVE

OLYMPIC

WYNOOCHEE
FALLS

NATL

FR 245

FOREST

FR 2204

Grisdale

BROWN
CREEK

LAKE
CUSHMAN
S.P.

Hoodsport

POTLATCH S.P.

Union

HOOD CANAL

106

SKOKOMISH
INDIAN RES

Humptulips

WYNOOCHEE R.

Matlock

LAKE NAHWATZEL
RESORT

3

Shelton

WYNOOCHEE
RIVERSIDE
PARK

SCHAFER
S.P.

108

McCleary

101

8

101

Satsop

Elma

CAPITOL STATE FOREST

0   5   10   15   20   25   miles

CAMP SIX LOGGING EXHIBIT, at Ft Defiance Park in Tacoma, is an elaborate reconstruction of an authenic logging camp. All of the railway equipment was actually used by loggers. You can take a 15-minute ride on a SHAY #7 that operates on Saturdays, Sundays and holidays from Memorial Day to Labor Day weekend. • Anyone passing through Seattle should definitely stop off at the SPACE NEEDLE. From the top, there's a magnificent view of Washington's great recreational areas: Mt Rainier, the Cascades, Olympic Natl Park and Puget Sound. • OLD MAN HOUSE, ½ mile SW of Suquamish, was once the home of Chief Sealth. A small section of the long house has been reconstructed to give you an idea of what it was like. • If you're in need of FERRY SERVICE to Puget Sound's islands, or for a pleasure cruise, write for information about schedules and routes to Washington State Ferries, Seattle Ferry Terminal (Pier 52), Seattle 98104.

BELFAIR STATE PARK (10') 3 mi west of Belfair on State 300. 147 tent sites, 47 trailer spaces, fee, hot showers. Warm pleasant swimming, fishing, clamming.

BIG QUILCENE (1400') 2 mi SW on US 101 from Quilcene then 4½ mi south on County 78 and FR 2812. 3 tent sites, May to Nov 1, no limit of stay, no water supply. Fishing 1 mi, hunting, hiking. Olympic NF.

BLAKE ISLAND STATE PARK (sea level) This is a marine island accessible only by private boat, 5 mi west of Seattle. 30 tent sites, fee, all year, 7 day limit. Salmon barbeque in summer, fishing, sailing, canoeing, motor-boating, swimming — no lifeguards, water skiing, hiking trails, clamming, deer. PO Box 287, Manchester 98353.

COLLINS (200') 2 mi south on US 101 from Brinnon then 5 mi west on FR 2515. 6 tent sites, 5 trailer spaces — 16' max, Mar 1 to Nov 20, no limit of stay. Fishing in the Duckabush River, hunting, trail 1½ mi west leads to Olympic NP. Olympic NF.

DASH POINT STATE PARK (10') 5 mi NE of Tacoma on State 509. 110 tent sites, 28 trailer spaces, fee. Swimming, surf fishing, clamming, hiking in a pleasant forest area.

DOSEWALLIPS STATE PARK (10') At Brinnon on US 101. 150 campsites for tents or trailers — 30' max, fee, all year, 7 day limit, all hookups, supplies ¼ mi north, hot showers. Fishing, boating, water skiing, hiking. Primary attraction is — cockels, oysters, clams, sea cucumbers, shrimp and crab. Not much shade on the west side of the hwy, a few grassy, shaded sites along the Canal. PO Box 97, Brinnon 98320.

FALLS VIEW (500') 3½ mi SW of Quilcene on US 101. 24 campsites for tents and trailers — 32' max, Apr 1 to Dec 31, no limit of stay. Rhododendrons in June, salt water activities 5 mi at Quilcene Bay. From a viewpoint at the camp you can see a waterfall spilling into Big Quilcene River. Olympic NF.

FAY-BAINBRIDGE STATE PARK (50') On the NE end of Bainbridge Island, accessible by ferry from Seattle. 10 tent sites, 28 trailer spaces — 30' max, fee, open all year, 7 day limit, supplies 6 mi, hot showers, playground, kitchen and shelters. Salt water fishing, boating, ramp, swimming, water skiing, nature trail, clamming, crabs. Ft Ward SP, at the south end of the island, is the remains of a World War II fort. Rt 7, Box 7635, Bainbridge Island 98110.

ILLAHEE STATE PARK (sea level) 1 mi north from Bremerton on State 303 then 1½ mi east on Sylvan Way. 25 campsites for tents or trailers — 32' max, group facilities — contact ranger in advance, open all year, 7 day limit, hot showers, supplies 2 mi, playground. Fishing, boat ramp, unguarded swimming, water skiing, hiking, clamming, coastal forest. Rt 5, Box 365, Bremerton 98310.

JARRELL COVE STATE PARK (10') On the north end of Hartstene Island off State 3. A car ferry takes you to the island. 10 tent sites, fee, boat mooring facilities, swimming, fishing, clamming.

KITSAP MEMORIAL STATE PARK (60') 4 mi south of the Hood Canal Floating Bridge on Hood Canal. 25 tent sites, 18 trailer spaces, fee, kitchen shelters, hot showers. Swimming, fishing, clamming.

KOPACHUCK STATE PARK (400') 5 mi west of Gig Harbor. 41 campsites for tents or trailers — 40' max, fee, open all year, 7 day limit, hot showers. Saltwater fishing, swimming, 1500-foot beach, clamming, hiking, 500 feet to Carr Inlet.

PENROSE POINT STATE PARK (48') 10 mi NW on State 16 from Tacoma, then 15 mi SW via State 302 to Lakebay. 82 campsites for tents and trailers — 30' max, fee, group facilities, open all year, 7 day limit, supplies 2 mi, hot showers. Saltwater fishing, boating, mooring facilities, swimming, water skiing, trails, clamming, gulls and cranes. PO Box 73, Lakebay 98349.

RAINBOW (800') 4½ mi SW of Quilcene off US 101. 7 wooded tent sites, Apr 1 to Dec 31, no limit of stay, fishing, hiking, salt water activities 6 mi. Olympic NF.

SALTWATER STATE PARK (5') 1 mi south of Des Moines on State 509, take Kent-Des Moines exit off Int 5. 58 campsites for tents or trailers — 30' max, fee, group facilities, open all year, 7 day limit, hot showers, no firewood, disposal station, kitchen shelters. Fishing, boating, swimming, water skiing, hiking, clamming. 25205 8th Pl So, Kent 98031.

SCENIC BEACH STATE PARK (10') 13 mi NW of Bremerton at Seabeck. 7 tent sites, 43 trailer spaces — 30' max, fee, all year, 7 day limit, all hookups, hot showers, supplies 2 mi. Fishing, boating, launch 1 mi, swimming, water skiing, hiking. Coastal forest, black bear and deer. The historic town of Seabeck was once larger than Seattle with one of the first logging mills in the Lower Puget Sound. PO Box 7, Seabeck 98380.

SEAL ROCK (100') 2 mi north of Brinnon on US 101. 32 campsites for tents and RVs — 22' max, Apr 1 to Nov 12, no limit of stay. Beach access, boat launch, sailing, swimming, water skiing, fishing, oyster picking. Olympic NF.

SQUAXIN ISLAND BOAT CAMP (10') On Squaxin Island, accessible by private boat only. 13 tent sites, boat mooring facilities, swimming, fishing, clamming beach. The island is an Indian Reservation.

TWANOH STATE PARK (10') 13 mi SW from Bremerton on State 3 then 8 mi west on State 106. 81 tent sites, 10 trailer spaces, fee, all year, 7 day limit, concession — food and supplies. Fishing, boat dock, launch, mooring float, swimming, beach access across the hwy, water skiing, hiking, clamming, dense woods. Salmon run up a small creek in Sep and Oct. Rt 1, Box 330, Union 98592.

VASA PARK RESORT (29') On the SW shore of Sammamish Lake, take Redmond exit from Int 90. 20 tent sites, 10 trailer spaces — 30' max, fee, group facilities, Apr 15 to Oct 15, reservations accepted, RV hookups, disposal station, snack bar, playground, games area. Fishing, row boat rentals, swimming, water skiing, nature trail, bicycling, autumn foliage. The park was founded by Swedish immigrants, in 1926, who still live nearby. There are 18 acres of woods and beach, and a creek lined with ferns and flowers. 3560 W Lake Sammamish Rd So, Bellevue 98008. Privately owned.

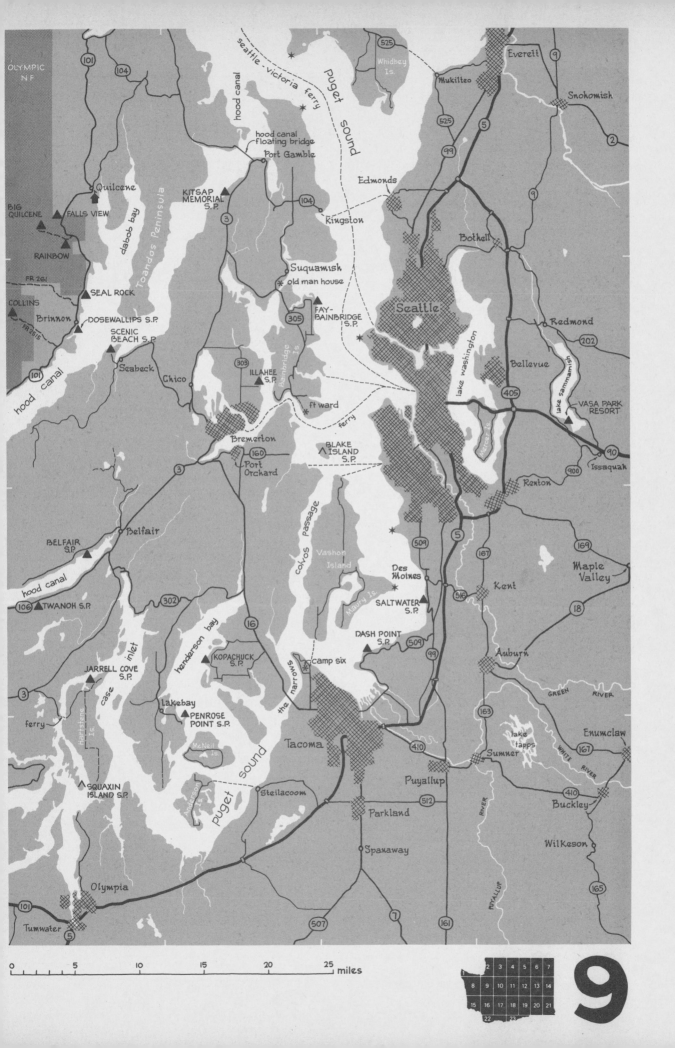

OLYMPIC
N F

OLYMPIC N F

101
104

hood canal

seattle - victoria ferry

puget sound

525
Whidbey Is.

Everett
9

Mukilteo

525

Snohomish

5

2

hood canal floating bridge
Port Gamble

104

Edmonds

99

Kingston

9

Bothell

Seattle

Redmond

202

Bellevue

405

lake sammamish

Vasa Park
Resort

Quilcene

BIG
QUILCENE

FALLS VIEW

RAINBOW

FR 261

dabob bay

Toandos Peninsula

KITSAP
MEMORIAL
S.P.

3

Suquamish
old man house

305

FAY-
BAINBRIDGE
S.P.

SEAL ROCK

COLLINS

FR 2515

Brinnon

DOSEWALLIPS S.P.

SCENIC
BEACH S.P.

Seabeck

Chico

303

ILLAHEE
S.P.

ft ward

ferry

lake washington

90

Issaquah

900

101

hood canal

Bremerton

160

Port
Orchard

BLAKE
ISLAND
S.P.

Renton

Belfair

3

BELFAIR
S.P.

hood canal

106

TWANOH S.P.

302

16

Vashon
Island

colvos passage

Maury Is.

Des
Moines

SALTWATER
S.P.

509

5

509

516

Kent

169

Maple
Valley

18

case inlet

henderson bay

KOPACHUCK
S.P.

camp six

DASH POINT
S.P.

99

163

Auburn

GREEN   RIVER

Enumclaw

167

WHITE   RIVER

JARRELL COVE
S.P.

3

ferry

Harstene Is.

lakebay

PENROSE
POINT S.P.

McNeil
Is.

the narrows

Anderson Is.

Tacoma

410

Sumner

lake
tapps

Puyallup

512

Buckley

410

SQUAXIN
ISLAND S.P.

Steilacoom

puget sound

Parkland

Wilkeson

165

Spanaway

Olympia

161

507

7

101

Tumwater

5

0   5   10   15   20   25   miles

1	2	3	4	5	6	7
8	9	10	11	12	13	14
15	16	17	18	19	20	21
22	23					

9

Ride the **STEAM TRAIN** at the Puget Sound Railroad Museum in Snoqualmie. It's a half-hour, 2-mile ride through the forest with a self-guided tour of an excellent collection of railway equipment. It operates only on Sundays and holidays, Memorial Day thru Oct. • For the most unique breakfast of your life, stop at **SNOQUALMIE FALLS LODGE** on the outskirts of Snoqualmie. You'll be served a magnificent family style meal with an endless variety of courses. Duck, when they serve the honey. Make reservations if you can. It's popular and not so cheap, but good things never are. **SNOQUALMIE FALLS** drops 270 feet just outside the windows. The surrounding area is a forested park and a good place to hike, relax or picnic. • **FEDERATION FOREST STATE PARK**, 17 miles east of Enumclaw, displays the variety of contrasts in nature that are found in Washington. Two nature trails wind through several distinct forest zones. The historic **NACHES TRAIL** passes through the park, and you can still see marks left by early pioneers.

ANNETTE LAKE TRAIL CAMP (4800') 17¼ mi SE on Int 90 from North Bend then 3½ mi south by trail. 3 campsites, June 1 to Oct 15, lake water. Swimming, fishing, hiking, mtn climbing. Snoqualmie NF.

BEAR LAKE TRAIL CAMP (3700') 4 mi SE on Int 90 from North Bend then 19 mi NE on FR 2445 then 4 mi east by trail. 6 campsites, June 15 to Oct 15, lake water. Swimming, fishing, hiking. Snoqualmie NF.

BECKLER RIVER (900') 1 mi east on US 2 from Skykomish then 1 mi north on FR 280. 21 campsites for tents or trailers — 22' max, May 15 to Nov 1, 14 day limit. Fishing. Snoqualmie NF.

BIG HEART LAKE TRAIL CAMP (5100') 2 mi east on US 2 from Skykomish, then 6 mi south on FR 2622, then 6 mi south by trail. 4 campsites, July 1 to Sep 15, lake water. Swimming, fishing, hiking. Snoqualmie NF.

CAMP JOY (1800') 13 mi SE on Int 90 from North Bend, then ¼ mi south on FR 2267 at Bandera Airstrip. 10 tent sites, May 1 to Nov 15, 14 day limit, river water. Fishing, hiking. Snoqualmie NF.

CLE ELUM RIVER (1100') 18¼ mi NW on State 903 from Cle Elum. 7 tent sites, 5 trailer spaces — 22' max, May 30 to Oct 1, 14 day limit, river water, supplies and horse rentals 3 mi. Fishing. Wenatchee NF.

COPPER LAKE TRAIL CAMP (3800') 2 mi east on US 2 from Skykomish, then 6 mi south on FR 2622, then 4 mi south by trail. 5 campsites, July 1 to Sep 15, lake water. Swimming, fishing, hiking. Snoqualmie NF.

CORRAL PASS (5700') 31 mi SE on State 410 from Enumclaw then 6 mi east on FR 185, road not suitable for trailers. 12 tent sites in an alpine setting, July 1 to Oct 30, 14 day limit, stream water. Berrypicking, riding, autumn foliage, trails lead to a Mountain Goat Reserve, Castle Mtn Trail. Snoqualmie NF.

COUGAR VALLEY (5400') 4 mi NW on State 410 from Cliffdell (see Map 17), then 2½ mi NW on FR 197, then ¼ mi SW on FR 1800, then 19½ mi west on FR 182. 4 tent sites, July 15 to Oct 15, 14 day limit, stream water. Fishing 3 mi, hunting, Pacific Crest Trail 2½ mi west. Snoqualmie NF.

CRYSTAL SPRINGS (2400') 20½ mi NW on Int 90 from Cle Elum, then ½ mi west on FR 212. 27 campsites beside the Yakima River, trailers — 22' max, May 15 to Oct 1, 14 day limit, community kitchen, supplies and boat rentals 5 mi. Water sports at Keechelus Lake, fishing, hunting, berrypicking. Wenatchee NF.

DECEPTION LAKE TRAIL CAMP (5100') 11 mi east on US 2 from Skykomish, then ½ mi SW on FR 2609, then 10 mi south on Trail 1060. 4 campsites, July 1 to Sep 15, lake water. Swimming, fishing, hiking, Deception Lakes Horse Camp 1 mi north. Snoqualmie NF.

DENNY CREEK (200') 17 mi SE on Int 90 from North Bend to Asahel Curtis Picnic Ground, then 2¼ mi NE on FR 2219. Several loops with 20 tent sites and 12 trailer spaces — 22' max, May 1 to Nov 1, 10 day limit. Interesting swimming holes north of the camp, fishing, hunting, Franklin Falls 1½ mi. A portion of an historic wagon road has been preserved nearby. Snoqualmie NF.

DINGFORD JUNCTION (1200') 4 mi SE on Int 90 from North Bend, then 15 mi NE on FR 2445, then 6 mi SE on FR 241. 3 tent sites, May 15 to Nov 30, 14 day limit, stream water. Fishing, hiking, mtn climbing. Snoqualmie NF.

ECHO LAKE TRAIL CAMP (3800') ½ mi east on FR 185 from Corral Pass Campground then 5¼ mi NE by trail. 6 campsites, July 1 to Sep 15, 14 day limit, lake water, shelter. Fishing, riding, access to the Pacific Crest Trail. Snoqualmie NF.

FISH LAKE (3400') 22 mi NW on State 903 from Cle Elum then 11 mi NE on FR 2405. 10 tent sites, July 1 to Oct 1, 14 day limit, stream water. Canoeing, Fishing, hunting, berrypicking, views of Cathedral Rock, mtn climbing, Pacific Crest Trail 2 mi NW. Wenatchee NF.

FOSS RIVER (1400') 2 mi east on US 2 from Skykomish then 4½ mi south on FR 2622. 4 campsites for tents and RVs, May 15 to Oct 1, 14 day limit, river water. Fishing, hiking.

GLACIER LAKE TRAIL CAMP (4900') 11 mi east on US 2 from Skykomish, then ½ mi SW on FR 2609, then 7 mi south on Trail 1060. 4 campsites, July 1 to Sep 15, no water supply. Swimming, fishing, hiking, riding. Snoqualmie NF.

GOVERNMENT MEADOW TRAIL CAMP (4900') 18½ mi SE on State 410 from Enumclaw, then 8 mi east on FR 197, then 6¼ mi SE on Trail 1175. 2 campsites, July 1 to Oct 30, stream water, shelter. Located on the Pacific Crest Trail. Historic Naches Trail, an old pioneer route, passes by the camp. Snoqualmie NF.

GREEN RIVER GORGE (400') 6 mi north of Enumclaw on State 169. 21 secluded campsites in dense woods, ferns and mossy growth. Hiking trail, hunting, fishing. Dept of Natural Resources.

GREENWATER PARK (1780') 18 mi east on Enumclaw on State 410. 46 wooded campsites for tents and RVs, several walk-in sites, open all year, 14 day limit, supplies and restaurant 1 mi, disposal station. Fishing in Greenwater River, hiking trails. Watch for logging trucks. Rt 3, Enumclaw 98022. Weyerhaeuser Co.

HUCKLEBERRY (5300') 4 mi NW on State 410 from Cliffdell (see Map 17), then 2½ mi NW on FR 197, then ¼ mi west on FR 1800, then 11 mi NW on FR 182. 8 tent sites, July 1 to Sep 30, 14 day limit, no water supply, not much shade. Fishing, hunting, riding, berrypicking, trail to Raven Roost Observation Point with a view of all the major peaks in Wash. Snoqualmie NF.

KACHESS (2300') 20½ mi NW on Int 90 from Cle Elum, then 5½ mi NE on FR 228. 164 campsites on a wooded peninsula, tents or trailers — 22' max, May 30 to Oct 1, 14 day limit, supplies, autumn foliage, boat launch and rentals. Swimming, water skiing, fishing, hunting, Big Tree Nature Trail, trail northward along the lakeshore, berrypicking, mushroom gathering in the area. Wenatchee NF.

LAKE DOROTHY INLET TRAIL CAMP (3100') 2¼ mi west on US 2 from Skykomish, then 7½ mi south on FR 2516, then 3 mi south by trail. 5 campsites, June 15 to Sep 30. Swimming, fishing. Snoqualmie NF.

LAKE EASTON RESORT (2000') 12 mi west of Cle Elum off Int 90 adjacent to Lake Easton SP. 10 tent sites, 75 trailer spaces, fee, Apr 15 to Nov 15, no limit of stay, reservations accepted, all hookups, disposal station, store, laundry, hot showers. Good trout fishing, row boat rentals, swimming, hiking, hunting, bicycle rentals and trails. Box 96, Easton 98925. Privately owned.

LAKE EASTON STATE PARK (2000') 14 mi west of Cle Elum off Int 90. 100 campsites for tents and RVs, fee, store, cafe, hot showers, boat launch. Swimming, good fishing, hiking, autumn foliage.

LAKE JANUS TRAIL CAMP (4200') 23 mi east on US 2 from Skykomish, then 2 mi NW on FR 2714, then 1½ mi NW on Trail 1590, then 2½ mi NW on the Pacific Crest Trail. 6 campsites, July 1 to Sep 15, lake water. Swimming, fishing, hiking, riding, facilities for campers with horses. Snoqualmie NF.

MILLER RIVER (1000') 2½ mi west on US 2 from Skykomish, then 3½ mi south on FR 2615. 6 tent sites, 6 trailer spaces — 22' max, May 15 to Oct 1, 14 day limit, river water. Swimming, fishing. Snoqualmie NF.

MONEY CREEK (900') 2¼ mi west of Skykomish on US 2 then south across the bridge. 6 tent sites, 11 trailer spaces — 22' max, pleasant well-shaded sites on both sides of the road — some beside the stream, May 1 to Nov 1, 14 day limit. River running on Skykomish R, swimming and fishing. Snoqualmie NF.

NECKLACE VALLEY TRAIL CAMP (4700') 2 mi east on US 2 from Skykomish, then 5 mi south on FR 2622, then 9 mi SE by trail. 4 campsites, July 1 to Sep 15, stream water. Swimming, fishing, hiking, berrypicking. Snoqualmie NF.

PRATT LAKE TRAIL CAMP (3400') 17¼ mi SE on Int 90 from North Bend, then 6 mi NW by trail. 6 campsites, June 1 to Oct 15, lake water. Swimming, fishing, hiking. Snoqualmie NF.

RED MOUNTAIN (2200') 19½ mi NW of Cle Elum on State 903. 4 campsites for tents and RVs along the Cle Elum River, May 30 to Oct 1, 14 day limit, river water, supplies and horse rentals 2 mi. Fishing. Wenatchee NF.

ROCKY RUN (2600') 27 mi NW of Cle Elum on Int 90. 18 tent sites along a swift flowing stream, May 15 to Oct 1, 14 day limit. Boat launch, water sports, fishing, hunting, trail above the camp, berrypicking. Wenatchee NF.

SALMON LA SAC (2400') 22 mi NW of Cle Elum on State 903. 45 tent sites, 11 trailer spaces — 22' max, heavily-used camp, May 30 to Oct 1, 14 day limit, supplies, playground, community kitchen, horse rental. Swimming, fishing, hunting, hiking, riding. Wenatchee NF.

(Continued on following page)

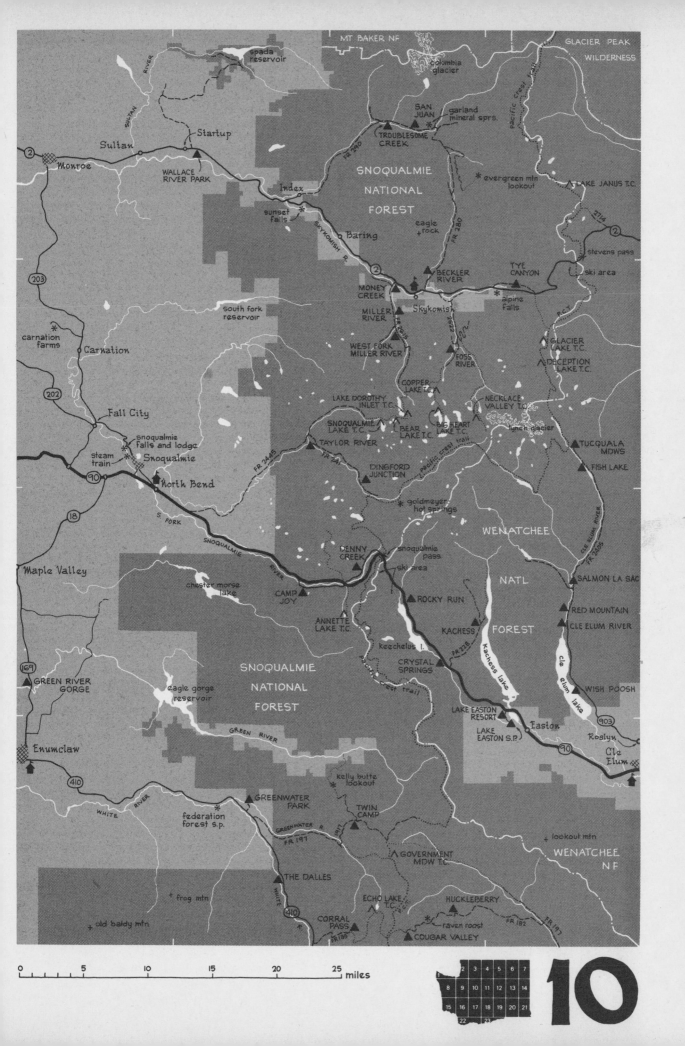

MT BAKER NF

GLACIER PEAK
WILDERNESS

spada
reservoir

*columbia
glacier*

SAN JUAN

garland
mineral sprs.

TROUBLESOME
CREEK

FR 280

Startup

Sultan

Monroe

WALLACE
RIVER PARK

SNOQUALMIE
NATIONAL
FOREST

*evergreen mtn
lookout*

LAKE JANUS T.C.

2714

203

Index

*sunset
falls*

SKYKOMISH R.

Baring

*eagle
+rock*

2

stevens pass

ski area

BECKLER
RIVER

TYE
CANYON

FR 280

P.C.T.

south fork
reservoir

MONEY
CREEK

Skykomish

MILLER
RIVER

*alpine
falls*

*carnation
farms*

Carnation

WEST FORK
MILLER RIVER

FOSS
RIVER

GLACIER
LAKE T.C.

DECEPTION
LAKE T.C.

202

COPPER
LAKE T.C.

LAKE DOROTHY
INLET T.C.

NECKLACE
VALLEY T.C.

Fall City

SNOQUALMIE
LAKE T.C.

BEAR
LAKE T.C.

BIG HEART
LAKE T.C.

lynch glacier

*snoqualmie
falls and lodge*

TAYLOR RIVER

FR 2445

FR 2421

TUCQUALA
MDWS

FISH LAKE

*steam
train*

Snoqualmie

DINGFORD
JUNCTION

pacific crest trail

90

North Bend

*goldmeyer
hot springs*

WENATCHEE

18

S. FORK

SNOQUALMIE RIVER

CLE ELUM RIVER

FR 2405

Maple Valley

chester morse
lake

DENNY
CREEK

snoqualmie
pass

ski area

NATL

SALMON LA SAC

CAMP
JOY

ROCKY RUN

RED MOUNTAIN

CLE ELUM RIVER

FOREST

ANNETTE
LAKE T.C.

keechelus l.

KACHESS

FR 228

kachess lake

cle elum lake

169

GREEN RIVER
GORGE

eagle gorge
reservoir

SNOQUALMIE
NATIONAL
FOREST

CRYSTAL
SPRINGS

crest trail

WISH POOSH

LAKE EASTON
RESORT

Easton

903

LAKE
EASTON S.P.

Roslyn

Cle
Elum

Enumclaw

GREEN RIVER

90

410

WHITE   RIVER

GREENWATER
PARK

*kelly butte
lookout*

TWIN
CAMP

lookout mtn

WENATCHEE
NF

*federation
forest s.p.*

GREENWATER R.

FR 197

FR 70

GOVERNMENT
MDW T.C.

HUCKLEBERRY

FR 182

FR 197

THE DALLES

frog mtn

ECHO LAKE
T.C.

old baldy mtn

410

WHITE R.

CORRAL
PASS

FR 7150

raven roost

COUGAR VALLEY

0   5   10   15   20   25 miles

10

SAN JUAN (1500') 14 mi NE of Index on County Rd 290. 12 tent sites, May 15 to Oct 1, 14 day limit, river water. Fishing in North Fork Skykomish. Snoqualmie NF.

SNOQUALMIE LAKE TRAIL CAMP (3200') 4 mi SE on Into 90 from North Bend, then 19 mi NE on FR 2445, then 2 mi east by trail. 8 campsites, June 1 to Oct 15, lake water. Swimming, fishing, hiking. Snoqualmie NF.

TAYLOR RIVER (1000') 4 mi SE on Int 90 from North Bend, then 15 mi NE on FR 2445, then 1¼ mi SE on FR 241, then ½ mi west on FR 2444. 20 tent sites on a river bar, no trailers, May 15 to Nov 30, 14 day limit, river water. Fishing in Snoqualmie R, hiking, mtn climbing. Strange limestone formations can be found along the river a few hundred yards north of the camp. Snoqualmie NF.

THE DALLES (2200') 25½ mi SE of Enumclaw on State 410. 19 tent sites, 26 trailer spaces — 22' max, May 15 to Sep 30, 14 day limit, stream water, picnic pavilion, community kitchen, horse rentals 5 mi. Fishing, John Muir Nature Trail in the picnic area. A small footbridge near campsite 27 leads to a 9½-foot diameter Douglas Fir that was the survivor of a forest fire about 300 years ago. Snoqualmie NF.

TROUBLESOME CREEK (1300') 12 mi NE of Index on County 290. 22 pleasantly wooded campsites for tents or trailers — 22' max, May 15 to Oct 1, 14 day limit, river water. Fishing, hiking, riding. Snoqualmie NF.

TUCQUALA MEADOWS (3400') 22 mi NW on State 903 from Cle Elum, then 13 mi north on FR 2405. 9 tent sites, July 1 to Oct 1, no limit of stay, stream water. Fishing, hunting, mtn climbing, Pacific Crest Trail. Wenatchee NF.

TWIN CAMPS (3700') 20 mi east on State 410 from Enumclaw then 7¼ mi east on FR 197 then 3 mi NE on FR 1917, (road not suitable for trailers). 3 tent sites, July 1 to Oct 30, 14 day limit, no water supply. Hunting, berrypicking, Pacific Crest Trail and Windy Gap 4 mi east. Snoqualmie NF.

TYE CANYON (2200') 6 mi east on US 2 from Skykomish then 2 mi east on FR 2607. 2 tent sites, June 1 to Oct 1, 14 day limit, stream water. Fishing in the Tye River, hiking. Snoqualmie NF.

WALLACE RIVER PARK (100') 13 mi east of Monroe on US 2 between Startup and Gold Bar. 22 campsites for tents or trailers, fee, group facilities, all year, no limit of stay, reservations accepted, all hookups, disposal station, hot showers, supplies, laundry. Fishing, swimming, hiking, blackberry picking, autumn foliage, panoramic view of Cascade Mtns. PO Box 167, Startup 98293. Privately owned.

WEST FORK MILLER RIVER (1700') 2½ mi west on US 2 from Skykomish then 5½ mi south on FR 2615. 4 secluded walk-in tent sites, no trailers, May 15 to Oct 1, 14 day limit, river water. Fishing. Snoqualmie NF.

WISH POOSH (2400') 10¼ mi NW on State 903 from Cle Elum then ¼ mi west on FR 2194. 34 campsites for tents or trailers — 22' max, May 1 to Nov 30, 14 day limit, supplies, cafe, horse rentals. Driftwood, boat launch, swimming, water skiing, fishing, riding. Wenatchee NF.

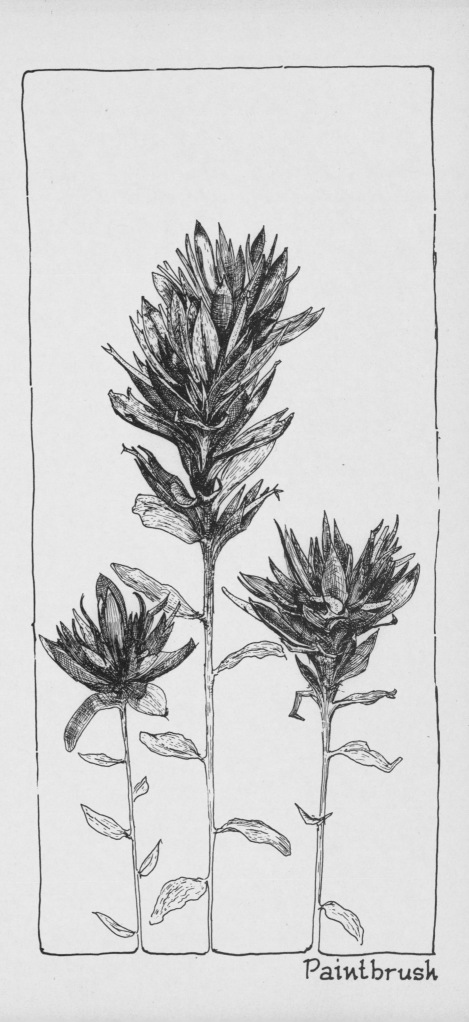

Paintbrush

11

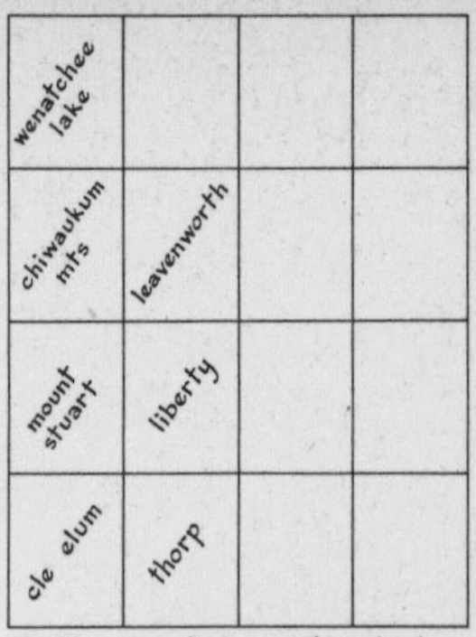

USGS 15-minute quadrangle key

BLEWETT MINING SITE, about 11 miles south of Leavenworth on US 97, has some interesting remains of an old timber stamp mill. It was used to crush ore and stands in a dilapidated and unsafe condition. Across the highway from the historical marker is an **ARRASTRE**, which was water powered and used for grinding ore. • **INDIAN CAVE** is reached by a short trail from the upper section of Swiftwater Picnicground, about 8 miles NW of Leavenworth. Seashells are scattered over the floor of the cave, and there is evidence of smoke from campfires on the ceiling. • If you're driving north on US 2 from East Wenatchee, watch for the **LINCOLN ROCK** Memorial Marker. On the mountainside to the west you'll see a natural rock formation that has a strong resemblance to Abe Lincoln's profile. • **OHME GARDENS** now occupy what was once a desolate hill, 3 miles north of Wenatchee. Fantastic displays of flowers and plants were created among the weathered rock formations on a craggy cliff overlooking the Columbia River. • **ROCKY REACH DAM** (See SEVERAL INTERESTING TOURS).

ANTILON LAKE (2300') 6 mi NW on State 150 from Chelan, then 5¼ mi north on County 10, then 3 mi north on FR 3001. 2 tent sites, Apr 15 to Nov 15, 14 day limit, stream water. Boating, swimming, fishing. Wenatchee NF.

ATKINSON FLAT (2500') 16 mi NW on US 2 from Leavenworth, then 4 mi north on State 207, then 1 mi east on County 22, then 15 mi NW on FR 311. 2 tent sites, 2 trailer spaces – 22' max, June 15 to Oct 15, 14 day limit, river water. Fishing, hiking, riding. Wenatchee NF.

BAKER (2600') 4 mi SE on US 10 from Cle Elum, then 12 mi NE on US 97. 3 tent sites, Apr 15 to Nov 30, 14 day limit, stream water, supplies and cafe 2 mi. Fishing, hunting, hiking, goldpanning in nearby creeks. Wenatchee NF.

BEEHIVE SPRINGS (4100') 10 mi south on County 4 from Wenatchee then 1½ mi NW on FR 2107. 4 tent sites, May 1 to Oct 31, 14 day limit, hunting, fishing. Wenatchee NF.

BEVERLY (3200') 4 mi SE on US 10 from Cle Elum, then 4¼ mi NE on US 97, then 13 mi north on County 107, then 4 mi NW on FR 232. 12 tent sites beside the river, June 1 to Nov 30, 14 day limit, river water. Fishing, hunting. Beverly Cr Trail just south of the camp leads to good mtn climbing on Mt Stuart. Wenatchee NF.

BIG HILL (6800') 29½ mi NW on County 371 from Entiat, then 8 mi north on FR 298, then 1½ mi north on FR 298A. 1 tent site, no trailers, July 1 to Sep 30. 14 day limit, no water supply, shelter. Hunting, riding, hiking, good views from the mtn top. Wenatchee NF.

BONANZA (2700') 4½ mi SE on US 2 from Leavenworth then 13 mi south on US 97. 4 tent sites, 1 trailer space – 16' max, Apr 15 to Nov 30, 14 day limit. Hunting. Wenatchee NF.

BRIDGE CREEK (1900') 3 mi south on County 71 from Leavenworth then 5½ mi west on FR 2451. 3 campsites, trailers – 22' max, May 1 to Oct 31, 14 day limit, stream water. Fishing, hunting, riding, mtn climbing. Wenatchee NF.

CHATTER CREEK (2800') 3 mi south on County 71 from Leavenworth then 12¼ mi NW on FR 2451. 11 tent sites, 1 trailer space – 22' max, other sites across the wooden footbridge, May 1 to Oct 31, 14 day limit, stream water, community kitchen. Fishing, hunting, riding, trail to Trout Lake. Wenatchee NF.

CHIWAUKUM CREEK (1400') 10¼ mi NW on US 2 from Leavenworth then 1½ mi west on FR 265. 5 tent sites, 2 trailer spaces – 22' max, May 1 to Oct 31, 14 day limit, stream water, horse corral. Fishing, hunting, trail to Chiwaukum Lake. Wenatchee NF.

CHIWAUKUM LAKE TRAIL CAMP (2400') 4 mi NW on Trail 1571 from Chiwaukum Creek Campground, then 4 mi NW on Trail 1591. 4 campsites, July 1 to Oct 15, 14 day limit, stream water. Fishing, riding, hiking. Wenatchee NF.

COUGAR CREEK TRAIL SHELTER (3000') 11¼ mi NW from Pine Flat Campground on Trail 1409. 1 campsite, July 15 to Sep 30, 14 day limit, river water, trail shelter. Hiking, riding, fishing in Mad River. Wenatchee NF.

DE ROUX (3800') 4 mi SE on US 10 from Cle Elum, then 4¼ mi NE on US 97, then 13 mi north on County 107, then 8 mi NW on FR 232. 2 tent sites, June 15 to Oct 31, 14 day limit, stream water. Fishing, riding, Teanaway Falls 1½ mi north on FR 232. De Roux Cr Trail just north of the camp leads to a series of small waterfalls. Wenatchee NF.

DICKEY CREEK (2600') 4 mi SE on US 10 from Cle Elum, then 4¼ mi NE on US 97, then 8 mi NW on Teanaway Valley Rd. Several campsites for tents and RVs, all year. 5 acres, fishing, hiking, hunting. Boise Cascade.

EIGHTMILE (1800') 3 mi south on County 71 from Leavenworth, then 4¼ mi west on FR 2451. 7 tent sites, 1 trailer space – 22' max, May 1 to Oct 31, 14 day limit, horse rental 5 mi, corral at the camp. Fishing, hunting. A trail just north of the camp leads to Eightmile Lake. Wenatchee NF.

EIGHTMILE LAKE TRAIL CAMP (4500') 3 mi south on County 71 from Leavenworth, then 5½ mi west on FR 2451, then 4½ mi SW on Trail 1552. 3 campsites, July 1 to Oct 31, 14 day limit, lake water. Fishing, hiking. Wenatchee NF.

FISH POND (1800') 16 mi NW on US 2 from Leavenworth then 1 mi north on State 207. 3 primitive tent sites, May 1 to Oct 31, 14 day limit, stream water, supplies 4 mi, cafe 1 mi, horse rental and boat launch 4 mi at Wenatchee Lake. Fishing, hunting. Wenatchee NF.

FOX CREEK (2300') 27¼ mi NW on County 371 from Entiat. 9 tent sites, May 15 to Oct 15, 14 day limit, river water. Fishing, hunting, trail ½ mi north. A forest fire swept thru this area during the summer of 1970. Wenatchee NF.

GLACIER VIEW (1900') 16 mi NW on US 2 from Leavenworth, then 3½ mi NE on State 207, then 5½ mi west on FR 290. 20 walk-in tent sites, May 15 to Oct 15, 14 day limit, horse rental 5 mi. Boating, swimming, water skiing, fishing, hunting, trail along the south shore of the lake. Wenatchee NF.

GOOSE CREEK (2200') 17½ mi north on State 209 from Leavenworth then 3¼ mi north on FR 2746. 2 tent sites, 2 trailer spaces – 32' max, June 1 to Oct 15, 14 day limit, stream water. Fishing, hunting. Wenatchee NF.

GRASSHOPPER MEADOWS (2000') 16 mi NW on US 2 from Leavenworth, then 8½ mi north on State 207, then 1 mi NW on County 22, then 8 mi NW on FR 293. 4 tent sites, June 1 to Oct 15, 14 day limit, river water. Fishing, hunting, berrypicking, pleasant meadow, trail to Glacier Peak Wilderness. Wenatchee NF.

GROUSE CREEK (2400') 16 mi NW on US 2 from Leavenworth, then 4 mi north on State 207, then 1 mi east on County 22, then 7 mi north on FR 311. 4 tent sites, June 1 to Oct 15, 14 day limit, stream water. Fishing in Chiwawa R, hunting, hiking. Wenatchee NF.

GROUSE MOUNTAIN (4500') 3 mi west on US 97 from Chelan, then 16 mi NW on County 10, then 8 mi west on FR 298 (road not suitable for trailers). 4 tent sites, June 15 to Nov 15, 14 day limit, no water supply. Hunting, hiking. Wenatchee NF.

HALF WAY SPRING (5000') 41½ mi NW on County 371 from Entiat then 4 mi north on FR 298; road not suitable for trailers. 5 tent sites, June 15 to Oct 15, 14 day limit. Hunting, hiking. Wenatchee NF.

HANDY SPRING CAMP (6000') 3 mi west on US 97 from Chelan, then 16 mi NW on County 10, then 14½ mi west on FR 298, then ¾ mi south on FR 298A. 1 tent site, July 1 to Oct 31, 14 day limit. Hunting, Junior Point Lookout 1 mi. Wenatchee NF.

IDA CREEK (1900') 3 mi south on County 71 from Leavenworth, then 10¼ mi NW on FR 2451. 3 tent sites, 1 trailer space – 22' max, stream water. Fishing, hunting, hiking. Wenatchee NF.

JOHNNY CREEK (2300') 3 mi south on County 71 from Leavenworth then 8 mi NW on FR 2451. 11 tent sites, 3 trailer spaces – 22' max, May 1 to Oct 31, 14 day limit. Fishing, hunting, hiking, berrypicking. Wenatchee NF.

JUNIOR POINT (6600') 3 mi west on US 97 from Chelan, then 16 mi NW on County 10, then 14¼ mi west on FR 298. 2 tent sites in an alpine setting, July 15 to Sep 30, 14 day limit. Hunting, wildflowers, Junior Point Lookout. Wenatchee NF.

LAKE CHELAN STATE PARK (1100') 9 mi west of Chelan off US 97. 176 tent sites, 25 trailer spaces, hot showers, disposal station, store, golf course nearby. Boat launch, mooring facilities, swimming, fishing, several hiking trails.

LAKE CREEK (2400') 29 mi NW on County 371 from Entiat. 9 campsites, May 15 to Oct 15, 14 day limit, stream water. Fishing, hunting, riding, horse corral, Little Wenatchee Tr. Vegetation around the camp was burned by a forest fire during the summer of 1970. Wenatchee NF.

LAKE JULIUS TRAIL CAMP (4900') 21 mi NW on US 2 from Leavenworth, then 1¼ mi SE on FR 2734, then 7 mi SW on Trail 1584. 2 campsites, July 1 to Oct 15, 14 day limit, stream water. Fishing, riding. The lakeshore is closed to horses within 200 yards. Wenatchee NF.

LAKE STUART TRAIL CAMP (6300') 3 mi south on County 71 from Leavenworth, then 5½ mi west on FR 2451, then 5½ mi SW on Trail 1552A. 7 campsites, July 1 to Oct. 31, 14 day limit, lake water. Fishing, hiking. Wenatchee NF.

LAKE WENATCHEE RANGER STATION (1900') 16 mi NW on US 2 from Leavenworth, then 7¼ mi north on State 207. 8 tent sites, May 1 to Oct 31, 14 day limit, cafe and supplies 1 mi, boat launch and rentals 1 mi. Water sports, fishing, hunting, trail to Dirtyface Lookout. Wenatchee NF.

LAKE WENATCHEE STATE PARK (1800') 15 mi NW on US 2 from Leavenworth, then 3½ mi NE on State 207, then 1 mi west on FR 290. 160 campsites, fee, hot showers, stores, boat launch. Swimming, fishing, hiking, riding, horse rentals, pack trips. Crowded in summer.

LION ROCK SPRING (6300') 12½ mi north on County 179 from Ellensburg, then 5¼ mi north on FR 2008, then 4½ mi north on FR 2101 (road not suitable for trailers). 3 tent sites, June 15 to Oct 15, 14 day limit, no water supply, horse corral. Hunting, hiking, riding, good views from the remains of Lion Rock Lookout, rockhounding. Wenatchee NF.

MAD LAKE TRAIL CAMP (5500') 10 mi NW on County 371 from Entiat, then 2½ mi NW on FR 2710, then 9 mi SW on FR 2615, then 16 mi NW on FR 2924, then 8 mi NW on Trail 1407. 3 campsites, July 15 to Sep 30, 14 day limit, stream water. Fishing, riding, trail leads to Larch Lakes and Glacier Peak Wilderness. Wenatchee NF.

MERRITT LAKE TRAIL CAMP (5000') 25½ mi NW on US 2 from Leavenworth, then 3 mi NW on Trail 1588. 2 campsites, May 15 to Oct 15, lake water. Fishing, riding. Horses aren't allowed within 200 yards of the lake shore. Wenatchee NF.

(Continued on following page)

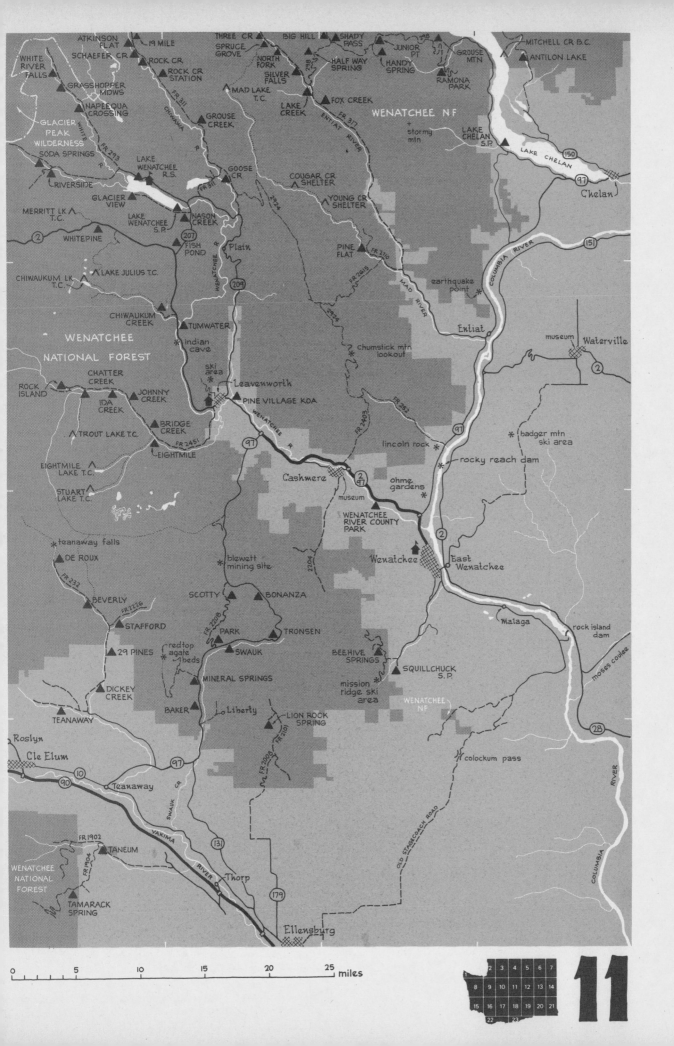

ATKINSON FLAT △   19 MILE △   THREE CR.   BIG HILL △   SHADY PASS   JUNIOR PT.   MITCHELL CR. B.C.   △ ANTILON LAKE
SCHAEFER CR. △   ROCK CR. △   SPRUCE GROVE   △   △   HALF WAY SPRING   △ HANDY SPRING   GROUSE MTN.   △
WHITE RIVER FALLS   ROCK CR STATION △   NORTH FORK △   SILVER FALLS   RAMONA PARK
GRASSHOPPER MDWS △   MAD LAKE T.C. △   LAKE CREEK △   FOX CREEK △   WENATCHEE N.F.
NAPEEQUA CROSSING △   GROUSE CREEK △   FR 317   + stormy mtn   LAKE CHELAN S.P. △   LAKE CHELAN   150
GLACIER PEAK WILDERNESS   97   Chelan ⊠
SODA SPRINGS   LAKE WENATCHEE R.S. △   GOOSE CR. △   COUGAR CR. SHELTER   FR 2100
RIVERSIDE   YOUNG CR. SHELTER   earthquake point *   COLUMBIA RIVER   151
MERRITT LK. T.C. △   GLACIER VIEW   LAKE WENATCHEE S.P. △   NASON CREEK   Plain   FR 2615   PINE FLAT △   FR 2924   Entiat   museum ⊠ Waterville   2
WHITEPINE   2   207   FISH POND △   209   MAD RIVER
CHIWAUKUM LK. T.C. △   △ LAKE JULIUS T.C.   chumstick mtn lookout *   97
CHIWAUKUM CREEK △   △ TUMWATER   * indian cave   badger mtn ski area *
WENATCHEE NATIONAL FOREST   ski area *   Leavenworth   FR 2403   rocky reach dam   rock island dam
CHATTER CREEK △   Leavenworth ▲ ⊠   △ PINE VILLAGE KOA   lincoln rock *   rocky reach dam *
ROCK ISLAND △   JOHNNY CREEK △   97   WENATCHEE R.   2 47   ohme gardens *
IDA CREEK △   BRIDGE CREEK △   Cashmere ⊠   museum
TROUT LAKE T.C. △   FR 2451   EIGHTMILE △   2204   WENATCHEE RIVER COUNTY PARK   2
EIGHTMILE LAKE T.C. △   badger mtn
STUART LAKE T.C. △   blewett mining site *   Wenatchee ▲ ⊠   East Wenatchee
teanaway falls *   SCOTTY △   BONANZA △   Malaga   rock island dam
DE ROUX △   FR 2208   PARK △   TRONSEN △   2B
BEVERLY △   FR 1226   redtop agate beds *   SWAUK △   BEEHIVE SPRINGS △   moses coulee
STAFFORD △   MINERAL SPRINGS △   SQUILLCHUCK S.P. △   COLUMBIA RIVER
29 PINES △   BAKER △   Liberty   LION ROCK SPRING   mission ridge ski area *   WENATCHEE NF
DICKEY CREEK △   FR 2101   colockum pass
TEANAWAY △   Roslyn ⊠   Cle Elum ⊠   97
10   90   Teanaway ⊙   SWAUK CR.   FR 2008   OLD STAGECOACH ROAD
FR 1902   131   YAKIMA   179
WENATCHEE NATIONAL FOREST   FR 1904   TANEUM △   Thorp ⊙   RIVER
TAMARACK SPRING △   Ellensburg ⊠   COLUMBIA RIVER

0   5   10   15   20   25 miles

MINERAL SPRINGS (2700') 4 mi SE on US 10 from Cle Elum then 14 mi NE on US 97. 5 tent sites in woods, Apr 15 to Nov 30, 14 day limit, supplies and cafe. Fishing, hunting, goldpanning in nearby streams, Mineral Springs Resort. Wenatchee NF.

MITCHELL CREEK BOAT CAMP (1100') 15 mi NW of Chelan on Lake Chelan, accessible by boat only. 4 campsites, May 1 to Oct 31, 14 day limit, stream water, boat dock. Water sports, sailing, fishing. Wenatchee NF.

NAPEEQUA CROSSING (2000') 16 mi NW on US 2 from Leavenworth, then 8½ mi north on State 207, then 1 mi NW on County 22, then 6 mi NW on FR 293. 3 tent sites, 2 trailer spaces — 32' max, May 15 to Oct 31, 14 day limit, river water. Fishing, hunting, berrypicking, Twin Lakes Trail leads to Glacier Peak Wilderness. Wenatchee NF.

NASON CREEK (1800') 16 mi NW on US 2 from Leavenworth, then 3½ mi NE on State 207, then ¼ mi west on FR 290. 27 tent sites, 40 trailer spaces — 32' max, overflow area, May 1 to Oct 31, 14 day limit, supplies 2 mi, boat launch and horse rentals 1 mi. Hunting, fishing. Nason Ridge Trail, just beyond the bridge, leads to Round Mtn Trail (6 mi) and Alpine Lookout (9½ mi). Wenatchee NF.

NINETEEN MILE (2600') 16 mi NW on US 2 from Leavenworth, then 4 mi north on State 207, then 1 mi east on County 22, then 18 mi NW on FR 311. 2 tent sites, 1 trailer space — 22' max, June 15 to Oct 15, 14 day limit, river water. Fishing, hunting, riding. Wenatchee NF.

NORTH FORK (2700') 33½ mi NW on County 371 from Entiat. 8 campsites, trailers — 22' max, June 15 to Oct 15, 14 day limit, river water. Fishing in Entiat R, hunting, trail to Duncan Hill. Wenatchee NF.

PARK (3000') 4 mi SE on US 10 from Cle Elum, then 16½ mi NE on US 97, then 1 mi NE on FR 2208. 3 tent sites, May 1 to Nov 30, 14 day limit, stream water, good shade, supplies and cafe 4 mi. Hunting. Wenatchee NF.

PINE FLAT (1900') 10 mi NW on County 371 from Entiat, then 3½ mi NW on FR 2710. 8 campsites, May 1 to Oct 31, 14 day limit, river water, supplies and cafe 4 mi. Fishing, hunting, trail along Mad River. Wenatchee NF.

PINE VILLAGE KOA (1100') ½ mi east from Leavenworth on US 2, then ½ mi north. 20 tent sites, 55 trailer spaces — 30' max, fee, May 1 to Oct 31, No limit of stay, reservations accepted, all hookups, store, laundry, hot showers, disposal station, snack bar. Swimming pool, square dancing, games area, bike rentals. Floating on the Wenatchee, fishing, hiking, Sat night hayrides during the summer, pines. US Hwy 2, Leavenworth 98826. Privately owned.

RAMONA PARK (2400') 3 mi west on US 97 from Chelan, then 16 mi NW on County 10, then 2½ mi SW on FR 298, then ½ mi south on FR 2805. 3 tent sites, Apr 15 to Nov 15, 14 day limit, stream water, supplies 4 mi, boat launch and water sports 4 mi. Fishing, nearby trail leads to Devils Backbone. You can catch the excursion tour boat at 25 Mile Creek Dock, 3 mi east. Wenatchee NF.

RIVERSIDE (2000') 16 mi NW on US 2 from Leavenworth then 9 mi north on State 207 then 7 mi west on FR 283. 6 campsites, trailers — 32' max, May 1 to Oct 31, 14 day limit, river water. Fishing, hunting, hiking, blackberries. Wenatchee NF.

ROCK CREEK (2500') 16 mi NW on US 2 from Leavenworth, then 4 mi north on State 207, then 1 mi east on County 22, then 13 mi NW on FR 311. 4 campsites, trailers — 22' max, June 15 to Oct 15, 14 day limit. Fishing, hunting, mtn climbing, trails to Estes Butte and along Rock Cr. Wenatchee NF.

ROCK CREEK STATION (2500') 16 mi NW on US 2 from Leavenworth, then 4 mi north on State 207, then 1 mi east on County 22, then 11 mi NW on FR 311. 3 campsites, trailers — 32' max, June 15 to Oct 15, 14 day limit. Fishing, hunting, Basalt Ridge trailhead. Wenatchee NF.

ROCK ISLAND (2900') 3 mi south on County 71 from Leavenworth, then 14 mi NW on FR 2451. 13 tent sites, 5 trailer spaces — 22' max, May 1 to Oct 31, 14 day limit. Fishing, hunting, hiking, riding, berrypicking, Icicle Cr Trail across the bridge. Wenatchee NF.

SCHAEFER CREEK (2600') 16 mi NW on US 2 from Leavenworth, then 4 mi north on State 207, then 1 mi east on County 22, then 14 mi NW on FR 311. 3 tent sites, June 15 to Oct 15, 14 day limit, river water. Fishing, hunting. Wenatchee NF.

SCOTTY (2800') 4½ mi SE on US 2 from Leavenworth, then 12 mi south on US 97, then 1¼ mi SW on FR 2208, then 1 mi SE on FR 223. 5 tent sites, May 1 to Nov 30, 14 day limit, stream water. Hunting, fishing in Scotty Cr. The remains of Blewett, an old mining camp, are about 3 mi north. Wenatchee NF.

SHADY PASS (5400') 29½ mi NW on County 371 from Entiat then 8 mi north on FR 298. 1 tent sites, July 1 to Sep 30, 14 day limit, no water supply. Hunting. Wenatchee NF.

SILVER FALLS (2400') 30½ mi NW of Entiat on County 371. 30 tent sites, 4 trailer spaces — 22' max, June 1 to Oct 15, 14 day limit, community kitchen. Fishing in Entiat R, hunting, hiking, Silver Falls just north of the camp. Wenatchee NF.

SODA SPRING (2000') 16 mi NW on US 2 from Leavenworth, then 9 mi north on State 207, then 9 mi west on FR 283. 5 tent sites, May 1 to Oct 31, 14 day limit, stream water. Fishing, hunting, nature trail, soda spring nearby. Just beyond the spring you can carve your name on Initial Rock. Wenatchee NF.

SPRUCE GROVE (2900') 35 mi NW on County 371 from Entiat. 2 tent sites, no trailers, June 15 to Oct 15, 14 day limit, river water. Fishing, hunting. Wenatchee NF.

SQUILLCHUCK STATE PARK (3200') 7 mi SW of Wenatchee via County 4. 25 campsites for tents or trailers — 22' max, fee, open all year, 7 day limit, hot showers. Hiking trails, skiing and sledding during the winter, lifts, equipment rentals. Rt 1, Box X237, Wenatchee 98801.

STAFFORD (2800') 4 mi SE on US 10 from Cle Elum, then 4¼ mi NE on US 97, then 13 mi north on County 107, then 1 mi north on FR 232, then 1 mi NE on FR 2226. 8 tent sites, 2 trailer spaces — 16' max, heavily-wooded area, June 1 to Nov 30, 14 day limit, stream water. Fishing, hunting, riding, mushroom gathering. Wenatchee NF.

SWAUK (3000') 4 mi SE on US 10 from Cle Elum then 18 mi NE on US 97. 16 tent sites, 3 trailer spaces — 22' max, Apr 15 to Nov 30, 14 day limit, supplies and cafe 4 mi, community kitchen, playground. Fishing, hunting, riding, Sculpture Rock Nature Trail. Wenatchee NF.

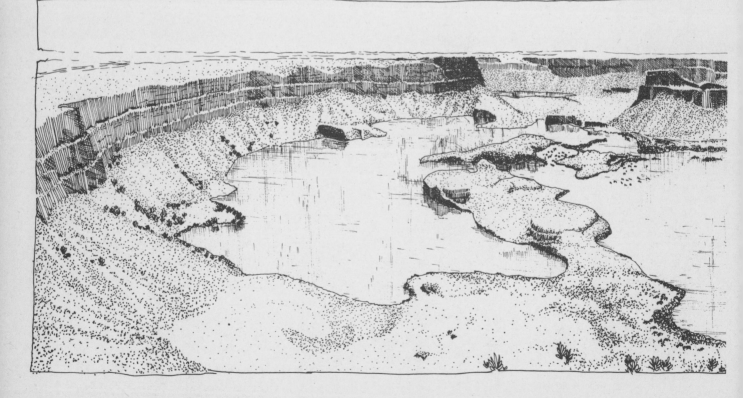

TAMARACK SPRING (4700') 15 mi SE on Int 90 from Cle Elum, then 1 mi south on County 3M, then 5½ mi NW on County 51, then 4½ mi NW on FR 1902, then 6½ mi SW on FR 1904. 1 tent sites, June 1 to Nov 30, 14 day limit. Hunting, riding, horse corral, spring nearby. Just east of the camp and off the road is the gravesite of a woman who died on a wagon train headed west. Wenatchee NF.

TANEUM (2200') 15 mi SE on Int 90 from Cle Elum, then 1 mi south on County 3M, then 5½ mi NW on County 51, then 4¼ mi NW on FR 1902. 11 tent sites, 2 trailer spaces — 22' max, May 1 to Nov 30, 14 day limit, community kitchen, sparse timber. Hunting, fishing, riding. Wenatchee NF.

TEANAWAY (2600') 4 mi SE on US 10 from Cle Elum, then 4¼ mi NE on US 97, then 9 mi NW via Teanaway Valley Rd. Several campsites for tents and trailers, open all year. Fishing, hiking, hunting. Boise Cascade.

THREE CREEK (2900') 36 mi NW on County 371 from Entiat. 3 tent sites, no trailers, June 15 to Oct 15, 14 day limit, river water. Fishing, hunting. Wenatchee NF.

TRONSEN (4000') 4½ mi SE on US 2 from Leavenworth, then 18 mi south on US 97. 12 tent sites, 5 trailer spaces — 22' max, heavily-wooded area, May 15 to Oct 30, 14 day limit, stream water. Meadow, hunting. Wenatchee NF.

TROUT LAKE TRAIL CAMP (4900') 6 mi south from Chatter Creek Campground by trail. 1 campsite, July 1 to Oct 31, stream water. Fishing. Wenatchee NF.

TUMWATER (2000') 10 mi NW of Leavenworth on US 2. 29 tent sites, 25 trailer spaces — 22' max, overflow area nearby, May 1 to Oct 31, 14 day limit, community kitchen. Fishing. The campsites are fairly secluded and some are beside Chiwaukum Cr and the Wenatchee R. Wenatchee NF.

TWENTYNINE PINES (2800') 4 mi SE on US 10 from Cle Elum, then 4¼ mi NE on US 97, then 11 mi NW on Teanaway Valley Rd. Several campsites for tents and RVs, all year. Fishing, hiking, hunting, berrypicking. Boise Cascade.

WENATCHEE RIVER COUNTY PARK (1000') 4 mi east of Cashmere on US 2 at Monitor. 40 overnight campsites for tents and RVs, fee, Apr 1 to Oct 15, all hookups, disposal station, hot showers, picnic shelter. Play fields, fishing and swimming. Grassy lawns, not much shade, near the hwy. PO Box 254, Monitor 98836.

WHITEPINE (1900') 25 mi NW on US 2 from Leavenworth then ½ mi west on FR 266. 5 campsites, trailers — 22' max, May 1 to Oct 31, 14 day limit, stream water, supplies and horse rentals 1 mi. Fishing, hunting, berrypicking. Wenatchee NF.

WHITE RIVER FALLS (2100') 16 mi NW on US 2 from Leavenworth, then 8½ mi north on State 207, then 1 mi NW on County 22, then 9 mi NW on FR 293. 5 tent sites, June 1 to Oct 15, 14 day limit, river water. Fishing, hunting, riding, berrypicking, hiking along the White River, waterfall nearby. Wenatchee NF.

YOUNG CREEK TRAIL SHELTER (2700') 10 mi NW on County 371 from Entiat, then 3½ mi NW on FR 2710 to Pine Flat Campground, then 8 mi NW on Trail 1409. 1 campsite, July 1 to Sep 30, 14 day limit, river water. Fishing, riding, hiking along Mad River. Wenatchee NF.

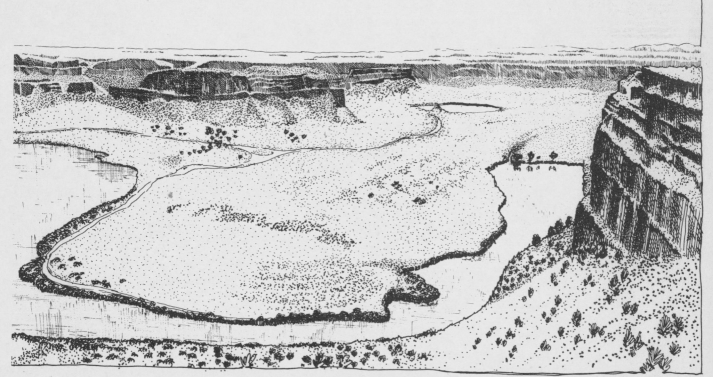

Dry Falls (see Map 12)

12

POTHOLES RESERVOIR created hundreds of small islands when an earth dam backed up water around sand dunes. It's an interesting place to go boating and to seek out a weekend island that's all your own. • **DRY FALLS** is one of the great natural attractions in the state, 2 miles south of Coulee City. In prehistoric times, this was one of the greatest waterfalls in geologic history. Niagara Falls would have looked small in comparison. The waterflow stopped after the ice age glaciers melted, but you can imagine what a sight it was then. • At the **WELLS DAM VISTA POINT** you can see some great examples of **INDIAN PICTOGRAPHS** that were salvaged from areas now underwater. There is a self-guided tour of the dam and a geological presentation of the Columbia River Basin. • **SOAP LAKE** is a highly mineralized body of water which is believed to have therapeutic values; even the early Indians thought so. Soap-like suds form along the shore in the spring and fall when the water temperature is cooler.

USGS 15-minute quadrangle key

BIG SUN RESORT (1500') On Marina Dr in the city of Moses Lake. Going west from town, take the second Moses Lake Exit 176. 13 tent sites, 35 trailer spaces — 36' max, fee, Apr 1 to Dec 1, reservations accepted, all hookups, disposal station, laundry. Fishing, sailing, motorboating, ramp, boat rentals, swimming, water skiing, bicycle trails. Shade trees, grass, ducks and geese. 2300 W Marina Dr, Moses Lake 98837. Privately owned.

BRIDGEPORT STATE PARK (1000') Just north of Bridgeport off State 17. 28 campsites, trailers — 28' max, fee, store, cafe, no firewood. Golf course, Chief Joseph Dam, fishing in Rufus Woods Lake. Box 846, Bridgeport 98813.

COULEE CITY COMMUNITY PARK (1575') At Coulee City on the south shore of Banks Lake. 75 tent sites, 10 trailer spaces — 24' max, fee, Apr 15 to Oct 15, 14 day limit, supplies ¼ mi, all hookups, disposal station. Fishing, boating, sailing, swimming, water skiing, hunting. Young locust, russian olive and willow trees, grassy lawns. Operated by Coulee City.

COULEE LODGE RESORT (1000') 7 mi south of Coulee City on Blue Lake. 28 tent sites, 29 trailer spaces, fee, Apr 15 to Oct 15, reservations accepted, all hookups, hot showers, store, laundry, playground. Sailing, canoeing, motorboating, launch, boat and motor rentals, fishing, swimming, water skiing, hiking and bicycle trails, hunting, caves and waterfalls in the area, interesting and colorful rock formations. Star Rt, Box 156, Coulee City 99115. Privately owned.

SUN LAKES STATE PARK (950') 7 mi south of Coulee City on State 17. 227 campsites for tents and trailers — 20' max, fee, all year, 7 day limit, RV hookups, disposal station, store, laundry, restaurant, hot showers. Fishing, sailing, canoeing, motorboating, launch, boat rentals, swimming, water skiing, games area, riding trails and horse rentals, bicycle paths and rentals, numerous hiking trails, stagecoach and hayrides, golf course, early cave shelters 2 mi, strange volcanic formations in the area, Summer Falls nearby. This is a very pleasant and highly popular beach area, separate areas for tents and trailers. Star Rt, Box 136, Coulee City 99115.

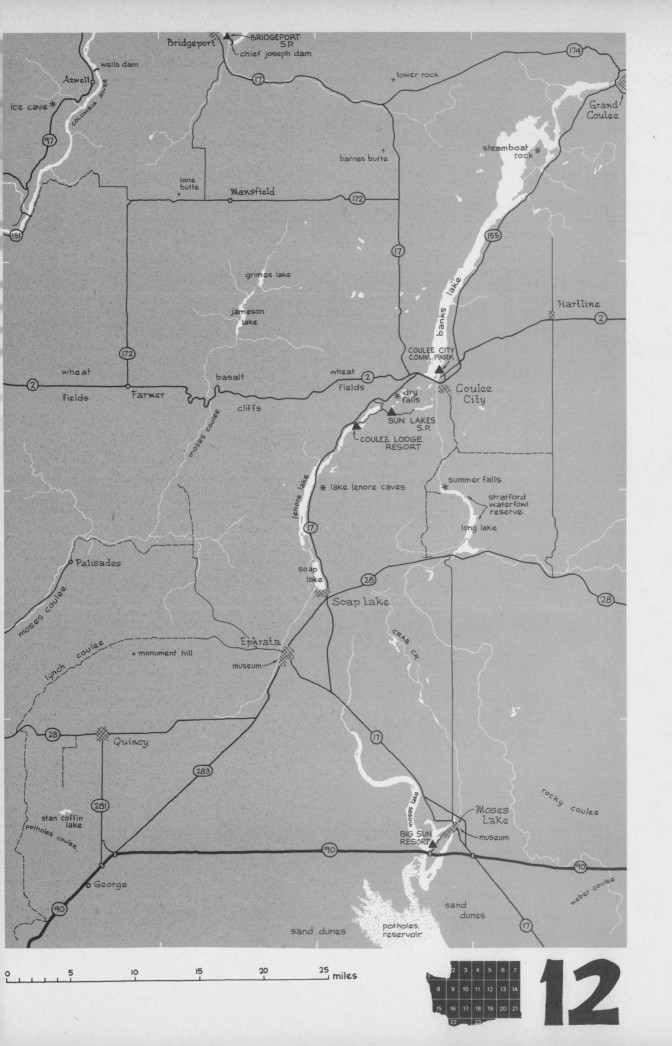

Bridgeport
BRIDGEPORT S.P.
chief joseph dam
wells dam
Azwell
ice cave *
COLUMBIA RIVER
97
151
17
tower rock +
174
Grand Coulee
steamboat rock *
barnes butte +
lone butte +
Mansfield
172
17
155
grimes lake
jameson lake
Hartline
2
banks lake
COULEE CITY COMM. PARK
wheat fields
2
Farmer
basalt cliffs
172
moses coulee
wheat fields
2
* dry falls
Coulee City
SUN LAKES S.P.
COULEE LODGE RESORT
lenore lake
* lake lenore caves
summer falls *
stratford waterfowl reserve
long lake
17
Palisades
moses coulee
soap lake
28
Soap Lake
28
Ephrata
lynch coulee
monument hill +
museum
CRAB CR
28
Quincy
283
17
281
stan coffin lake
potholes coulee
rocky coulee
moses lake
Moses Lake
museum
BIG SUN RESORT
90
90
George
weber coulee
90
sand dunes
17
sand dunes
potholes reservoir

0   5   10   15   20   25 miles

12

	2	3	4	5	6	7
1	8	9	10	11	12	13	14
	15	16	17	18	19	20	21
		22		23		

13

COULEE DAM NATL RECREATION AREA is full of things to see; the giant COULEE DAM, fascinating VOLCANIC GEOLOGY along the highways, a variety of WILDLIFE, and the water-carved canyon of the GRAND COULEE. (Also, see the heading to Map 6.) • FORT SPOKANE, 24 miles north of Davenport, was established to protect settlers and miners in the Colville and Okanogan Valleys. There is an old guardhouse, a museum full of frontier history and self-guiding trails. • KELLER FERRY, 14 miles north of Wilbur, is a free means of getting across Roosevelt Lake to the Colville Indian Reservation. It's a scenic drive on the northern side along the Sanpoil River to Republic, an old gold mining town.

USGS 15-minute quadrangle key

DETILLION BOAT CAMP (1300') 6 mi NE of Miles up the Spokane River, accessible by boat only. 12 campsites shaded by Ponderosa Pines, open all year, no limit of stay, boat dock. Swimming in warm shallow water, water skiing, fishing. This was the site of a small farming community before Lake Roosevelt was formed. Coulee Dam NRA.

FORT SPOKANE (1300') 26 mi north of Davenport off State 25. Modern campground with 62 well-developed campsites for tents and RVs, open all year, 14 day limit, 1 group campsite, supplies at Miles, boat ramp and dock, playground. Swimming beach with lifeguard, water skiing, fishing, campfire programs. Boaters will have to carry their gear about 500 feet to the sites. Old Ft Spokane and museum is a short distance from the camp. Coulee Dam NRA.

HAWK CREEK (1300') 14 mi NE of Creston. 7 tent sites, all year, no limit of stay, bring your own drinking water, boat dock. Water sports, fishing, Hawk Cr Falls. Across the channel from the camp are the remains of a railroad bed started during the mining rush of 1892. Coulee Dam NRA.

JONES BAY BOAT CAMP (1300') 5 mi east of Keller's Ferry on the south shore of Lk Roosevelt, accessible by boat only. 43 tent sites, all year, no limit of stay, no drinking water, boat dock. Fishing, hiking, deer and coyotes. The campsites are nestled under Ponderosa pines at the head of the bay. Coulee Dam NRA.

KELLER FERRY (1300') 14 mi north of Wilbur on State 21. 17 campsites for tents and RVs, all year, no limit of stay, boat ramp and dock, marina and supplies at the ferry landing, picnic shelter. Water skiing, swimming beach, fishing. Coulee Dam NRA.

PIERRE BOAT CAMP (1300') 4½ mi NE of Miles on the Spokane River, accessible by boat only. 11 tent sites in Ponderosa pines, open all year, no limit of stay, no drinking water — closest water at Detillion Campground. Boat dock, sandy beach, swimming, water skiing, fishing. Coulee Dam NRA.

PORCUPINE BAY (1300') 12½ mi north on State 2? from Davenport then 6½ mi NE to the Spokane River. 3? campsites under Ponderosa pines, May 1 to Oct 15, 1-day limit. Boat dock and ramp, sandy beach, swimming lifeguard, water skiing, fishing for walleye. During the summer, you'll find perch and spawning carp in Laughbon's Bay. Coulee Dam NRA.

SPRING CANYON (1350') 3 mi east of Grand Coulee on State 174. 78 well-developed campsites, all year, 14 day limit, group facilities, boat dock, low water launching ramp. Swimming, fishing. The campsites are located on grassy lawns under a variety of exotic trees. Coulee Dam NRA.

THREE MILE BOAT CAMP (1300') 4½ mi NW from Miles on the west shore of Lake Roosevelt, accessible by boat only. 2 campsites on a narrow neck of land, open all year, no limit of stay, no drinking water. Fishing. Screeching kingfishers and honking geese serve as alarm clocks in the mornings. The inlet behind the camp will protect you from the wind. Coulee Dam NRA.

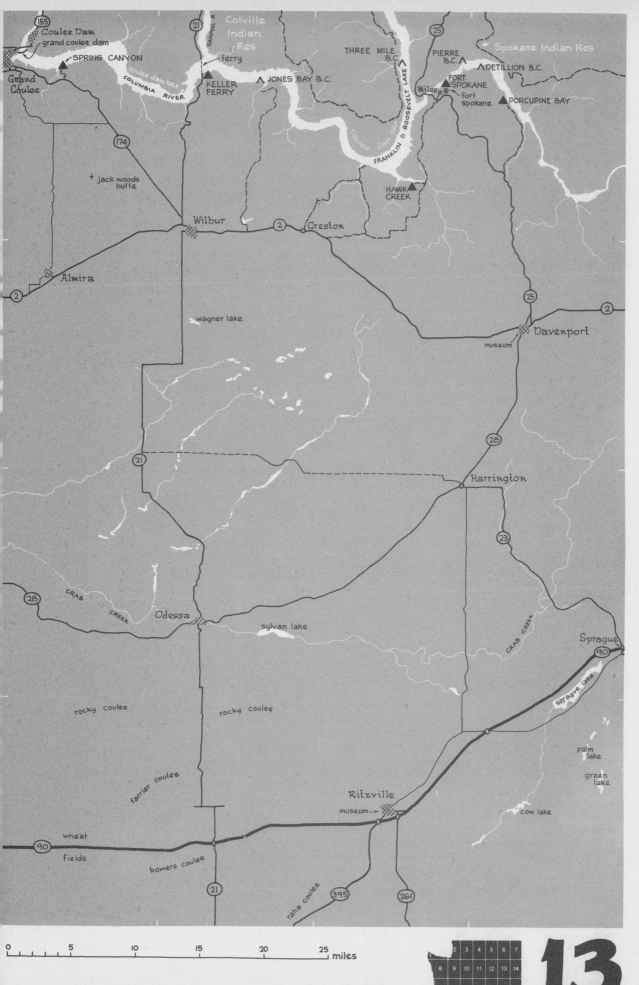

155 Coulee Dam
grand coulee dam
SPRING CANYON
Grand Coulee
coulee dam N.R.A.
COLUMBIA RIVER

21 SANPOIL R
Colville Indian Res
ferry
KELLER FERRY
JONES BAY B.C.

THREE MILE B.C.
FRANKLIN D ROOSEVELT LAKE
coulee dam N.R.A.

25
Spokane Indian Res
PIERRE B.C.
DETILLION B.C.
FORT SPOKANE
Miles
fort spokane
PORCUPINE BAY

174
+ jack woods butte

HAWK CREEK

Wilbur
2 Creston

2
25
Davenport
museum

wagner lake

28

21
Harrington

23

28
CRAB CREEK
Odessa
sylvan lake

CRAB CREEK

Sprague
90
Sprague lake

rocky coulee
rocky coulee

palm lake

green lake

farrier coulee

Ritzville
museum

cow lake

90 wheat
fields

bowers coulee

21

raha coulee
395
261

0   5   10   15   20   25 miles

13

TURNBULL NATL WILDLIFE REFUGE, just south of Cheney, has a Visitor Use Area for wildlife observation, nature study, photography, sightseeing, hiking and an interesting self-guiding tour (see page 82). • In the early days, SPOKANE HOUSE was a trading post and one of the first white settlements in Washington. A Visitor Center contains relics and artifacts from an archeological dig, along with other historical material. Located 9 miles NW of Spokane. • A few early INDIAN PAINTINGS can be seen on a protected rock surface, NW of Spokane on Indian Trail Rd. The reddish designs might have meant something to the Indian who painted them, but they are meaningless to anyone today. • RIVER RAFT TRIPS take you over the calm waters and thrashing currents of the Spokane River. Three types of trips are available, depending on the number of thrills you want. Spokane River Expeditions, Inc, West 3433 Taft Dr, Spokane 99208.

wallpinit	clayton	deer park	mt. spokane
reardon	medical lake	spokane	greenacres
sprague	cheney	spangle	fairfield

USGS 15-minute quadrangle key

FISHTRAP LAKE RESORT (2000') 8 mi NE on Int 90 from Sprague to the Fishtrap exit, then east to the lake. 10 tent sites, 20 trailer spaces — 28' max, fee, Apr 15 to Oct 1, no limit of stay, reservations accepted, small store, RV hookups, disposal station. Fishing dock, row boats, swimming, hiking. The lake is stocked with 130,000 Rainbow Trout each year. Sprague 99032. Privately owned.

LEWIS BROTHERS RESORT (2300') 12 mi south of Cheney at Badger Lake. 80 campsites for tents and trailers, fee, Apr 15 to Sep 31, no limit of stay, reservations accepted, disposal station, laundry, hot showers. Fishing, boat rentals, ramp, swimming, water skiing, trails, pine trees. Rt 1, Amber 99002. Privately owned.

LITTLE FALLS (1400') 12 mi north on State 231 from Reardon then 5 mi west on a county rd. 3 campsites in a stand of Ponderosa pines, open all year, no limit of stay, no drinking water, boat ramp. Fishing. The camp is located in a peaceful area and not heavily used. Coulee Dam NRA.

MOUNT SPOKANE STATE PARK (5100') 34 mi NE of Spokane off State 290 via Evergreen, Forker and Deadman Creek Rds. 12 campsites for tents or trailers — 24' max, fee, June to Oct, 7 day limit, picnic shelter, supplies 25 mi. Ski lodge with equipment rentals, ski touring trails, lifts. Hiking and riding trails. Views of Spokane, 8 lakes, 2 mtn ranges, 3 states and Canada.

PEACEFUL PINES (2400') 1 mi west of Cheney on State 904. 20 tent sites, 8 trailer spaces — 30' max, fee, open all year, 30 day limit, RV hookups, hot showers. Pine trees, 9 lakes within 15 mi, tours of Turnbull Natl Wildlife Refuge 5 mi. Rt 1, Box 111, Cheney 99004. Privately owned.

RIVERSIDE STATE PARK (2300') 3 mi NW of Spokane on Aubrey White Parkway. 110 tent sites in a wooded area near the Spokane River, fee, open all year, hot showers. Fishing, trails to the river, lava rock outcroppings, Nine Mile Falls north of the camp.

SMOKEY TRAIL CAMPSITE (1800') 6 mi SW on Int 90 from Spokane to the Medical Lake exit, then 1 mi east on Hallet Rd, then ½ mi south on Flint Rd. 70 campsites for tents and trailers — 30' max, fee, May 1 to Sep 30, no limit of stay, reservations accepted, supplies, disposal station, RV hookups, hot showers. Almost all of the campsites are shaded by Ponderosa pines, fishing and water sports 5 mi, hiking trails. The campground used to be the site of an Indian camp during a period of Indian wars in the area. Rt 1, Spokane 99204. Privately owned.

WEBBERT'S LANDING (2400') Just south of the town of Medical Lake on the north shore of Silver Lake. 5? campsites for tents and trailers, fee, group facilities, Apr 15 to Sep 30, no limit of stay, reservations accepted supplies ½ mi. Boating, ramp, swimming, duck hunting excellent trout fishing. Rt 1, Box 267, Medical Lake 99022. Privately owned.

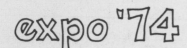

The folks in Spokane decided it was about time that an event of major importance focused on the problems of the environment. So, they set out to put together a meaningful World's Fair, EXPO '74, with a six month run (May 4 thru Oct 31, 1974). The theme became "Celebrating Tomorrow's Fresh, New Environment." The exhibits and entertainment were designed to "reflect man's awakening concern about his place in nature's cycle and to show what steps he is taking to restore and preserve his environment."

Located on two islands in the Spokane River, you'll find all the fun and entertainment that a fair is all about — major performing events from rock bands to symphonic orchestras, experimental theaters, international pavilions, a Smithsonian exhibit, tramways over the churning river, a turn-of-the-century carousel and exciting rides for the kids. Education is a major feature of the Exposition, and the problems and solutions related to the environment are intertwined in the exhibits and events (environmental symposia, films, and hopefully, a permanent center for residual programs).

For the duration of the fair, lodging reservations, and info about the fair, will be handled by HOSPITALITY SERVICES, Box 1974, Spokane 99210 (Telephone: 509-456-1974). They'll keep track of the availability of rooms, RV sites and campgrounds within a 2½-hour drive of Spokane. For those who plan to camp out, there will be a selection from about 6000 RV sites and 560 campsites in public campgrounds.

Getting to the fair without your car will be no hassle, since Spokane is served by AMTRAK, Greyhound busses and major airlines.

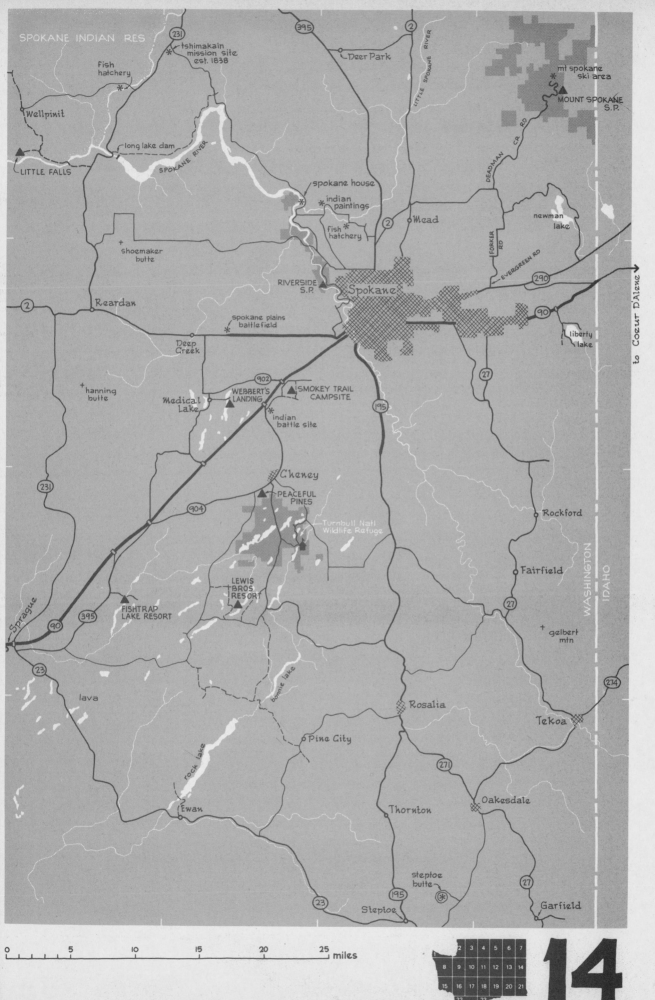

SPOKANE INDIAN RES

Wellpinit

LITTLE FALLS

fish hatchery

tshimakain mission site est. 1838

long lake dam

SPOKANE RIVER

shoemaker butte

RIVERSIDE S.P.

Deer Park

LITTLE SPOKANE RIVER

mt spokane ski area

MOUNT SPOKANE S.P.

DEADMAN C.P. RD

spokane house

indian paintings

fish hatchery

Mead

FORKER RD

newman lake

EVERGREEN RD

Spokane

liberty lake

to Coeur D'Alene

Reardan

Deep Creek

spokane plains battlefield

hanning butte

Medical Lake

WEBBERT'S LANDING

SMOKEY TRAIL CAMPSITE

indian battle site

Cheney

PEACEFUL PINES

Turnbull Nat'l Wildlife Refuge

Rockford

Fairfield

WASHINGTON IDAHO

Sprague

FISHTRAP LAKE RESORT

LEWIS BROS RESORT

gelbert mtn

lava

bonnie lake

Rosalia

Tekoa

rock lake

Pine City

Ewan

Thornton

Oakesdale

steptoe butte

Steptoe

Garfield

0   5   10   15   20   25 miles

2	3	4	5	6	7
8	9	10	11	12	13	14
15	16	17	18	19	20	21
22	23					

14

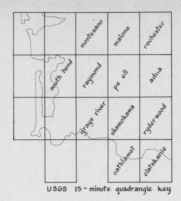

USGS 15-minute quadrangle key

MIMA MOUNDS are thousands of mysterious earth mounds only a few feet high that cover the prairies near Mima. No one has yet come up with a definite explanation for their existence. You can see the mounds off State 121, SW of Littlerock. • One mile east of the town of Gray's River is the last COVERED BRIDGE in use in the state. It's a picturesque, weathered wooden bridge dating back to 1905. It is 158 feet long, 14 feet wide and has a load limit of 4 tons. • There is a variety of wildlife to be seen at the WILLAPA NATL WILDLIFE REFUGE, 12 mi NE of Ilwaco. The main part of the refuge is located on LONG ISLAND, where you can explore a sand spit, "High Point" Meadow and the sites of old logging camps. • FORT COLUMBIA, near Chinook, was one of 3 forts built to guard the mouth of the Columbia River. You can still visit some of the old buildings and explore gun emplacements. • The SHIPWRECK of the SS Catala is easily accessible at the end of Point Brown Ave south of Ocean Shores. It was grounded during a winter storm, and the giant hulk now protrudes from the sands.

BAY CENTER KOA (15') At Bay Center, 3 mi west of US 101. 18 tent sites, 30 trailer spaces — 40' max, fee, open all year, no limit of stay, reservations accepted, supplies, hot showers, all hookups, laundry, playground. Boating and fishing 1 mi, bicycle trails and rentals, hiking and clamming along the beaches, beachcombing. Shady campsites on Willapa Bay. Box 315, Bay Center 98527. Privately owned.

BRUCEPORT (100') 6 mi west of South Bend on US 101. 20 tent sites, 10 trailer spaces, fee, group facilities, open all year, no limit of stay, disposal station, laundry, restaurant. Fishing, sailing, swimming, oyster beds, Willapa Bay. South Bend 98586. Operated by Pacific County.

BUSH PIONEER PARK (25') In Bay Center, 3 mi off US 101. 29 wooded campsites for tents or trailers, fee, open all year, no limit of stay, reservations accepted, playground. Fishing, swimming, bicycle and hiking trails, clamming. Located on a rugged peninsula at the mouth of the Palix River. Good exploring up and down the beaches. Box 303, Bay Center 98527. Pacific County.

CHINOOK PARK (10') At Chinook near the mouth of the Columbia River. 100 campsites for tents or trailers — 50' max, fee, May 1 to Oct 1, no limit of stay, supplies 1 mi, hot showers, firewood can be gathered on the beach. Fishing, boating, swimming, Ft Columbia SP 1 mi, salmon fishing port 1 mi. Chinook 98614. Pacific County.

FORT CANBY STATE PARK (20') Just south of Ilwaco off US 101. 90 tent sites, 60 trailer spaces, fee, open all year, RV hookups, store, snack bar, hot showers, boat launch. Driftwood collecting, winter storm watching, surf fishing, sand dunes, clamming, beachcombing, swimming in mild surf, sea caves, Light House nearby.

LAKE SYLVIA STATE PARK (500') 2 mi north of Montesano off US 12. 35 campsites for tents or trailers — 30' max, fee, group facilities, open all year, 7 day limit, hot showers, disposal station. Fishing, sailing, canoeing, ramp, no motor boats allowed, trail along the east side of the lake, bicycling, swimming (life guard). Raccoons, beaver and otter in the area. Lake Sylvia is narrow and a mile long. PO Box 701, Montesano 98563.

LONG ISLAND BOAT CAMPS (10') mi NE of Ilwaco off US 101, accessible by boat only — bring your own. 7 primitive campgrounds with 37 campsites, no limit of stay, no drinking water. Canoeing, hiking and bicycle trails, archery hunting in the fall, clamming, bird-watching, beachcombing, agate and rock collecting. Willapa Natl Wildlife Refuge, Ilwaco 98624.

RAINBOW FALLS STATE PARK (500') 16 mi west of Chehalis on State 6. 45 campsites for tents or trailers — 25' max, fee, open all year, 7 day limit, supplies 3 mi. Fishing, swimming, nature trail. Rt 4, Box 457, Chehalis 98532.

TWIN HARBORS STATE PARK (sea level) 2 mi south of Westport on State 105. 419 campsites for tents and trailers — 30' max, fee, all year, 7 day limit, supplies. RV hookups. Fishing, swimming, horse rentals, sand dunes, clamming beaches ¼ mi, boating 4 mi, salmon charters available. Westport 98595.

WILLIAMS PARK (15') 20 mi SW on US 101 from South Bend then 1 mi east. 25 tent sites, 40 trailer spaces, fee, May to Feb, no limit of stay, reservations accepted, supplies 1 mi, hot showers, all hookups, laundry. Silver Salmon fishing Aug to Dec, canoeing on the N Nemah River, swimming, hunting, hiking and riding trails. Elk, otter and black bear in the area. Star Rt, South Bend 98586. Privately owned.

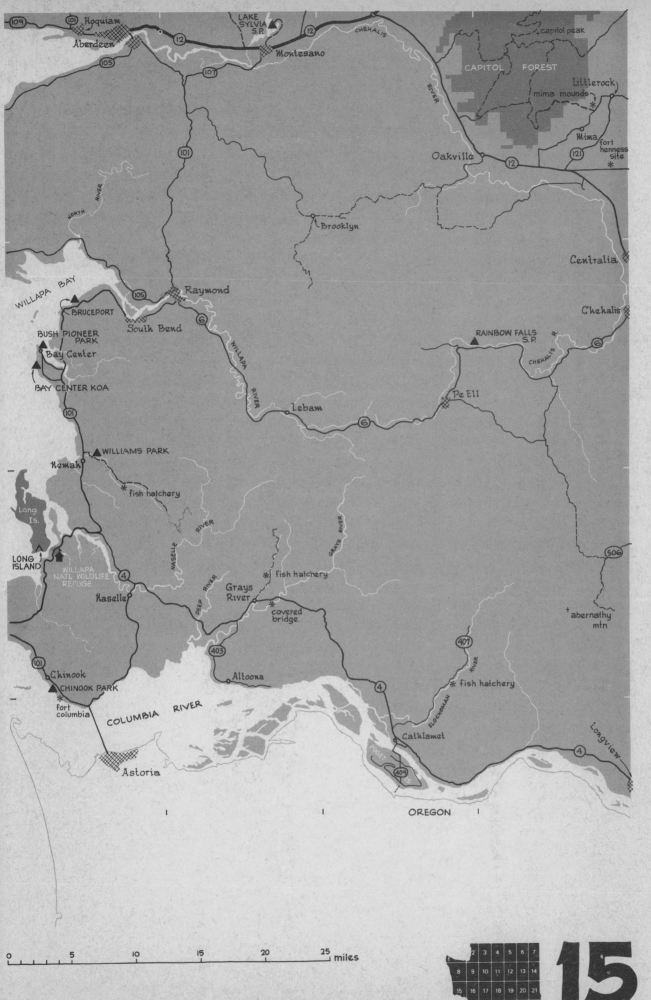

101 Hoquiam
Aberdeen

LAKE
SYLVIA
S.P.

12

12

CHEHALIS

RIVER

CAPITOL   FOREST

capitol peak

littlerock

mima mounds

Mima

fort
henness
site

105

107

101

107

Montesano

Oakville

12

121

NORTH RIVER

Brooklyn

Centralia

WILLAPA   BAY

105

Raymond

BRUCEPORT

South Bend

6

C'hehalis

6

BUSH PIONEER
PARK

Bay Center

BAY CENTER KOA

WILLAPA

RIVER

Lebam

6

RAINBOW FALLS
S.P.

Pe Ell

CHEHALIS

101

WILLIAMS PARK

Nemah

* fish hatchery

RIVER

GRAYS RIVER

506

Long
Is.

NASELLE

RIVER

* fish hatchery

abernathy
mtn

LONG
ISLAND

WILLAPA
NAT'L WILDLIFE
REFUGE

4

Naselle

DEEP RIVER

Grays
River

* covered
bridge

407

ELOCHOMAN RIVER

* fish hatchery

101

Chinook

CHINOOK PARK

*
fort
columbia

Altoona

403

4

Cathlamet

Longview

4

COLUMBIA   RIVER

PUGET IS.

409

Astoria

OREGON

0   5   10   15   20   25 ⌐ miles

1	2	3	4	5	6	7
8	9	10	11	12	13	14
15	16	17	18	19	20	21
22	23					

15

tenino	yelm	chop valley	kapowsin
centralia	onalaska	morton	mineral
castle rock	toutle	elk rock	spirit lake
	pigeon springs	cougar	mt. st. helens

USGS 15-minute quadrangle key

APE CAVE is the longest single lava tube in the U.S. (over 2 miles long). It was formed when molten lava flowed down the slopes of Mt St Helens. The outer surface started to cool, but the inner core kept flowing. Consequently, a hollow tube was formed. The cave is open for exploration, but you'll need a flashlight, heavy shoes and warm clothes. • **MT ST HELENS** is probably Washington's most beautiful volcano. It's 9,677 feet high, very symetrical and a favorite with mountain climbers. The mountain last erupted in 1842, but steam jets were seen near the summit in the 1940's. • On the **ANCIENT FOREST NATURE TRAIL**, at Spirit Lake Campground, you can see what's left of an ancient forest that existed prior to being covered by pumice deposits during eruptions on Mt St Helens.

BEAVER BAY (500') 2 mi NE of Cougar on FR N90. 100 campsites for tents or trailers, fee, 1 group site for 15 persons — reservations required, open all year, 14 day limit, hot showers, disposal station, lake water. Fishing, sailing, canoeing, motorboating, launch, swimming, water skiing, Ape Caves 5 mi NE. Pacific Power and Light Rec Dept, Public Service Bldg, Portland Ore 97204.

CEDAR CREEK TRAIL CAMP (3200') 46 mi east on State 504 from Castle Rock, then 1½ mi north by trail. 12 campsites, June 15 to Oct 15, 14 day limit, lake water, supplies and boat rentals 2 mi. Swimming, water skiing, sailing, fishing, hunting, riding. Gifford Pinchot NF.

CLEARWATER (1500') 18¼ mi east on N90 from Cougar, then 4½ mi north on FR 125, then 3½ mi north on FR N92. 24 tent sites, 9 trailer spaces — 16' max. Fishing, hunting, hiking along Muddy R. Gifford Pinchot NF.

COUGAR (500') At Cougar on the north shore of Yale Lake. 45 tent sites only, fee, Mem Day to Labor Day, 14 day limit, reservations accepted, supplies 1 mi, hot showers. Fishing, sailing, canoeing, motorboating, launch, swimming beach, water skiing. Pacific Power and Light Rec Dept, Public Service Bldg, Portland Ore 97204.

COUGAR PARK GROUP CAMP (500') At Cougar on Yale Lake. 1 group site for campers with tents only, 15 tent capacity, $15 per night, reservations required, Mem Day to Labor Day, 14 day limit. Swimming, fishing, water sports. Pacific Power and Light Rec Dept, Public Service Bldg, Portland Ore 97204.

DONNYBROOK TRAIL CAMP (3200') 46 mi east on State 504 from Castle Rock then 1 mi north by trail. 12 campsites, June 15 to Oct 15, 14 day limit, lake water, supplies and boat rentals 2 mi. Water sports, sailing, fishing, riding. Gifford Pinchot NF.

GRIZZLY LAKE TRAIL CAMP (4300') 46 mi east on State 504 from Castle Rock, then 6 mi north on Trail 211 from Spirit Lake. 7 campsites, July 1 to Oct 15, lake water. Swimming, fishing, riding. Gifford Pinchot NF.

KALAMA SPRING (2800') 1 mi west on County 503 from Cougar then 12¼ mi north on FR N818. 18 campsites for tents or trailers — 16' max, June 15 to Nov 15, 14 day limit, stream water. Fishing, hunting, hiking, mineral springs. Gifford Pinchot NF.

LEWIS AND CLARK STATE PARK (500') 9 mi SE on Int 5 from Chehalis, then 2½ mi east on US 12, then 1½ mi south. 32 campsites for tents and trailers — 16' max, fee, group facilities, Apr to Nov, 7 day limit, supplies 5 mi, 2 sheltered kitchens. Trails for nature study, historic John R Jackson House nearby. Rt 1, Box 520, Winlock 98596.

MILLERSYLVANIA STATE PARK (200') 12 mi north on Int 5 from Centralia to the Maytown exit then 3 mi east. 189 tent sites, 52 trailer spaces, fee, open all year, hot showers, RV hookups, disposal station, store, cafe, snack bar, golf course nearby, horse rentals, boat rentals and launch at Deep Lk, mooring facilities. Swimming, lifeguard, fishing for rainbow trout.

PANHANDLE LAKE TRAIL CAMP (4500') 46 mi east on State 504 from Castle Rock then 8 mi north on Trail 211. 5 campsites, July 1 to Sep 15, lake water. Swimming, fishing, riding. Gifford Pinchot NF.

RYAN LAKE (3200') 9 mi SW on FR 125 from Randle (see Map 17), then 12¼ mi SW on FR 115, then ¼ mi west on FR 1203. 4 tent sites, June 1 to Sep 15, no limit of stay, lake water. Fishing, hunting, riding, berrypicking. Gifford Pinchot NF.

SEAQUEST STATE PARK (800') 5 mi NE on State 504 from Castle Rock. 70 campsites for tents and trailers — 24' max, fee, Apr to Nov, 7 day limit, RV hookups, disposal station, hot showers, supplies ½ mi. Fishing in Silver Lk, hiking and bicycle trails. Box 3030 Spirit Lk Hwy, Castle Rock 98611.

SPIRIT LAKE (3200') 46 mi east of Castle Rock on State 504 on the south shore of Spirit Lake. 114 tent sites, 29 trailer spaces — 22' max, June 15 to Sep 15, 14 day limit, heavily-used, supplies and boat rentals 1 mi. Visitor Center, campfire programs at the amphitheater, water sports, fishing, hiking, riding, Ancient Forest Nature Trail, Botanical Trail, climbing on Mt St Helens. Horsemen's camp nearby. Gifford Pinchot NF.

ST HELENS LAKE TRAIL CAMP (4500') 46 mi east on State 504 from Castle Rock then 3½ mi north on Trail 207. 5 campsites, July 1 to Sep 15, lake water, supplies 4 mi. Swimming, fishing, riding. Gifford Pinchot NF.

SWIFT CAMP (500') 18 mi east from Cougar on FR N90 to the east end of Swift Reservoir. 100 campsites for tents or trailers, fee, Mem Day to Labor Day, 14 day limit, supplies 2 mi. Fishing, sailing, canoeing, motorboating, launch, swimming, water skiing. Pacific Power and Light Rec Dept, Public Service Bldg, Portland Ore 97204.

TIMBERLINE (4200') 50 mi east of Castle Rock on State 504. 10 tent sites, no trailers, June 15 to Sep 15, 14 day limit, supplies and water sports at Spirit Lake. Hiking trails. Good base camp for climbing on Mt St Helens. Gifford Pinchot NF.

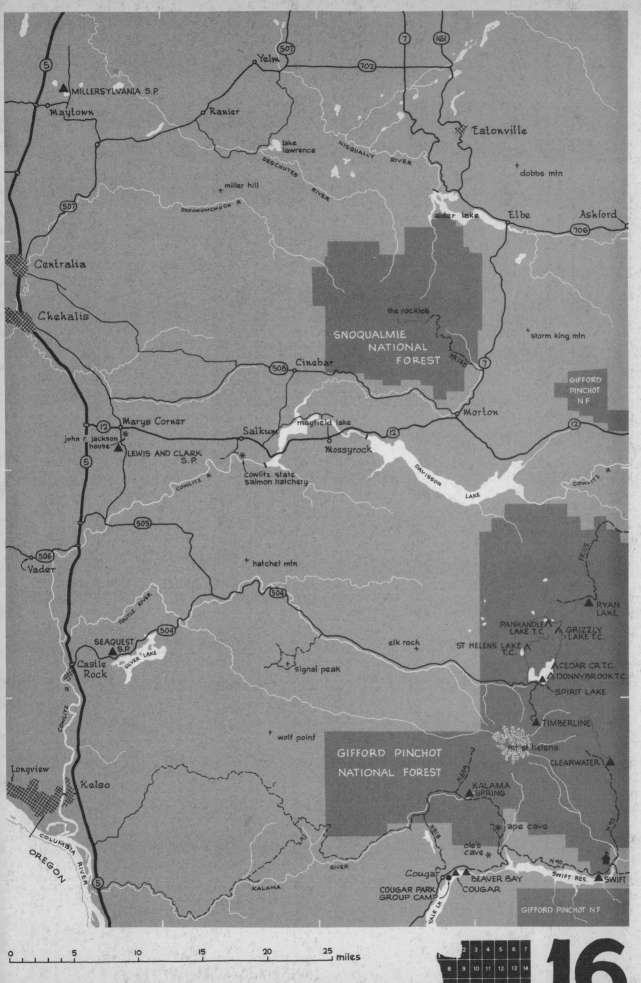

MILLERSYLVANIA S.P.

Maytown

Ranier

Yelm

Eatonville

lake
lawrence

NISQUALLY RIVER

dobbs mtn

DESCHUTES RIVER

alder lake

Elbe

Ashford

miller hill

SKOOKUMCHUCK R

Centralia

the rockies

storm king mtn

Chehalis

SNOQUALMIE
NATIONAL
FOREST

GIFFORD
PINCHOT
N F

Cinebar

Morton

FR 138

Marys Corner

mayfield lake

Salkum

john r. jackson
house

LEWIS AND CLARK
S.P.

Mossyrock

DAVISSON LAKE

COWLITZ R

cowlitz state
salmon hatchery

COWLITZ R

FR 115

Vader

hatchet mtn

RYAN
LAKE

TOUTLE RIVER

SEAQUEST
S.P.

SILVER LAKE

elk rock

PANHANDLE
LAKE T.C.

GRIZZLY
LAKE T.C.

St HELENS LAKE
T.C.

CEDAR CR T.C.

Castle
Rock

signal peak

DONNYBROOK T.C.

SPIRIT LAKE

COWLITZ R

wolf point

TIMBERLINE

GIFFORD PINCHOT

mt st helens

CLEARWATER

Longview

NATIONAL FOREST

KALAMA
SPRING

N 838

Kelso

COLUMBIA RIVER

ape cave

ole's
cave

N 90

OREGON

RIVER

SWIFT RES.

SWIFT

Cougar

KALAMA

COUGAR PARK
GROUP CAMP

BEAVER BAY
COUGAR

YALE LK.

GIFFORD PINCHOT N F

0   5   10   15   20   25   miles

16

17

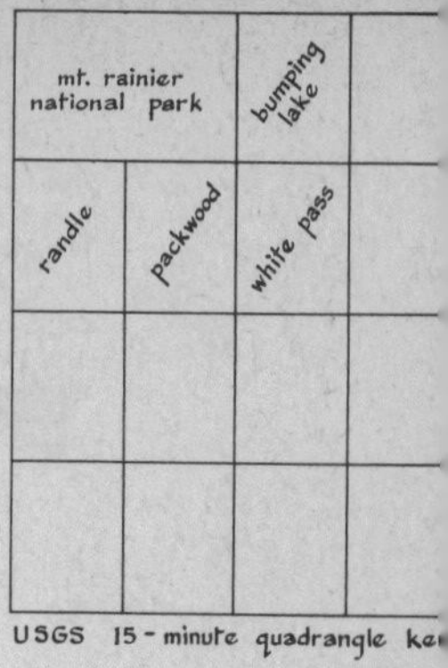

USGS 15-minute quadrangle ke

In Mt Rainier Natl Park, take time to explore the **GROVE OF THE PATRIARCHS, PARADISE ICE CAVES** (not open every year), **NISQUALLY GLACIER VISTA TRAIL** and the **WILDFLOWERS** at Sunrise. If you have the time, hike the **WONDERLAND TRAIL**, which encircles Mt Rainier • **PALISADES VIEWPOINT**, 10 miles NE of Packwood, has a picnic ground and a view of the spectacular **BASALT COLUMNS** across the river. The cliffs are made up of vertical columns of rock formed during the cooling of molten lava. • **SAWTOOTH HUCKLEBERRY FIELDS** (See CAMPING CALENDAR – Summer). • **WILDFLOWER** freaks will appreciate knowing that more than 400 species have been identified in the Bird Creek Meadows area north of the town of Trout Lake. It's a delicate alpine environment that deserves the utmost protection. • **BOULDER CAVE** is about ¾ mile west of Boulder Cave Campground, accessible by a trail along Devils Creek. A large overhanging mass of rock marks the mouth of the cave, which should only be explored by qualified spelunkers.

ADAMS FORK (2580') 18½ mi SE on FR 123 from Randle, then 4½ mi SE on FR 1302. 8 tent sites, 15 trailer spaces – 16' max, June 1 to Sep 30, no limit of stay. Dense firs, fishing, hunting, berrypicking. Gifford Pinchot NF.

AMERICAN FORKS (2800') 7½ mi NW on State 410 from Cliffdell then ¼ mi SW on FR 174. 35 campsites along the river, June 1 to Oct 31, 14 day limit, water well with hand pump, picnic pavilion, community kitchen, firewood dispenser. Rocky river bed, fishing, hunting. Snoqualmie NF.

BENCH LAKE (4850') 4½ mi north on County 17 from Trout Lake, then 4½ mi NE on FR N700, then 10 mi north on FR N80 (rough and narrow road). 30 tent sites, July 1 to Sep 30, 14 day limit, boat launch. Swimming, fishing, trail around the lake, mtn climbing, many species of wildflowers. Gifford Pinchot NF.

BIG BASIN TRAIL CAMP (6000') 4½ mi west on Trail 970 from Upper Bumping Campground, then 5½ mi north on Trail 958. 2 campsites, July 1 to Sep 15, no water supply. Hiking. Snoqualmie NF.

BIG CREEK (1800') 2¼ mi east from Ashford on State 706, then 1½ mi south on County 1504, then ½ mi east on Skate Cr Rd (FR 152). 22 tent sites, 8 trailer spaces – 22' max, Apr 15 to Sep 30, 14 day limit. Fishing in Big Cr, hunting, trail to Osborne Mtn. Gifford Pinchot NF.

BIG CROW BASIN TRAIL CAMP (5800') 28 mi NW on State 410 from Cliffdell, then 10½ mi NE on the Pacific Crest Trail, then ¼ mi east. 2 campsites, July 1 to Sep 15, stream water. Fishing. Snoqualmie NF.

BIG TWIN SISTER LAKE TRAIL CAMP (5200') 2 mi SW on Deep Creek Campground by trail. 6 campsites, July 1 to Sep 15, lake water. Swimming, fishing, Pacific Crest Trail 1 mi. Snoqualmie NF.

BIRD LAKE (5100') 4½ mi north on County 17 from Trout Lake, then 4½ mi NE on FR N700, then 5½ mi north on FR N80, then 1 mi west on FR N808. 18 tent sites, 2 trailer spaces – 16' max. Boating, fishing, hiking, mtn climbing. Trail to Bird Cr Mdws, where you'll find over 400 species of wildflowers in the surrounding area. Gifford Pinchot NF.

BLANKENSHIP MEADOW TRAIL CAMP (5200') ¾ mi north on FR 162 from Deep Creek Campground then 2½ mi south by trail. 3 campsites, July 1 to Sep 15, 14 day limit, no water supply. Hiking, riding. An old sheep herder's cabin is available for public use. Snoqualmie NF.

BLUE LAKE CREEK (1800') 16½ mi SE of Randle on FR 123. 6 campsites for tents or trailers – 16' max, dense lush foliage, Apr 15 to Sep 15, no limit of stay. Fishing, hunting, berrypicking, High Log Trail across the road, trail to Blue Lake 1 mi south. Gifford Pinchot NF.

BLUE LAKE TRAIL CAMP (4900') 17 mi SE from Randle on FR 123, then 3¼ mi NE on Trail 271. 3 campsites, June 15 to Sep 15, lake water. Fishing, hunting, riding. Gifford Pinchot NF.

BOULDER CAVE (2400') 1 mi north on State 410 from Cliffdell then 1¼ mi NW on FR 175. 22 campsites, June 1 to Oct 31, 14 day limit, river water, picnic pavilion, community kitchen. Hunting, fishing in swift flowing Naches River. Boulder Cave is about ¾ mi west by trail. Snoqualmie NF.

BUMPING BOAT LANDING (3400') 7½ mi NW on State 410 from Cliffdell, then 11 mi SW on FR 174, then ¼ mi north on FR 1740. 4 tent sites, 2 trailer spaces – 16' max, May 1 to Oct 31, 14 day limit, lake water, supplies and horse rentals 3 mi. Boating, launch, swimming, water skiing, fishing, hunting. Snoqualmie NF.

BUMPING CROSSING (3200') 7½ mi NW on State 410 from Cliffdell then 9½ mi SW on FR 174. 7 informal tent sites, June to Oct, 14 day limit, river water, horse rentals and supplies 1 mi. Boating and water sports 1 mi, fishing in Bumping R. Snoqualmie NF.

BUMPING LAKE (3400') 7½ mi NW on State 410 from Cliffdell, then 11 mi SW on FR 174, then ½ mi north on FR 1602. 31 wooded tent sites, June 1 to Sep 30, 14 day limit, stream water, cafe and horse rentals 3 mi. Water sports 1 mi, fishing, hunting. Snoqualmie NF.

CAT CREEK (3000') 19 mi SE from Randle on FR 123 then 6 mi SE on FR 1302. 3 tent sites, June to Nov, no limit of stay, stream water. Fishing, hunting, berrypicking. Gifford Pinchot NF.

CEDAR SPRINGS (2800') 7½ mi NW on State 410 from Cliffdell then ½ mi SW on FR 174. 14 tent sites, 4 trailer spaces – 16' max, June to Nov, 14 day limit, river water, fishing, hunting. Snoqualmie NF.

CHAMBERS LAKE (4500') 2½ mi SW on US 12 from Packwood, then 13½ mi SE on FR 1302, then 3½ mi NW on FR 1104. 7 tent sites, June 25 to Sep 30, 15 day limit, lake water. Fishing, hunting, mtn climbing, trailhead to Goat Rocks Wilderness. Gifford Pinchot NF.

CLEAR LAKE (3100') 25½ mi NE on US 12 from Packwood, then ½ mi south on FR 143, then ¾ mi south on FR 1312. 58 tent sites, 14 trailer spaces – 22' max, May 1 to Oct 31, 14 day limit, lake water, supplies and boat rentals 3 mi. Boat launch, hunting, horse rentals 2 mi. Snoqualmie NF.

CLOVER SPRINGS (6300') 16 mi NW on State 410 from Naches (see Map 18), then 1¼ mi south on county rd, then 18½ mi NW on FR 161. 8 tent sites, July 1 to Sep 30, 14 day limit, spring water, hunting, hiking, observation point. Trail 1 mi north of the camp leads to Flatiron Lake. Snoqualmie NF.

COLD SPRINGS (5700') 17 mi north of Trout Lake on Morrison Cr Rd (FR N81). 2 tent sites, July 1 to Sep 30, 14 day limit, shelter. Hiking, riding, mtn climbing on Mt Adams, spectacular views. Gifford Pinchot NF.

CORA LAKE TRAIL CAMP (4000') 2¼ mi east on State 706 from Ashford, then 3 mi south on county rd, then 4½ mi SE on FR 149, then 1½ mi south on FR 149C, then ½ mi south on Trail 914. 4 tent sites, June 15 to Sep 30, shelter, lake water. Swimming, fishing, mtn climbing, trail to Sawtooth Ridge. Gifford Pinchot NF.

COTTONWOOD (2300') 3 mi south of Cliffdell on State 410. 14 tent sites, 1 trailer space – 22' max, May to Nov, 14 day limit, water well with hand pump. Fishing in the Naches R, hunting. Snoqualmie NF.

COUGAR FLAT (3100') 7½ mi NW on State 410 from Cliffdell then 6 mi SW on FR 174. 2 tent sites, 6 trailer spaces – 16' max, June 1 to Sep 30, 14 day limit. Fishing, hunting, horse rental 3 mi, trail to Goat Peak. Snoqualmie NF.

COUGAR LAKES TRAIL CAMP (5000') 5 mi SW by trail from Upper Bumping Campground. 3 campsites, July 1 to Sep 15, lake water. Boating, swimming, fishing. Snoqualmie NF.

COUGAR ROCK (3180') 3 mi north of Longmire on State 706. 200 campsites with several pull-thru trailer sites, June to mid-Oct, 14 day limit, disposal station, supplies and Visitor Center at Longmire. Campfire programs, Wonderland Trail across the hwy. Mt Rainier NP.

COUNCIL LAKE (4300') 34 mi SE from Randle on F 123, then ½ mi north on FR N925. 15 tent sites, July to Sep 15, no limit of stay, lake water. Boating, huntin fishing, berrypicking, Council Bluff Trail starts ju beyond the camp. Gifford Pinchot NF.

CRANE PARK (3000') 35 mi NE on US 12 fro Packwood, then 3 mi south on FR 143, then 1 mi west c FR 1431. 4 tent sites, Apr 15 to Oct 31, 14 day limi lake water. Water sports, fishing, hunting, hikin Snoqualmie NF.

CROW CREEK (2000') 4½ mi NW on State 410 fro Cliffdell, then 2½ mi NW on FR 197, then ¼ mi NW c FR 1800, then ¼ mi NW on FR 182. 4 campsites, June to Oct 31, 14 day limit, river water. Fishing, huntin hiking. Snoqualmie NF.

CULTUS CREEK (4000') 18 mi NW of Trout Lake o FR 123. 60 tent sites, 6 trailer spaces – 16' max, June 1 to Sep 30, 14 day limit, info station. Hunting, berry picking, Pacific Crest Trail 1½ mi west, trailhead to India Heaven Backcountry. Gifford Pinchot NF.

DEEP CREEK (4338') 7½ mi NW on State 410 fror Cliffdell, then 13¼ mi SW on FR 174, then 7 mi south o FR 162. 6 campsites, July to Oct, 14 day limit, strear water. Hunting, riding, fishing 1 mi, trailhead to Twi Sister Lakes and Pacific Crest Trail. Good base camp fc horsemen. About a mile north is the site of old Coppe City – take the spur road west for a short distance to th ruins. Snoqualmie NF.

DEWEY LAKE TRAIL CAMP (5200') 28 mi NW on Stat 410 from Cliffdell then 2½ mi south on the Pacific Cres Trail. 3 campsites, July 1 to Sep 15, lake wate Swimming, fishing, hiking. Snoqualmie NF.

DOG LAKE (4300') 22¼ mi NE of Packwood on US 12 10 campsites, June to Nov, 14 day limit, lake water supplies 3 mi. Boat launch and rentals, water sports fishing, hunting, trail northward to Cramer Lake, Pacifi Crest Trail 1 mi west. Snoqualmie NF.

EAST POINT (3000') 35 mi NE on US 12 fron Packwood, then 3 mi south on FR 143, then 1½ mi wes on FR 1431. 4 tent sites, Apr 15 to Oct 31, 14 day limit lake water, not much shade. Boating, swimming, wate skiing, fishing, hunting, hiking. Snoqualmie NF.

GRANITE LAKE (5000') 7½ mi NW on State 410 fron Cliffdell, then 14 mi SW on FR 174, then 3½ mi SW o FR 163. 8 tent sites in an alpine environment, July tc Oct, 14 day limit, lake water. Boating, swimming, fishing hunting, hiking. Miners Ridge Lookout 1 mi SW Snoqualmie NF.

GREY CREEK (4000') 35 mi NE on US 12 fron Packwood, then 4½ mi south on FR 143, then 5½ mi SW on FR 133. 5 tent sites, June 1 to Nov 15, 14 day limit Hunting, fishing in the Tieton R. Snoqualmie NF.

HALFWAY FLAT (2500') 1 mi north on State 410 fron Cliffdell then 3 mi NW on FR 175. 12 campsites, June 1 to Oct 31, 14 day limit, river water, cafe 3 mi. Hunting fishing in the Naches River. Snoqualmie NF.

HAUSE CREEK (2500') 35½ mi NE of Packwood on US 12. 19 tent sites, 28 trailer spaces – 22' max, Apr 15 tc Nov 30, 14 day limit, supplies 3 mi. Water sports 5 mi fishing, hunting, hiking. Snoqualmie NF.

(Continued on the following page)

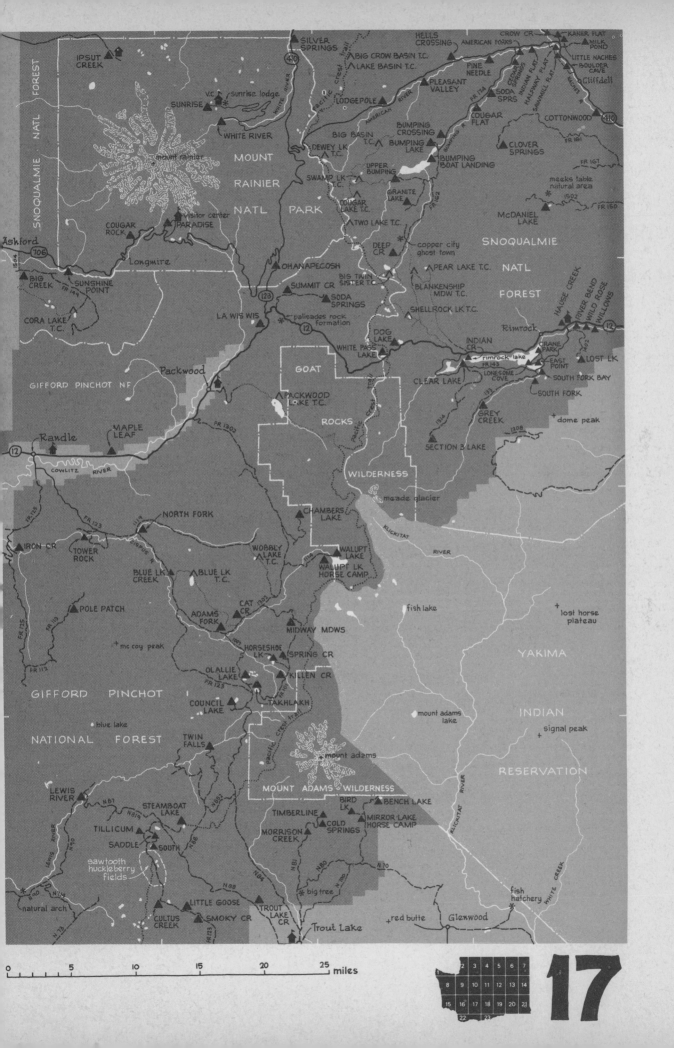

SNOQUALMIE NATL FOREST

IPSUT CREEK

SILVER SPRINGS

HELLS CROSSING
CROW CR
KANER FLAT
MILK POND
AMERICAN FORKS
LITTLE NACHES
BIG CROW BASIN T.C.
LAKE BASIN T.C.
BOULDER CAVE
CliffdelI
PLEASANT VALLEY
PINE NEEDLE
FR 174
CEDAR SPRINGS
INDIAN FLAT
HALFWAY FLAT
SAWMILL FLAT
V.C.   sunrise lodge
SUNRISE
LODGEPOLE
COUGAR FLAT
SODA SPRS
COTTONWOOD
410

WHITE RIVER
BIG BASIN T.C.
DEWEY LK T.C.
BUMPING CROSSING
BUMPING LAKE
CLOVER SPRINGS
FR 167

MOUNT
RAINIER
NATL PARK
mount rainier
SWAMP LK T.C.
UPPER BUMPING
BUMPING BOAT LANDING
meeks table natural area
1502
FR 150

COUGAR LAKE T.C.
GRANITE LAKE
FR 162
McDANIEL LAKE
SNOQUALMIE

Ashford
706
1504
visitor center
PARADISE
COUGAR ROCK
Longmire
TWO LAKE T.C.
DEEP CR
copper city ghost town
PEAR LAKE T.C.
NATL
FOREST

BIG CREEK
SUNSHINE POINT
FR 144
OHANAPECOSH
SUMMIT CR
BIG TWIN SISTER T.C.
BLANKENSHIP MDW T.C.
HAUSE CREEK
RIVER BEND
WILD ROSE
WILLOWS
12

CORA LAKE T.C.
128
LA WIS WIS
SODA SPRINGS
palisades rock formation
12
SHELLROCK LK T.C.
Rimrock
Packwood
DOG LAKE
WHITE PASS LAKE
INDIAN CR
rimrock lake
CRANE PARK
LOST LK
EAST POINT
1402

GIFFORD PINCHOT NF
GOAT
PACKWOOD LAKE T.C.
CLEAR LAKE
FR 143
LONESOME COVE
SOUTH FORK BAY
SOUTH FORK

Randle
MAPLE LEAF
FR 1302
ROCKS
GREY CREEK
1214
dome peak
1208

12
COWLITZ RIVER
SECTION 3 LAKE
WILDERNESS

NORTH FORK
FR 123
CHAMBERS LAKE
meade glacier
KLICKITAT
RIVER
lost horse plateau

IRON CR
TOWER ROCK
WOBBLY LAKE T.C.
WALUPT LAKE
WALUPT LK HORSE CAMP
fish lake

BLUE LK CREEK
BLUE LK T.C.
CAT CR
FR 1202
MIDWAY MDWS
YAKIMA

POLE PATCH
ADAMS FORK
HORSESHOE LK
SPRING CR
KILLEN CR
mount adams lake
INDIAN

mc coy peak
OLALLIE LAKE
FR 123
signal peak

COUNCIL LAKE
TAKHLAKH
RESERVATION

GIFFORD PINCHOT
blue lake
TWIN FALLS
mount adams

NATIONAL FOREST
MOUNT ADAMS WILDERNESS
BIRD LK
BENCH LAKE

LEWIS RIVER
N87
TIMBERLINE
MIRROR LAKE HORSE CAMP
KLICKITAT RIVER

STEAMBOAT LAKE
N819
MORRISON CREEK
COLD SPRINGS

TILLICUM
SADDLE
SOUTH
N88
N80
N10

sawtooth huckleberry fields
N81
big tree
fish hatchery

natural arch
LITTLE GOOSE
N88
TROUT LAKE CR
red butte
Glenwood
WHITE CREEK

CULTUS CREEK
SMOKY CR
FR 123
Trout Lake

0   5   10   15   20   25 miles

17

2	3	4	5	6	7
8	9	10	11	12	13	14
15	16	17	18	19	20	21
22	23					

HELLS CROSSING (3200') 12½ mi NW of Cliffdell on State 410. 12 tent sites, 5 trailer spaces — 16' max, June to Nov, 14 day limit. Fishing in the American R, hunting. Campsites are fairly secluded along the river, facing a high rock wall on the far side. Snoqualmie NF.

HORSESHOE LAKE (4200') 19 mi SE from Randle on FR 123, then 4½ mi SE on FR 1302, then 13 mi east on FR 101. 10 tent sites, 4 trailer spaces — 16' max, July 1 to Sep 15, no limit of stay, lake water. Mtn climbing, views of Mt Adams, boat launch, canoeing, fishing, riding, berrypicking, Mt Adams Wilderness 2 mi SE. Gifford Pinchot NF.

INDIAN CREEK (3000') 26½ mi NE of Packwood on US 12. 42 tent sites in a wooded area, 4 trailer spaces — 22' max, May 1 to Nov 15, 14 day limit, supplies. Boat and horse rentals 1 mi, meadows, fishing, hunting. Snoqualmie NF.

INDIAN FLAT (2600') 7 mi NW of Cliffdell on State 410. 12 campsites, June to Nov, 14 day limit, river water. Fishing in Swift running Bumping R, Indian Flat Trail across the hwy. Snoqualmie NF.

IPSUT CREEK (2100') 5¼ mi east of the NW entrance to Mt Rainier NP, accessible from Buckley (see Map 9). 33 campsites, May thru Oct, 14 day limit, Ranger Sta. supplies at Wilkeson 18 mi. Weekend campfire programs, Wonderland Trail leads to Moraine Park and Mowich Lake. Mt Rainier NP.

IRON CREEK (1200') 9½ mi SW of Randle on FR 125. 6 tent sites, 21 trailer spaces — 16' max, June to Sep 15, no limit of stay, pleasant woods. Hunting, fishing, trails along the Cispus R and Iron Cr. Gifford Pinchot NF.

KANER FLAT (2600') 4 mi NW from Cliffdell on State 410 then 2½ mi north on FR 197. 22 tent sites, 17 trailer spaces — 22' max, May 15 to Nov 15, 14 day limit. Fishing, hunting. This was once an old wagon train campsite on the Naches Trail. Snoqualmie NF.

KILLEN CREEK (4400') 19 mi SE from Randle on FR 123, then 4½ mi SE on FR 1302, then 13½ mi east on FR 101. 5 tent sites, July 1 to Sep 15, no limit of stay, stream water. Fishing, riding, hunting, trailhead to the north face of Mt Adams, mtn climbing. Gifford Pinchot NF.

LAKE BASIN TRAIL CAMP (5800') 28 mi NW on State 410 from Cliffdell, then 10 mi NE on the Pacific Crest Trail, then ½ mi east. 3 campsites, July 1 to Sep 15, lake water. Fishing. Snoqualmie NF.

LA WIS WIS (1460') 7 mi NE from Packwood on US 12 then ½ mi west on FR 1407. 93 tent sites, 13 trailer spaces — 16' max, all year, 15 day limit, supplies 3 mi. Hunting, fishing, Purcell Falls, trail along the Cowlitz R. Gifford Pinchot NF.

LEWIS RIVER (1500') 1½ mi west on State 141 from Trout Lake, then 12¼ mi NW on FR N88, then 7 mi north on FR 819, then 5 mi west on FR N87. 2 tent sites, June 15 to Sep 30, 14 day limit. Fishing, hunting, riding, hiking trail parallels the Lewis R. Gifford Pinchot NF.

LITTLE GOOSE (4021') 15½ mi west of Trout Lake on FR 123. 27 tent sites. 5 trailer spaces — 16' max, June 1 to Oct 31, 14 day limit. Hunting, berrypicking, Filloon Trail, access to Indian Heaven Backcountry. Corral and 5 campsites at the far end of the camp for horsemen. Gifford Pinchot NF.

LITTLE NACHES (2550') 4 mi NW of Cliffdell on State 410. 17 tent sites, May 1 to Oct 31, 14 day limit. Fishing, hunting, volcanic basalt features. Snoqualmie NF.

LODGEPOLE (3500') 19½ mi NW of Cliffdell on State 410. 22 tent sites, 7 trailer spaces — 22' max, June 1 to Oct 31, 14 day limit, river water, semi-dense stand of pines. Hunting, fishing in the American River. Snoqualmie NF.

LONESOME COVE (3000') 35 mi NE on US 12 from Packwood, then 3 mi south on FR 143, then 2 mi SW on FR 1431. 4 tent sites on a peninsula, Apr 15 to Oct 31, 14 day limit, lake water. Water sports, fishing. Snoqualmie NF.

LOST LAKE (3500') 35 mi NE on US 12 from Packwood, then ¼ mi south on FR 143, then 4½ mi SE on FR 1402. 5 tent sites, June 1 to Nov 15, 14 day limit, lake water. Boating, swimming, fishing, hunting, hiking. Snoqualmie NF.

MAPLE LEAF (1000') 6½ mi east of Randle on US 12. 15 tent sites, 3 trailer spaces — 16' max, open all year, supplies and cafe 5 mi. Hunting, fishing and riding 1 mi. Gifford Pinchot NF.

McDANIEL LAKE (3200') 12½ mi NW on State 410 from Naches (see Map 18) then 14¼ mi west (on county rd, FR 150 and FR 1502). 2 tent sites, June 1 to Oct 31, 14 day limit, lake water. Boating, fishing, hunting, hiking. Meeks Table Natural Area 1 mi north — no established trails, watch for rattlesnakes while hiking. Snoqualmie NF.

MIDWAY MEADOWS (4400') 19 mi SE from Randle on FR 123, then 4½ mi SE on FR 1302, then 9 mi east on FR 101. 4 tent sites, July 1 to Sep 15, no limit of stay, stream water. Fishing, riding, berrypicking, Pacific Crest Trail 1 mi east. Gifford Pinchot NF.

MILK POND (3000') 3½ mi NW on State 410 from Cliffdell then 1½ mi east on FR 173. 5 tent sites, June 1 to Oct 31, 14 day limit. Boating, fishing, rockhounding. Snoqualmie NF.

MIRROR LAKE HORSE CAMP (5200') 4½ mi north on County 17 from Trout Lake, then 4½ mi NE on FR N700, then 5¼ mi north of FR N80. 6 tent sites for horsemen, July to Oct, 14 day limit. Mtn climbing, fishing, riding, Bird Cr Falls 2 mi south. Gifford Pinchot NF.

MORRISON CREEK (4600') 11 mi north of Trout Lake on Morrison Cr Rd (FR N81). 9 tent sites, July 1 to Sep 30, 14 day limit, stream water, shelter. Hunting, hiking, base camp for mtn climbing, Crofton Ridge Trail just south of the camp. Gifford Pinchot NF.

NORTH FORK (1500') 12 mi SE of Randle just off FR 123. 16 tent sites, 27 trailer spaces — 16' max, Apr 15 to Sep 30, no limit of stay, dense shade. Hunting, fishing in N Fork Cispus River which flows thru the camp. USFS Guard Sta at the far end. Gifford Pinchot NF.

OHANAPECOSH (1914') 7 mi NE from Packwood on US 12 then 4 mi north on State 123. 232 heavily wooded campsites, several walk-in sites, mid-May to late Oct, 14 day limit, disposal station, supplies 7 mi at Coal Cr. Visitor Center, campfire programs, nature walks, amphitheater, Silver Falls Loop Trail, hot mineral springs nearby, fly fishing in the Ohanapecosh R. One of the most pleasant camps in the park. Mt Rainier NP.

OLALLIE LAKE (3700') 32 mi SE from Randle on FR 123, then 1 mi north on FR 101, then ½ mi north on FR 1007. 6 tent sites in a lightly-timbered area, July 1 to Sep 15, no limit of stay, lake water. Boating, canoeing, hunting, hiking, fishing, excellent view of Mt Adams. Gifford Pinchot NF.

PACKWOOD LAKE TRAIL CAMP (2900') 5¼ mi east on FR 1320 from Packwood then 4¼ mi east on Trail 78. 8 tent sites, June 25 to Sep 30, 15 day limit, rental boats at Packwood Resort on the north side of the lake. Fishing, hunting, boating, swimming, small island, trailhead to Goat Rocks Wilderness. Gifford Pinchot NF.

PARADISE (5300') 12 mi NE of Longmire. 65 campsites in a pleasant alpine environment, mid-July to mid-Sep, 10 day limit, very little shade. Visitor Center, snack bar, lodge. Wildflowers, trails to Mt Rainier summit and Nisqually Glacier. Mt Rainier NP.

PEAR LAKE TRAIL CAMP (4700') 26½ mi NE on US 12 from Packwood, then 2 mi north on FR 1410 to Muddy Cr, then 4 mi north on Trail 1105, then 1½ mi north on Trail 1148. 4 campsites, June 15 to Sep 15, lake water. Fishing, hiking. Snoqualmie NF.

PINE NEEDLE (3000') 10 mi NW of Cliffdell on State 410. 6 tent sites, small camp not suitable for trailers, June 1 to Oct 31, 14 day limit, river water. Fishing, hunting. Snoqualmie NF.

PLEASANT VALLEY (3300') 16 mi NW of Cliffdell on State 410. 6 campsites, July to Nov, 14 day limit, river water, community kitchen, picnic pavilion. Meadow, hunting, fishing. A log footbridge over the river is the beginning of the Kettle Cr Trail. Snoqualmie NF.

POLE PATCH (4400') 22¼ mi south on FR 125 from Randle, then 3 mi east on FR 112, then 6 mi north on FR 113. 4 tent sites, 8 trailer spaces — 16' max, July 1 to Sep 15, no limit of stay. Hunting, huckleberries, 1 mi from a viewpoint with an excellent view of 3 snowcapped mtns. Gifford Pinchot NF.

RIVER BEND (2500') 36 mi NE of Packwood on US 12. 6 tent sites, Apr 15 to Nov 30, 14 day limit, supplies 3 mi. Water sports 5 mi, fishing. Snoqualmie NF.

SADDLE (4200') 24 mi NW of Trout Lake on FR 123, then 1¼ mi east on FR N705. 10 tent sites, 2 trailer spaces — 16' max, June 15 to Sep 30, 14 day limit, no water supply. Hunting, fishing, good berrypicking area. A road leads to West Twin Butte Lookout site. Gifford Pinchot NF.

SAWMILL FLAT (2500') 3 mi NW of Cliffdell on State 410. 19 campsites, trailers — 22' max, May to Nov, 14 day limit, firewood dispenser, picnic pavilion. Fishing, hunting, volcanic basalt cliffs. Snoqualmie NF.

SECTION 3 LAKE (6000') 25½ mi NE on US 12 from Packwood, then 5½ mi south on FR 143, then 5½ mi south on FR 1311, then 4 mi SW on FR 1314. 3 tent sites, July 1 to Oct 31, 14 day limit, no water supply. Trail to Bear Cr Mtn. Snoqualmie NF.

SHELLROCK LAKE TRAIL CAMP (5500') 24½ mi NE on US 12 from Packwood, then 2½ mi NW on Trail 110 (trailhead is ½ mi west of Silver Beach Resort on Hwy 12), then 3 mi west on Trail 1142. 4 campsites, June 1 to Sep 15, 14 day limit, lake water. Fishing, trail to Cowlitz Pass. Snoqualmie NF.

SILVER SPRINGS (2600') 1 mi north of the NE entrance to Mt Rainier Natl Park on State 410. 16 tent sites, trailer spaces — 22' max, May 15 to Sep 30, 14 day limit, supplies and cafe 1 mi, shelter, horse rentals 1 mi. Fishing, bubbling springs near the center of camp, berrypicking. Snoqualmie NF.

SMOKY CREEK (3700') 12 mi west of Trout Lake on FR 123. 3 tent sites, June 15 to Oct 31, 14 day limit. Hunting, berrypicking, hiking trails cross the road just south of the camp. Gifford Pinchot NF.

SODA SPRINGS/Snoqualmie (3100') 7½ mi NW on State 410 from Cliffdell then 5 mi SW on FR 174. 20 tent sites, June to Nov, 14 day limit, river water, supplies and horse rentals 4 mi, community kitchen. Fishing, hunting. Natural mineral springs across the bridge at the south end of the camp. Snoqualmie NF.

SODA SPRINGS/Gifford Pinchot (3200') 9 mi NE on US 12 from Packwood then 5½ mi west on FR 1400. 8 tent sites, June 25 to Sep 30, 15 day limit. Bubbling springs near the camp entrance, trail to Cowlitz Pass and numerous mtn lakes. Gifford Pinchot NF.

SOUTH (4000') 24 mi NW on FR 123 from Trout Lake, then ¼ mi east on FR N705. 8 tent sites, 2 trailer spaces — 16' max, June 15 to Sep 30, 14 day limit. Riding, hunting, berrypicking. Gifford Pinchot NF.

SOUTH FORK (3000') 35 mi NE on US 12 from Packwood, then 4 mi south on FR 143, then ½ mi south on FR 1326. 12 campsites, Apr 15 to Nov 15, 14 day limit, river water, boat launch. Swimming, fishing, hunting. Snoqualmie NF.

SOUTH FORK BAY (2900') 35 mi NE on US 12 from Packwood, then 4 mi south on FR 143, then ¼ mi south on FR 1326. 5 tent sites, Apr 15 to Nov 15, 14 day limit, river water. Boating, water skiing, fishing. Snoqualmie NF.

SPRING CREEK (4000') 19 mi SE from Randle on FR 123, then 4½ mi SE on FR 1302, then 12 mi east on FR 101. 3 tent sites, July 1 to Sep 15, no limit of stay, stream water. Hunting, berrypicking, Mt Adams Wilderness 2 mi SE. Gifford Pinchot NF.

STEAMBOAT LAKE (4000') 1½ mi west on State 141 from Trout Lake, then 13¼ mi NW on FR N88, then 3½ mi NW on FR N819, then 3 mi SE on FR 123. 3 tent sites, very primitive camp — no tables or fireplaces, July 1 to Sep 30, 14 day limit, river water. Rough boating access, fishing, riding, berrypicking. Gifford Pinchot NF.

SUMMIT CREEK (2400') 9 mi NE from Packwood on US 12 then 2 mi north on FR 1400. 5 tent sites, June 15 to Sep 30, 15 day limit, stream water. Fishing, hunting. Gifford Pinchot NF.

SUNRISE (6500') 14½ mi west on Sunrise Hwy from the NE entrance to Mt Rainier NP. 85 campsites in an alpine environment, mid-July to early Oct, 14 day limit, some supplies at Sunrise Lodge. Wildflowers, Wonderland Trail nearby. Several campsites are near the Visitor Center, others are about 1½ mi down a dirt road near Shadow Lake. Mt Rainier NP.

SWAMP LAKE TRAIL CAMP (4800') 3½ mi west by trail from Upper Bumping Campground. 2 campsites, trail shelter beside the lake, July 1 to Sep 15, lake water. Boating, swimming, fishing. Snoqualmie NF.

TAKHLAKH (4500') 32 mi SE from Randle on FR 123 then 1½ mi north on FR 101. 33 tent sites, 9 trailer spaces — 16' max, July 1 to Sep 15 no limit of stay. Fishing in Takhlakh Lake, boat launch, canoeing, swimming, hunting, hiking around the lake, berrypicking, mtn climbing, excellent view of Mt Adams across the lake. Unusual volcanic rock formations 1 mi east. Gifford Pinchot NF.

TILLICUM (4300') 24½ mi NW of Trout Lake on FR 123. 37 tent sites, 12 trailer spaces — 16' max, June 15 to Sep 30, 14 day limit, stacked firewood around the camp. Hunting, huckleberry fields. Gifford Pinchot NF.

(Continued on following page)

TIMBERLINE (6300') 18 mi north of Trout Lake on Morrison Cr Rd (FR N81). Road is rough and narrow and not recommended for trailers. 3 tent sites, July 1 to Sep 30, 14 day limit, no water supply. Good views of peaks, mtn climbing, trailhead to Mt Adams Wilderness, Round-the-Mountain Trail leads westward. Gifford Pinchot NF.

TOWER ROCK (1100') 8½ mi SE from Randle on FR 123, then 1 mi SW on FR 1131, then ½ mi south on FR 1117. 10 tent sites, 1 trailer space — 16' max, Apr 15 to Sep 15. Fishing in Yellowjacket Cr, hunting, Tower Rock looms above the camp — a favorite for rock climbing. Gifford Pinchot NF.

TROUT LAKE CREEK (2100') 1½ mi west on State 141 from Trout Lake, then 4 mi NW on FR N85, then ½ mi north on FR N85. 8 tent sites, 1 trailer space — 16' max, June 15 to Sep 30, 14 day limit, stream water, dense woods. Fishing, hunting, berrypicking. Gifford Pinchot NF

TWIN FALLS (2700') 1½ mi west on State 141 from Trout Lake, then 16¼ mi NW on FR N88, then 5¼ mi north on FR 123 (Rough, narrow rd not recommended for trailers). 7 tent sites, July 1 to Sep 30, 14 day limit, stream water. Hunting, fishing in the Lewis River, Twin Falls nearby. Gifford Pinchot NF.

TWO LAKE TRAIL CAMP (5400') 28 mi NW on State 410 from Cliffdell then 10¼ mi south just off the Pacific Crest Trail. 2 campsites, July 1 to Sep 15, 14 day limit, lake water. Swimming, fishing, hiking. Snoqualmie NF.

UPPER BUMPING (3600') 7½ mi NW on State 410 from Cliffdell then 17 mi SW on FR 174. 4 tent sites, no trailers, July to Oct, 14 day limit, no drinking water. Trailhead to Cougar Lakes and the Pacific Crest Trail. Snoqualmie NF.

WALUPT LAKE (3900') 3 mi SW from Packwood on US 12 then 16½ mi SE on FR 1302 then 4½ mi east on FR 1114. 20 tent sites, 15 trailer spaces — 16' max, June 15 to Sep 30, 15 day limit, not much shade. Hunting, fishing, swimming, boating, launch, Pacific Crest Trail 4 mi east, access to Goat Rocks Wilderness. Gifford Pinchot NF.

WALUPT LAKE HORSE CAMP (3900') 3 mi SW from Packwood on US 12, then 11½ mi SE on FR 1302, then 3½ mi east on FR 1114. 6 campsites, trailers — 16' max, June 15 to Sep 30, 14 day limit, stream water, horse facilities. Riding. Gifford Pinchot NF.

WHITE PASS LAKE (4500') 21 mi NE on US 12 from Packwood then ¼ mi north on FR 1310. 15 campsites, June 1 to Nov 15, 14 day limit, lake water, supplies 1 mi, shelter, boat launch. Swimming, fishing, hunting, Pacific Crest Trail passes thru the camp. Snoqualmie NF.

WHITE RIVER (4400') 5 mi SW on Sunrise Hwy from the NE entrance to Mt Rainier NP, then 2 mi west. 125 campsites on 4 wooded loops, open late June to late Oct, 14 day limit, Ranger Sta, Wonderland Trail at Loop C, glacier climbing. Trails lead from Loop D to Emmons Glacier (1½ mi) and Glacier Basin (3¼ mi). Mt Rainier NP.

WILD ROSE (2400') 37 mi NE of Packwood on US 12. 11 campsites, trailers — 32' max, Apr 15 to Nov 30, 14 day limit, river water, supplies 3 mi. Hunting, fishing. Snoqualmie NF.

WILLOWS (2400') 37½ mi NE of Packwood on US 12. 16 campsites, Apr 15 to Nov 30, 14 day limit, river water, cafe and supplies 3 mi. Hunting, fishing in the Tieton R. Snoqualmie NF.

WOBBLY LAKE TRAIL CAMP (3400') 11½ mi SE on FR 123 from Randle, then 8¼ mi east on FR 1111, then 2½ mi east on FR 1124, then 2 mi south by trail. 3 tent sites, June 15 to Sep 15, 14 day limit, lake water. Riding, hiking, fishing, huckleberries. Gifford Pinchot NF.

Mount Rainier

USGS 15 - minute quadrangle key

There are some **INDIAN PAINTINGS** on a large rock cliff about 5 miles west of Yakima on the south side of US 12. The rock face has been pretty well vandalized, but some of the primitive paintings are still visible. This cliff was on an old Indian trail to the Wenas Mtns. • If you're interested in botany or zoology, visit the **MOXEE PREHISTORIC BOG**, 6 miles SE of Yakima on Birchfield Rd. This fragile bog was once the sanctuary of a prehistoric butterfly species. • **FORT SIMCOE**, 28 miles west of Toppenish, was established in 1856 to keep the lid on Indian hostilities. Five of the original and architecturally interesting buildings have been restored. There is a museum with displays of Indian crafts and an excellent picnic area in a grassy oak grove. • **GINKGO PETRIFIED FOREST** (see heading to Map 19.)

AHTANUM MISSION CAMPGROUND (1500') 14 mi west of Union Gap on Ahtanum Rd. 40 campsites for tents or trailers along 2 creeks, many sites well shaded under cottonwoods and locust, fee, group camping, Apr 15 to Oct 31, no limit of stay, reservations accepted, supplies 4 mi, some RV hookups, stream water, baseball, fishing 1 mi. This is the site of restored Ahtanum Mission, built in 1847 by Jesuit priests. Privately owned. Wiley Station 98906.

HANGING TREE (2000') 27 mi NW from Yakima on State 410 to Eagle Rock Store, then 3 mi SW, then 2 mi south on Rattlesnake Rd. 20 campsites for tents and RVs, fee, all year. Fishing, hunting, hiking. Boise Cascade.

NACHES (1800') 21 mi NW of Yakima on State 410. 14 campsites for tents and RVs, open all year. Fishing in the Naches River, hunting, hiking. Boise Cascade.

NILE CREEK (2500') 16 mi NW on State 410 from Naches, then 1¼ mi south on county rd, then 3¼ mi NW on FR 161. 2 campsites for tents and RVs — 16' max, June 1 to Oct 31, 14 day limit, stream water. Fishing, hunting. Snoqualmie NF.

RATTLESNAKE FORKS (2800') 12½ mi NW on State 410 from Naches, then 10½ mi west on county rd and FR 150. 6 tent sites, June 1 to Oct 31, 14 day limit, river water. Fishing, hunting. Snoqualmie NF.

RATTLESNAKE SPRINGS (2800') 12½ mi NW on State 410 from Naches then 9½ mi west on county rd and FR 150. 4 tent sites, June 1 to Oct 31, 14 day limit, no water supply. Fishing 2 mi, hunting. Snoqualmie NF.

WENAS (2800') 28 mi NW of Yakima on Wenas Valley Rd. 50 campsites for tents and RVs, open all year. This camp is considered a nature campground and suited primarily to those involved in nature study. Horses and motorbikes are not allowed. The Audubon Society holds its Memorial Day camp-out here. So far, its members have identified, in and around the camp, 184 species of birds, 45 species of mammals, 21 species of reptiles, 78 species of wildflowers, 36 species of edible mushrooms, 18 species of trees and 36 species of shrubs. Operated by Boise Cascade.

WINDY POINT (2000') 13 mi west of Naches on US 12. 15 campsites for tents and RVs, Apr 1 to Nov 30, 14 day limit, cafe 5 mi. Hunting, fishing. There are several caves once used by Indians just west of the camp above the river. Watch for rattlesnakes. Snoqualmie NF.

YAKIMA SPORTSMEN'S STATE PARK (1050') In Yakima. From Int 82 take Nob Hill and Moxee exit (State 24) east ¾ mi to Keyes Rd, then 1¼ mi north to the park. 30 tent sites, 34 trailer spaces, fee, group facilities, Apr 15 to Oct 15, 7 day limit, supplies 2 mi, hot showers, RV hookups, childrens playground, fishing in the Yakima River. Grassy lawns, ponds with ducks, geese and lily pads. A pleasant camping area shaded by cottonwoods, elms and willows. Separate tent and trailer areas. Rt 1, Box 49-B, Yakima 98901.

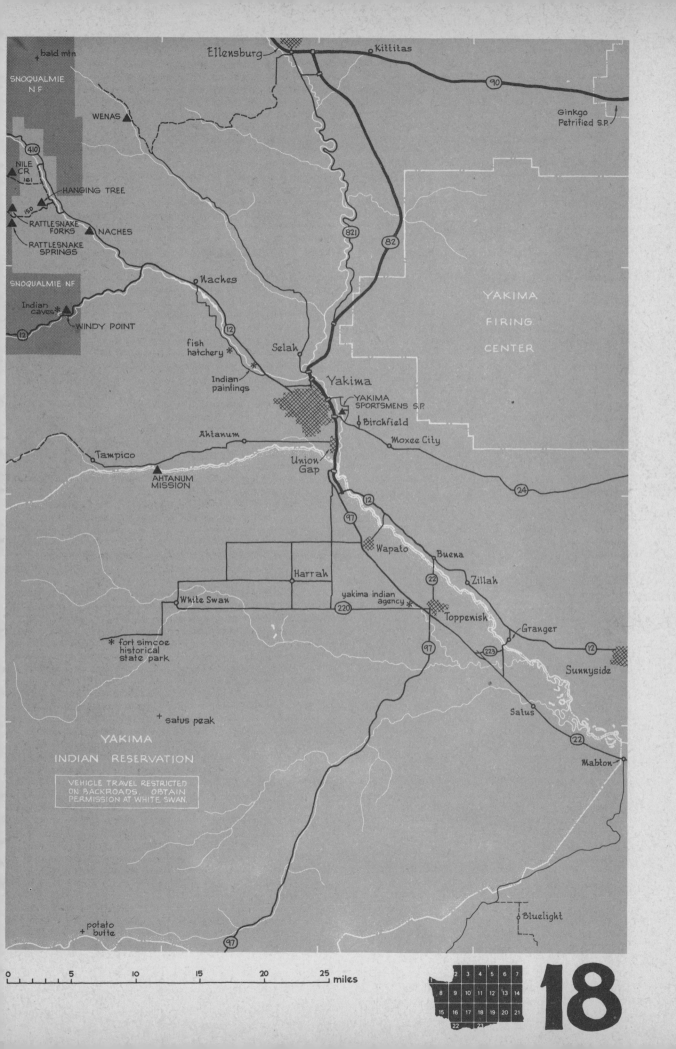

bald mtn

SNOQUALMIE
N F

WENAS ▲

410

NILE
CR
161

HANGING TREE

150

RATTLESNAKE
FORKS   ▲ NACHES

RATTLESNAKE
SPRINGS

SNOQUALMIE NF

Indian
caves ✱ ▲

WINDY POINT

12

Ellensburg   Kittitas

90

Ginkgo
Petrified S.P.

821   82

YAKIMA

FIRING

CENTER

Naches

12

fish
hatchery ✱

Indian
paintings ✱

Selah

Yakima

YAKIMA
SPORTSMENS S.P. ▲

Birchfield

Ahtanum   Moxee City

Tampico

▲ AHTANUM
   MISSION

Union
Gap

24

12

97

Wapato   Buena

Harrah

Zillah

22

White Swan

yakima indian
agency ✱

220

Toppenish

Granger

✱ fort simcoe
historical
state park

97

223

12

Sunnyside

Satus

+ satus peak

22

YAKIMA

INDIAN   RESERVATION

Mabton

VEHICLE TRAVEL RESTRICTED
ON BACKROADS. OBTAIN
PERMISSION AT WHITE SWAN.

Bluelight

potato
+ butte

97

0   5   10   15   20   25
                                                                    miles

2	3	4	5	6	7
8	9	10	11	12	13	14
15	16	17	18	19	20	21
22	23

18

beverly	smyrna	corfu	othello
priest rapids	coyote rapids	hanford	mesa
grandview	corral canyon	richland	eltopia
prosser	whitstran	badger mtn	pasco

USGS 15-minute quadrangle key

GINKGO PETRIFIED FOREST, at Vantage, is one of the most unusual fossil locations in the world. Over 200 varieties of petrified wood have been identified, and this is one of the few known sites where fossilized Ginkgo wood has been found. At the **INTERPRETIVE CENTER**, you can see a fantastic display of polished specimens, and learn how trees became petrified. Behind the Center are several rocks with **INDIAN PETROGLYPHS** chiseled into their surfaces. These were collected from basalt cliffs along inundated sections of the Columbia River. Partially excavated **PETRIFIED LOGS** can be seen in their natural state along trails 2½ miles east of the Interpretive Center. • **POTHOLES RESERVOIR** (see the heading to Map 12). • **WANAPUM DAM**, 2 miles south of Vantage, has a tour center with a good collection of Indian artifacts uncovered in villages, caves and fishing camps. In the fish viewing room, you can watch salmon making their way upstream. (Closed Nov. through Mar.)

C & R COLUMBIA CAMPGROUND (370') 4 mi west of Kennewick off Columbia Ave. 300 tent sites, 22 trailer spaces, fee, 7 day limit, hot showers, no firewood, supplies ½ mi, RV hookups, laundry. Fishing, boating, ramp, swimming, water skiing, hiking and bicycle trails, hunting. Ducks, geese and pheasants. Locust and Cottonwood trees. PO Box 6283, Kennewick 99336. Privately owned.

MAR-DON RESORT (1040') 11½ mi north on State 17 from Othello then 10 mi west to the west end of O'Sullivan Dam. 100 tent sites, 130 trailer spaces — 60' max, fee, all year, no limit of stay, grocery, disposal station, all hookups, laundry, restaurant, taxi boat for duck hunters. Fishing for walleye, bass and trout. Duck and pheasant hunting, sailing, canoeing, motorboating, rentals, ramp, swimming, water skiing, hiking, sand dunes, 50 lakes within 20 mi. Hot, dry summer environment. Royal Star Rt, Othello 99344. Privately owned.

POTHOLES STATE PARK (1060') 11½ mi north on State 17 from Othello then 10 mi west on O'Sullivan Dam Rd. 60 spaces suitable for RVs, trailers — 35' max, fee, open all year, 7 day limit, all hookups, disposal station, hot showers, playground. Fishing, sailing, canoeing, motorboating, launch, swimming, water skiing, hunting, hundreds of small sand dune islands in the lake. Hot, dry summer environment. Royal Star Rt, Othello 99344.

Petroglyphs at Ginkgo State Park

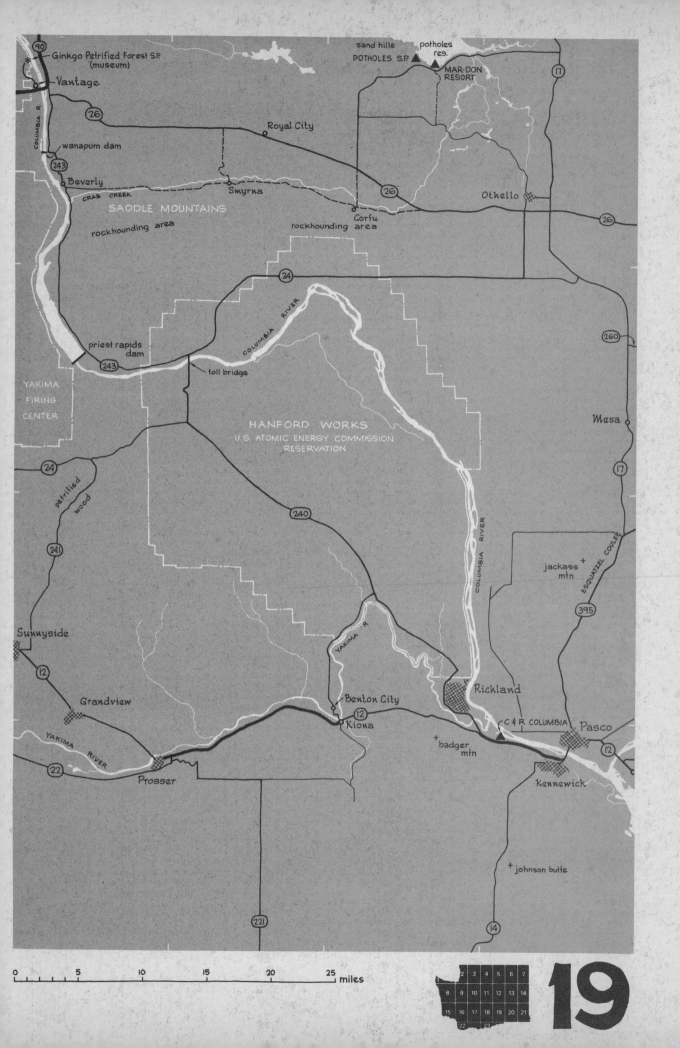

Ginkgo Petrified Forest S.P. (museum)

Vantage

sand hills
POTHOLES S.P.

potholes res.

MAR·DON RESORT

90

26

17

243

wanapum dam

Royal City

Beverly

CRAB CREEK

Smyrna

26

Othello

26

SADDLE MOUNTAINS

rockhounding area

Corfu area

rockhounding area

COLUMBIA R.

24

COLUMBIA RIVER

260

priest rapids dam

243

toll bridge

Mesa

YAKIMA FIRING CENTER

HANFORD WORKS
U.S. ATOMIC ENERGY COMMISSION
RESERVATION

24

petrified wood

240

COLUMBIA RIVER

jackass mtn

ESQUATZEL COULEE

17

241

395

Sunnyside

YAKIMA R.

Richland

12

Benton City

Grandview

12

Kiona

C & R COLUMBIA

Pasco

YAKIMA RIVER

badger mtn

12

22

johnson butte

Prosser

Kennewick

221

14

0   5   10   15   20   25   miles

2	3	4	5	6	7
8	9	10	11	12	13	14
15	16	17	18	19	20	21
		22	23		

19

MARMES MAN ARCHEOLOGICAL SITE, was the source of some of the oldest human remains and artifacts in the Western Hemisphere. The site is mostly submerged by backwaters from Lower Monumental Dam, but you can still see the mouth of the cave above the water line. The area is reached by a rough and rutty, 3-mile road from Lyons Ferry State Park. • **FORT WALLA WALLA MUSEUM COMPLEX** is a collection of early wooden buildings that have been restored and moved to the site to form a genuine pioneer village. You can see old cabins, a school, country store, train station, blockhouse and wagons of all kinds. It's open on Sunday afternoons during the summer. This preservation project deserves any contribution you can make. PO Box 1616, Walla Walla 99362. • **WHITMAN MISSION** was an important station on the Oregon Trail and the site of the massacre of Dr Whitman and 12 others in 1847. From the museum, trails lead to a memorial shaft, mission site, the grave, and a pleasant picnic area.

USGS 15-minute quadrangle key

FISHHOOK PARK (450') 16 mi NE from Burbank on State 124 then 4 mi north on county rd. 40 campsites for tents and RVs — 20' max, Apr 1 to Oct 1, 14 day limit, supplies 21 mi. Fishing in Lake Sacajawea, boating, ramp, swimming, water skiing, hunting 1 mi, grassy lawns, locust trees, waterfowl. Corps of Engineers.

FORT WALLA WALLA PARK (1000') 1 mi SW of Walla Walla on Dalles Military Rd. 100 campsites for tents or camp trailers (27' max) in a grassy tree-shaded area near Garrison Cr, fee, May 1 to Sep 30, 7 day limit, reservations accepted, hot showers, RV hookups, free firewood. Riding and hiking trails, archery range, Fort Walla Walla historical suite, museum. Box 478, Walla Walla 99362. City of Walla Walla.

LEWIS & CLARK TRAIL STATE PARK (1400') 5 mi east of Waitsburg on US 12. 30 tent sites, fee, open all year. Swimming, good fishing. Lewis and Clark camped near here on the Touchet River in 1806.

LYONS FERRY STATE PARK (540') 6 mi SW from Washtucna on State 260 then 14 mi SE on State 261. 50 campsites for tents or trailers — 30' max, fee, open all year, 10 day limit, supplies 8 mi, disposal station, concession stand in summer, hot showers, driftwood for campfires. Fishing, sailing, canoeing, motorboating, ramp, water skiing, swimming, Marmes Archeological site 3 mi north, variety of planted trees, waterbirds, pheasants. Box 447, Starbuck 99359.

PALOUSE FALLS STATE PARK (750') 6 mi SW from Washtucna on State 260 then 11 mi SE on State 261. 11 campsites for tents and RVs, fee, open all year, 10 day limit, planted trees, no firewood. Fishing, hiking trails, Palouse Falls. The surrounding area is full of interesting geological and rock formations. Watch for rattlesnakes when hiking. Box 447, Starbuck 99359.

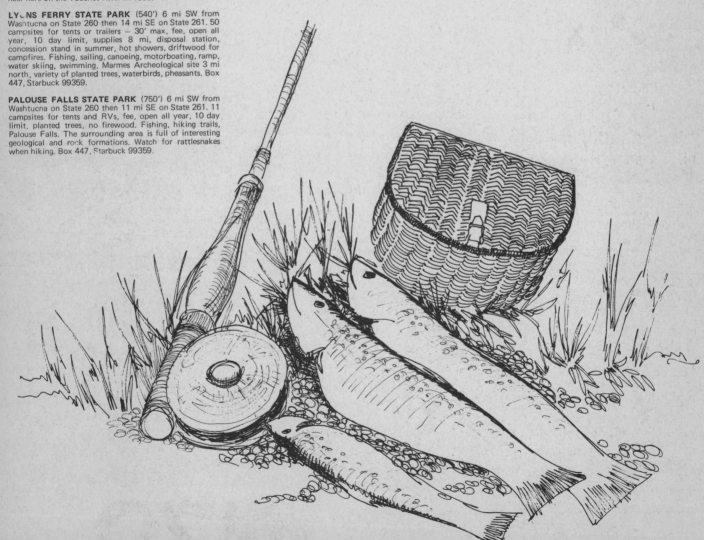

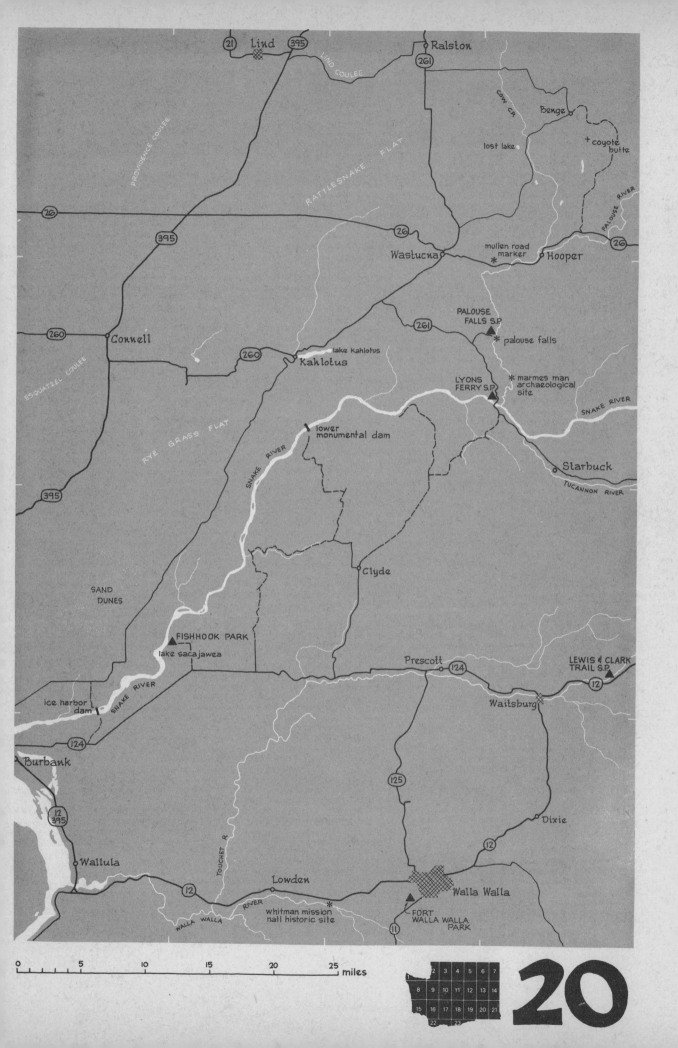

21 Lind 395 Ralston
261

LIND COULEE

COW CR

Benge
+ coyote butte

lost lake

PROVIDENCE COULEE

RATTLESNAKE FLAT

26

395

26

PALOUSE RIVER

26

mullen road marker *
Washucna   Hooper

ESQUATZEL COULEE

260 Connell   261
PALOUSE FALLS S.P. ▲
* palouse falls

260
260   lake kahlotus
Kahlotus

* marmes man archaeological site

RYE GRASS FLAT

LYONS FERRY S.P. ▲

SNAKE RIVER

lower monumental dam

SNAKE RIVER

Starbuck

TUCANNON RIVER

395

Clyde

SAND DUNES

FISHHOOK PARK ▲
lake sacajawea

Prescott
124   LEWIS & CLARK TRAIL S.P. ▲
12

SNAKE RIVER
ice harbor dam
124

125   Waitsburg

Burbank

12
395

Dixie

12

TOUCHET R

Wallula

12   Lowden   Walla Walla
WALLA WALLA RIVER   * whitman mission
nat'l historic site   FORT WALLA WALLA PARK ▲
11

0   5   10   15   20   25 miles

20

21

You can sign up for one, two or three-day **RIVER CRUISES** on the Snake River. Jet boats will speed into the great canyon where you'll see mountain goats and waterfalls, visit historical sites, shoot white water rapids, play on sandy beaches and explore gold mines. The tours are available at Asotin, Wash and Lewiston, Idaho. Write to the Chambers of Commerce for info. • At Buffalo Eddy, on the Snake River, Indians chipped **PETROGLYPHS** on the flat surfaces of rocks. This was once an early Nez Perce winter camp-site. • **WENAHA BACKCOUNTRY AREA**, in the Umatilla Natl Forest, is a roadless stretch of rugged basaltic ridges, deep canyons and rapid flowing streams. Trails, suitable for long or short hikes, criss-cross stream valleys, ridge tops and scattered stands of timber.

USGS 15-minute quadrangle key

ALDER THICKET (5100') 9 mi south on State 128 from Pomeroy, then 7½ mi south on County 107, then 3½ mi south on FR N911. 2 tent sites, June 15 to Nov 15, 10 day limit, no water supply. Hunting, berrypicking. Umatilla NF.

BIG SPRINGS (5300') 15 mi SE from Pomeroy on State 128, then 3½ mi south on County 191, then 5 mi south on FR N94. 6 tent sites, June 15 to Nov 15, 10 day limit, shelter. Hunting, hiking, berrypicking. Umatilla NF.

BOYER PARK AND MARINA (650') 15 mi SW from Colfax to Almota then 1 mi east. 39 campsites for tents or trailers — 30' max, fee, Mar to Nov, 14 day limit, store, restaurant, disposal station, RV hookups, laundry, hot showers. Fishing, sailing, canoeing, motorboating, launch, moorage facilities, sail and motorboat rentals, swimming, water skiing, Indian archeological site. Located on Lake Bryan and the Lower Snake River Canyon. Massive basalt cliffs, interesting geological features, hot summer environment. Rt 3, Box 69, Colfax 99111. Privately owned.

CABIN SADDLE (5500') 9 mi south on State 128 from Pomeroy, then 26 mi SE on County 107 and FR N911. 3 tent sites, June 15 to Nov 15, 10 day limit, no water supply. Hunting, riding, fishing 2 mi. Umatilla NF.

EDMISTON (5300') 14 mi SE from Dayton on County 118 then 6 mi south on FR N910. 6 tent sites, 3 trailer spaces — 16' max, June 15 to Nov 15, 10 day limit, spring water. Hunting, riding, berrypicking. Umatilla NF.

FIELDS SPRING STATE PARK (3800') 24 mi south of Asotin on State 129. 11 tent sites, open all year. Hiking and riding trails, views of the snake-like Grande Ronde River canyon, sledding and cross-country skiing in winter.

FOREST BOUNDARY (4400') 9 mi south on State 128 from Pomeroy then 7½ mi south on County 107. 2 tent sites, June 15 to Oct 15, 10 day limit, no water supply. Hunting, berrypicking. Umatilla NF.

GODMAN (5600') 14 mi SE from Dayton on County 118 then 11 mi south on FR N910. 5 tent sites, June 15 to Oct 15, 10 day limit, shelter, spring water. Hunting, riding, hiking. Umatilla NF.

GOVERNMENT SPRING (4600') 9 mi south from Pomeroy on State 128 then 9½ mi south on County 107. 2 tent sites, June 15 to Oct 15, 10 day limit, spring water. Hunting, riding, berrypicking. Umatilla NF.

INDIAN (5800') 2 mi east on State 12 from Walla Walla (see Map 20), then 16 mi SE on county rd, then 12½ mi east on FR N62, then 6½ mi NE on FR N910. 2 tent sites, July 15 to Nov 25, no limit of stay, stream water. Hunting, hiking, riding. Umatilla NF.

KAMIAK BUTTE (2800') 4 mi south on State 27 from Palouse then 2 mi west. 8 tent sites, 4 trailer spaces, fee, Apr 1 to Oct 31, 7 day limit. Good trails to the top of the butte, views of the countryside, interesting geological formations, Douglas fir and Ponderosa pine. Rt 1, Box 190, Palouse 99161. Operated by Whitman county.

MISERY SPRING (6000') 9 mi south on State 128 from Pomeroy, then 7½ mi SE on County 107, then 16½ mi SE on FR N911. Access road is rough and narrow and not recommended for trailers. 2 tent sites, June 15 to Nov 15, 10 day limit, spring water. Hunting, riding, hiking, views of the Wenaha Backcountry. Umatilla NF.

PATAHA (4200') 10½ mi south on State 128 from Pomeroy, then 5 mi south on County 185, then ½ mi south on Pataha Creek Rd (FR N906). 3 tent sites, June 15 to Nov 15, 10 day limit, stream water. Fishing in Pataha Cr, hunting, riding, hiking. Umatilla NF.

SEVEN SISTERS SPRING (5200') 24 mi SW on County 105 from Asotin, then 4 mi SW on FR N812, then 1 mi east on FR N800. 3 tent sites, June 15 to Nov 15, 10 day limit, spring water. Hunting, berrypicking. Umatilla NF.

SPRUCE SPRING (5700') 9 mi south on State 128 from Pomeroy, then 7½ mi south on County 107, then 11 mi SE on FR N911 (road not recommended for trailers). 2 tent sites, June 15 to Nov 15, 10 day limit. Hunting, riding, hiking, berrypicking. Umatilla NF.

STOCKADE SPRING (4650') 14 mi SE from Dayton on County 118 then 2 mi south on FR N910. 2 tent sites, June 15 to Nov 15, 10 day limit. Hunting, berrypicking. Umatilla NF.

TEAL SPRING (5600') 9 mi south on State 128 from Pomeroy, then 7½ mi south on County 107, then 9 mi south on FR N911. 5 tent sites, 2 trailer spaces — 16' max, June 15 to Nov 15, 10 day limit, shelter. Hunting, riding, hiking, berrypicking. Umatilla NF.

TEEPEE (5700') 14 mi SE from Dayton on County 118, then 11 mi south on FR N910, then 5 mi NW on FR N817. 5 tent sites, 3 trailer spaces, June 15 to Oct 15, 10 day limit, spring water. Hunting, berrypicking, riding, trails to Wenaha Backcountry and Oregon Butte. Umatilla NF.

TUCANNON (2600') 17 mi SW on County 101 from Pomeroy, then 4 mi SW on FR N98. 11 tent sites, 5 trailer spaces — 16' max, June 15 to Nov 15, 10 day limit, community kitchen, picnic shelter. Fishing in the Tucannon River, hunting, riding and hiking trail. Umatilla NF.

WICKIUP (6000') 24 mi SW on County 105 from Asotin, then 4 mi SW on FR N812, then 4 mi NW on FR N800. 6 tent sites, 3 trailer spaces — 16' max, June 15 to Nov 15, 10 day limit, spring water. Hunting, riding, hiking, berrypicking. Umatilla NF.

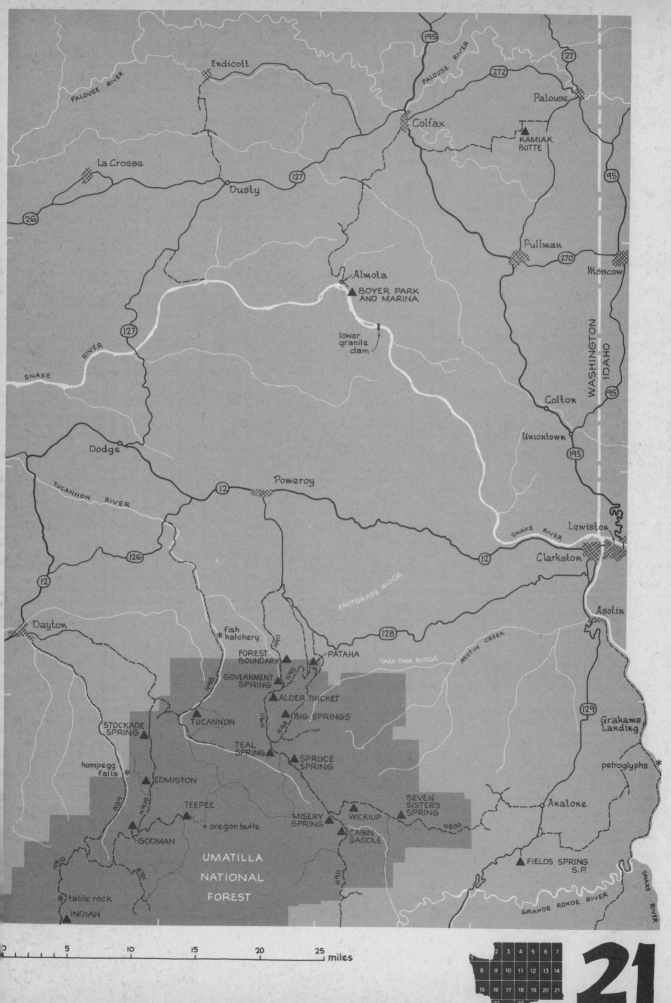

PALOUSE RIVER

Endicott

195

27

272

Palouse

Colfax

KAMIAK
BUTTE

PALOUSE RIVER

La Crosse

127

Dusty

95

26

127

Pullman

270

Moscow

Almota
BOYER PARK
AND MARINA

lower
granite
dam

Colton

Uniontown

SNAKE

RIVER

195

WASHINGTON

IDAHO

95

Dodge

Pomeroy

TUCANNON RIVER

12

Lewiston

SNAKE RIVER

126

12

128

Clarkston

KNOTGRASS RIDGE

Asotin

Dayton

* fish
hatchery

FOREST
BOUNDARY

PATAHA

TAM TAM RIDGE

ASOTIN CREEK

129

Grahams
Landing

N8lu

GOVERNMENT
SPRING

N80

ALDER THICKET

STOCKADE
SPRING

TUCANNON

N11u

BIG SPRINGS

N64

petroglyphs *

hompegg
falls *

N82

TEAL
SPRING

SPRUCE
SPRING

EDMISTON

N40

TEEPEE

+ oregon butte

MISERY
SPRING

WICKIUP

SEVEN
SISTERS
SPRING

N800

Anatone

GODMAN

N10

CABIN
SADDLE

N11u

UMATILLA

NATIONAL

FOREST

FIELDS SPRING
S.P.

N4701

* table rock

INDIAN

GRANDE RONDE RIVER

SNAKE

RIVER

0   5   10   15   20   25
miles

21

1 2 3 4 5 6 7
8 9 10 11 12 13 14
15 16 17 18 19 20 21
22 23

GIFFORD PINCHOT
NATIONAL FOREST

+ devils peak

lake merwin

YALE LK

CANYON CREEK
JAKES CREEK

Woodland

fish hatchery

Amboy

LEWIS

Yacolt

N508

PARADISE
POINT S.P.

SUNSET

N413

COLUMBIA R

502

Battleground

silver star mtn

* Indian pits

vancouver
lake

5

503

500

fish hatchery

BEACON ROCK
S.P.

Vancouver

Skamania

ft vancouver

14

140

Camas

Washougal

Portland

COLUMBIA

RIVER

OREGON

Beacon Rock

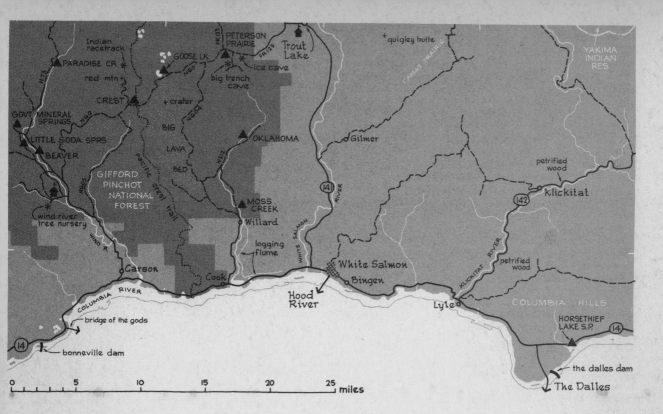

USGS 15-minute quadrangle key

BIG LAVA BEDS, between Carson and Trout Lake, cover 12,500 acres with interesting cracks, crevices, rock towers, small caves and weird lava formations. It's a fascinating place to explore and photograph, but beware of getting lost. • An historical **INDIAN RACETRACK** can be reached by a 1½-mile trail from Red Mountain, north of Carson. A ten-foot wide groove is visable where Indians raced their ponies while camped in the area. • **ICE CAVE**, near the wotn of Trout Lake, is not developed as a tourist facility, but you can explore at your own risk. Walk down the wooden stairs a few feet and you'll feel as if you're in a refrigerator. • At **GOVERNMENT MINERAL SPRINGS**, north of Carson, there is a well (Iron Mike) where you can pump mineral spring water for your own use. A sign indicates the various, and supposedly, curative minerals found in the water. Across the road and down a short trail, a small spring bubbles out of the ground. • **BEACON ROCK** was a dominant landmark for early explorers along the Columbia River. It's a state park now, and a twisting switchback trail leads to the top of the 848-foot "rock."

BEACON ROCK STATE PARK (100') 2 mi east of Skamania on State 14. 31 tent sites, camp trailers — 16' max, fee, group facilities, Mar to Nov, 7 day limit, reservations for group camping only, hot showers, laundry. Fishing, boating, ramp, boat moorage ½ mi west, swimming, water skiing, riding trails, Rodney Falls and Hardy Falls nearby. Trail to the top of Beacon Rock offers spectacular viewpoints and evidence of volcanic activity. Skamania 98646.

BEAVER (1100') 12 mi NW of Carson on the Wind River Hwy (State 135). 17 tent sites, 4 trailer spaces — 22' max, May 15 to Sep 15, no limit of stay, supplies and cafe 5 mi. Swimming, fishing in the Wind River. Good mushroom hunting in season. Gifford Pinchot NF.

CANYON CREEK (1200') 3 mi east from Amboy on State 503, then 3 mi east on county rd, then 12½ mi SE on FR N56. 8 tent sites, 3 trailer spaces — 16' max, May 1 to Oct 15, 14 day limit, stream water. Fishing in Canyon Creek, hunting. Gifford Pinchot NF.

CREST (3500') 6 mi NW from Carson on County 135, then 10¼ mi NW on FR 605, then 2½ mi east on FR 60. 3 tent sites, May to Nov, 14 day limit, horse corral and truck dock, no water supply. Hunting, lava beds. The Pacific Crest Trail leads northward to the site of an old Indian racetrack. Gifford Pinchot NF.

GOOSE LAKE (3200') 8 mi SW on State 141 from Trout Lake then 5¼ mi SW on FR N60. Rough, narrow road not recommended for trailers. 28 tent sites on the side of a hill overlooking the lake, June 15 to Sep 30, 14 day limit. Boat launch, canoeing, swimming, fishing, hunting, Lakeshore Trail, strange lava formations in the surrounding area. A maiden's footprints can be seen at low water on the NE shore. Gifford Pinchot NF.

GOVERNMENT MINERAL SPRINGS (1200') 14½ mi NW of Carson on the Wind River Hwy (State 135). 40 tent sites, 18 trailer spaces — 32' max, May 15 to Sep 30, no limit of stay, secluded campsites in dense woods. Fishing and hunting, trail to Observation Peak at the north end of the camp. Iron Mike Well and Bubbling Mike mineral spring. The camp is being phased out due to the hazard of decaying trees among the campsites. Gifford Pinchot NF.

HORSETHIEF LAKE STATE PARK (400') 8 mi west of Wishram on State 14. 10 campsites for tents or trailers, open all year, very little shade, grassy lawns by the lake, boat launch. Swimming, fishing, interesting rock bluffs. Ancient Indian village site downstream from the camp, petroglyphs on high rocks facing the Columbia R. Hiking trail up Horsethief Butte.

JAKES CREEK (1400') 3 mi east from Amboy on State 503, then 3 mi east on county rd, then 14½ mi SE on FR N56. 5 tent sites, May 1 to Sep 15, 14 day limit, stream water. Fishing, hunting. Gifford Pinchot NF.

LITTLE SODA SPRINGS (1100') 13 mi NW of Carson on State 135 then 1 mi south on FR N511. 5 walk-in tent sites across a footbridge in dense woods, May 15 to Sep 15, no limit of stay, supplies 5 mi. Fishing, hunting, soda-mineral water spring. Gifford Pinchot NF.

MOSS CREEK (1400') 8 mi north of Cook on Little White Salmon Rd (3087). 8 tent sites, 2 trailer spaces — 32' max, May 15 to Sep 15, no limit of stay, supplies 1 mi. Fishing and hunting. Gifford Pinchot NF.

OKLAHOMA (1700') 14½ mi north of Cook on Little White Salmon Rd (3087). 8 tent sites, 2 trailer spaces — 22' max, May 15 to Sep 15, no limit of stay. Fishing, swimming, hunting. Gifford Pinchot NF.

PARADISE CREEK (1500') 14 mi NW from Carson on State 135 then 6¼ mi north on FR N73. 25 tent sites, 6 trailer spaces — 32' max, May 15 to Sep 15, no limit of stay. Hiking along the river, trail to Lava Butte, fishing and hunting. Gifford Pinchot NF.

PARADISE POINT STATE PARK (300') 3 mi south of Woodland off Int 5. 70 campsites for tents and RVs, fee, all year, 7 day limit, disposal station, hot showers. Swimming holes, fishing, boat launch nearby. Campsites are located on a shady bluff overlooking the Lewis River.

PETERSON PRAIRIE (2896') 8 mi SW of Trout Lake on FR 123. 10 tent sites, 9 trailer spaces — 16' max, June 1 to Sep 30, supplies at Trout Lake. Hunting, hiking, berrypicking, ice and lava caves nearby. Gifford Pinchot NF.

SUNSET (1000') 3 mi SE from Yacolt on County 16 then 8 mi east on County 12. 17 tent sites, little shade, May 1 to Oct 15, 14 day limit. Fishing in E Fork Lewis River, hunting, Sunset Falls nearby. Gifford Pinchot NF.

22

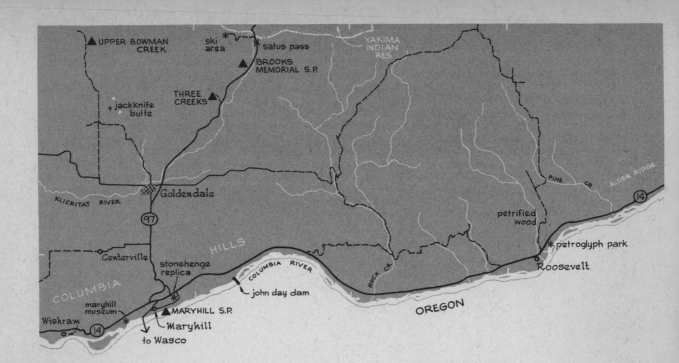

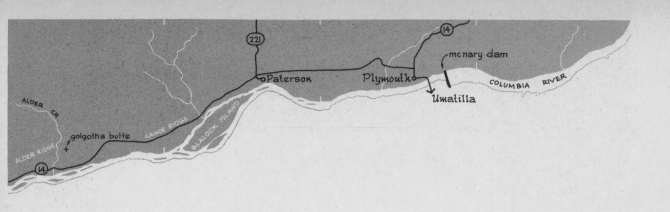

0 ⊢⊢⊢⊢⊢ 5 ⊢⊢⊢⊢ 10 ⊢⊢⊢⊢ 15 ⊢⊢⊢⊢ 20 ⊢⊢⊢⊢ 25 ⊢ miles

INDIAN PETROGLYPHS, which were salvaged from areas now submerged by backwaters along the Columbia River, are displayed at Petroglyph Park, 1½ miles east of Roosevelt. • A full scale replica of the mysterious **STONEHENGE,** in England, sits on a hill overlooking the Columbia River near Maryhill. It was built as a memorial to the men from Klickitat County who died in World War I. • At **McNARY DAM and LOCK,** near Plymouth, you can visit the exhibit room and fish counting station, and watch fish behind viewing windows. Outside, there is picnicking and swimming at McNary Beach and a good viewpoint on the south shore. • **MARYHILL MUSEUM** (see SEVERAL INTERESTING TOURS).

BROOKS MEMORIAL STATE PARK (3000') 12 mi north of Goldendale on US 97. 22 tent sites, 23 trailer spaces — 24' max, fee, June 1 to Oct 1, 7 day limit, supplies and coffee shop across the hwy, hot showers, picnic pavilion, all hookups. Winter skiing 2 mi north at Satus Pass. Hiking trails, ball field. The campsites are scattered in a pine forested area — used primarily as an overnight stopover, since there are no special recreational attractions. Rt 1, Box 87, Goldendale 98620.

MARYHILL STATE PARK (400') At Maryhill off state 14. Several campsites for tents and RVs overlooking the Columbia River, fee, very little shade at present, grassy lawns, swimming beach, old train engine on display. Stonehenge replica sits on a hill overlooking the park.

THREE CREEKS (2400') 9 mi north of Goldendale on US 97. Several campsites for tents and RVs, open all year, hunting, 4 acres located on West Prong Creek. Boise Cascade.

UPPER BOWMAN CREEK (3000') 14½ mi north of Goldendale on Cedar Valley Rd. Several campsites for tents and RVs, no fee, open all year, hunting, 3 acres located on Bowman Creek. Boise Cascade.

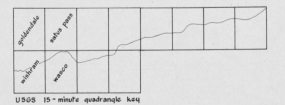

USGS 15-minute quadrangle key

23

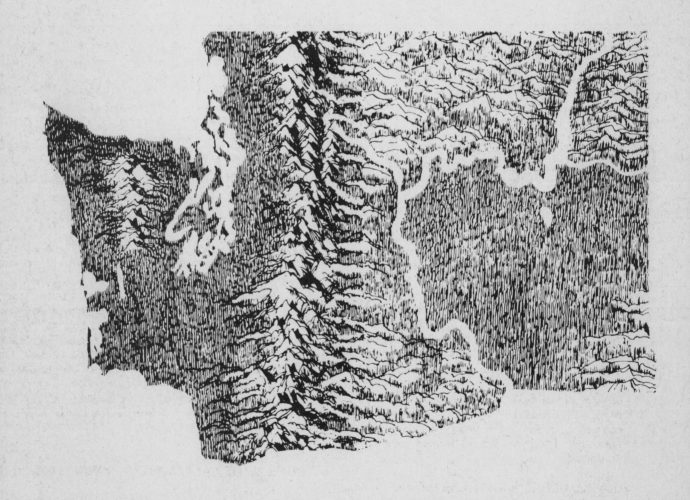

We ran across this map-sketch of Washington at Pacific First Federal Savings and Loan Association. The duck's-eye view of the topography is highly exaggerated, but gives a fair idea of where the mountains lie.

the map trip

ABOUT MAPS

This book is about maps — those visual, fascinating mind instruments that take you on a flying carpet tour of the land. They can help you plan ahead, think ahead and fill in the missing gaps about your destination or its alternatives. Absorb from them what you can and you'll know more about where you're going. Generally, they will serve you well in two ways: (1) they can let you plan a camping trip in detail before you ever set foot out the front door, and (2) once you're in the wilderness, maps can tell you just what kind of terrain lies ahead, the names of natural features, and the locations of points of interest worth exploring.

MAP RELATIONSHIPS

There are two series of US Geological Survey maps that are very useful to hikers and backpackers, anyone who travels the wilderness. These are the 7½-minute series and the 15-minute series. The 15-minute map is a compilation of four 7½-minute maps. It shows practically the same amount of information, covers four times as much area, and costs less. The 7½-minute map is theoretically more up-to-date and sometimes preferred by backpackers, but it's all a matter of choice. The maps in this book are keyed to the 15-minute series. If you've never carried one of these USGS maps on a camping trip — try it. The show all kinds of detail (trails, landmarks, lakes, springs, woods) that can be useful if you're hiking, hunting, fishing or whatever. To understand these maps better, here is an explanation of terms:

DEGREES AND MINUTES. The "degree" is the basic unit of measurement in mapmaking. A "minute" is a sub-division of a degree — 60 minutes equal one degree. All of our full-page Maps cover one degree of latitude and of longitude. Each of our Maps is then divided into four equal parts along each side using small tick marks, usually in white. Each division covers 15 minutes of latitude and longitude. By connecting opposite tick marks with vertical and horizontal lines, a grid is formed creation 16 "quadrangles."

QUADRANGLES. Any rectangular area of land shown as a map is called a quadrangle. Each of the quadrangles on our Maps corresponds to a USGS 15-minute topographic map. The scale of the maps is one inch equals approximately one mile, and the terrain is represented by "contour lines," usually at intervals of 80 and 40 feet.

CONTOUR LINES. The squirming lines on the maps, that look like loose vermicelli, are contour lines. These are imaginary lines used as a way of showing the topography in the third dimension. Each line connects all points of equal elevation above sea level. The closer the lines, the steeper the terrain — the further apart, the flatter. With a little practice, you can read them like a book and visualize the exact lay of the land.

USGS MAPS

There are several kinds available including special maps of National Parks and Recreation Areas, some with shaded-relief overprinting that makes the topography appear three-dimensional. A description of all the maps and how to order them is given in the "Index to Topographic Maps of Washington," which is free from the Distribution Section, US Geological Survey, Federal Center, Denver Colorado 80225. To order the 15-minute series maps, send the name of the map, the series, the state (e.g., Glacier Peak, 15-minute, Wash) and 75¢ for each to the above address. The maps are also sold at map shops and over-the-counter at the USGS sales office in Spokane. Some camping stores carry them for major recreation areas. It's cheaper to get them from government sources — at other places you pay a retailer's markup. (A free, 22-page booklet, "Topographic Maps," explains the symbols, colors and contours found on the maps.)

FOREST SERVICE MAPS

These are good, detailed maps for all 9 National Forests in the state, showing campgrounds, Ranger Stations, trails, boat launches, picnic areas and interesting attractions. A list of the Forests and the address for each is on page 79. Maps for as many as five Forests are free from Pacific Northwest Region, US Forest Service, PO Box 3623, Portland Ore 97208. Additional maps are 15¢ each. Colville and Kaniksu National Forests are in the Northern Region and those maps are available from US Forest Service, Federal Bldg, Missoula Montana 59801. The maps can also be picked up at Ranger Stations in the Forests.

BUREAU OF LAND MANAGEMENT MAPS

BLM publishes a series of maps that cover the entire state. Just tell them which specific area you need a map for, and they'll send it free. Available from Bureau of Land Management, PO Box 2965, Portland Oregon 97208. The maps show good detail as far as roads go, but campgrounds and recreation areas are hard to identify.

STATE HIGHWAY MAPS

AUTOMOBILE CLUB OF WASHINGTON. The AAA provides a good selection of maps to its members, covering the most popular parts of the state. There are regional maps for the Olympic Peninsula, Mt Baker, Mt Rainier, Okanogan and Central Basin areas. The "Explore and Enjoy" series offers several driving tours with maps and mile-by-mile descriptions of things to see and do. The AAA offices are also good sources of Forest Service, nautical and USGS maps, and a number of books (hiking and touring) are sold. Members get a discount, non-members pay regular prices.

OFFICIAL STATE HIGHWAY MAPS. Now that free service station maps are getting harder to find, try writing to the address under VACATION INFORMATION, on page 79, for a free Washington State Highway Map. This is an elaborate tourist guide that shows all of the federal and state parks, recreation areas, scenic points of interest and other information useful to travelers and visitors. This map can also be picked up at State Information Centers and Chambers of Commerce.

Here's a way to make this map a valuable tool. If you find the KEY MAP, on page 8, difficult for orienting yourself to various parts of the state, then create your own highly detailed key map as follows:

ALTERNATE KEY MAP. The maps in this book are bounded by degrees, as you can see by looking at the KEY MAP. Take your Official State Map and look for the degree indicators along the edge of the map (for example, 46° 00' or 47° 00', NOT 46° 30' — these are half degrees — ignore them). Make each section stand out by going over the degree lines with a felt pen to form a grid outlining the sections that correspond to the ones on our KEY MAP. Be careful — some of our sections cover more than one degree horizontally (1, 8, 15, 22 and 23). Write our Map numbers in each section of your highway map, and you will have a very detailed guide to the maps in this book. When finished, your highway map will look "gridded" like our KEY MAP.

NAUTICAL MAPS

Boating enthusiasts can get nautical maps giving depths and landmarks along the Washington coast, offshore islands, Puget Sound and the San Juan Islands, Franklin D. Roosevelt Lake (Coulee Dam NRA), and the length of the Columbia River from Pasco to the ocean. "National Chart Catalog 2" is your guide to these maps and includes a list of nautical chart agents. It's free on request from National Ocean Survey, 1801 Fairview Ave E., Seattle 98102.

COUNTY MAPS

Some county Chambers of Commerce can provide a free one; write to the county seat. The Metsker Map Company produces a good series of highly detailed maps for each county in Washington ($1.50 each). A price list for their complete selection is available from 111 South 10th St, Tacoma 98402.

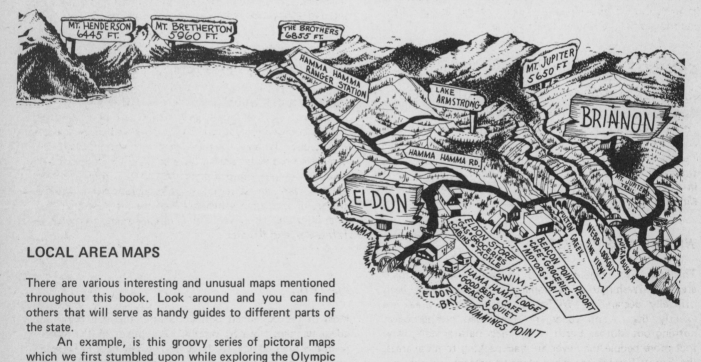

LOCAL AREA MAPS

There are various interesting and unusual maps mentioned throughout this book. Look around and you can find others that will serve as handy guides to different parts of the state.

An example, is this groovy series of pictoral maps which we first stumbled upon while exploring the Olympic Peninsula. WEST END MAP is our favorite. It's a pen and ink sketch map of Neah Bay and Cape Alava which shows all the backroads, trails, facilities and interesting features in the area — a good explorer's map because of the detail shown. Other maps in the series are: HOOD CANAL MAP; WESTPORT; GRAYLAND/NORTHCOVE/TOKELAND; LA PUSH/FORKS; and LONG BEACH/ILWACO. They were drawn by Pastor Esko Rentola, who is currently ministering among the Klallam Indians on the Little Boston Indian Reservation. (This sketch shows his unique style). The maps can be purchased at resort stores in each area or by sending 25¢, for each, to Pastor Esko Rentola, Little Boston Indian Reservation, Rt 2, Kingston Wash 98346.

stuff everyone should know

GOLDEN EAGLE PASSPORT

This is a handy gadget. It's a card that costs $10 and provides free one-year access to Federal recreation areas where entrance fees are charged. It's extremely useful because National Parks and many National Recreation Areas charge entry fees of $1 to $3 per day. However, it does not get you a discount at any Federal campgrounds, and it does not cover concessionaires' fees for services or facilities. If you visit a lot of National Recreation Areas it's a bargain, and the money from these permits is used only for buying more recreational land. Get the Passport at entrances to Federal recreational areas, major post offices, National Forest headquarters or write directly to the Bureau of Outdoor Recreation, Operation Golden Eagle, Box 7763, Washington DC 20044.

GOLDEN AGE PASSPORT

Anyone over 62 years of age can get one of these free. Good for a calendar year, it allows you free entry to National Parks and a half-price rate for any Federal recreation site, including campgrounds (if the fee system is in use). Inquire in person, with proof of age, at the offices mentioned for the Golden Eagle, above.

CAMPSITE AVAILABILITY

If the Toll Free Number (1-800-526-8200), at the State Parks Department, is given annual approval by the legislature, you can get up-to-the-minute information about campsite availability. There is also limited info about Federal, county and private campgrounds, weather, fishing, tides and other data valuable to the camper. The number is in operation 9-6, Mon-Sat (May 1 to Sep 15), and 9-5, Mon-Fri (Sep 16 to Apr 30).

WILDERNESS PERMIT

This is a newly created means of controlling access to the 4 areas in Washington's National Forests that have been officially declared as Wilderness Areas. These areas are exactly that — no roads, no developed campgrounds, nothing but Mother Earth in her most natural state. Now that more people than ever are backpacking to these areas, the Forest Service has taken steps to protect and preserve the values that make these areas wilderness. At the present time, the permits are required for overnight trips, free, and not rationed. They are issued for a single trip for a specified period of time. Apply in person at Ranger Stations and Forest Service offices or on a special form which is available from the appropriate National Forest headquarters. If your trip extends through more than one Wilderness, or through more than one National Forest, or starts in a National Park, get the permit from the point of origin. You may be advised that the area you plan to visit is overused and be asked to choose another section of the Wilderness. The necessary campfire permit is included. If you're taking pack or saddle stock along, ask about livestock permits and restrictions. (For a list of WILDERNESS AREAS, see page 79.)

BACKCOUNTRY USE PERMIT

These camping permits are required for all overnight trips into the backcountry at Mt Rainier, North Cascades and Olympic National Parks. Registration (which includes a campfire permit) is also required for overnight trips along the wilderness beaches of Olympic Natl Park. The permits are free and can be obtained in advance from the parks, or picked up at Ranger Stations. They serve as a means of advising backpackers about ecological restrictions, campfire safety and fire danger in specific areas. Horses are rough on meadows and therefore not allowed into some areas. If you plan to take stock with you, check in advance with the Park.

CAMPGROUND FACILITIES

You can expect all of the developed campgrounds, in this book, to have the following facilities: pit or flush type toilets, cooking grill or fire pit, an approved water supply and tables. If any of these facilities are missing, the campground descriptions will say so. You'll find that many privately owned campgrounds provide a combination of electric, water and sewer hookups for anyone traveling with trailers or recreation vehicles. All of the included trail and boat-in camps have, as minimum development, pit toilets, a few tables, and fire pits.

WATER

Most of the developed campgrounds in this book have an adequate piped water supply, but some of the more primitive ones do not. At these, you usually have to depend on a nearby spring, stream or lake as the source. If so, always boil the water or purify it with chemical tablets, otherwise discomforting things can happen. Keep in mind that some springs and streams run full force during the spring and early summer when the snows are melting, but tend to go dry later in the year. If you have doubts about finding water, carry your own.

FIREWOOD

In National Parks, it's usually OK to use downwood for fuel, if you can find any. Around heavily used camps, it's scarce. If you're passing through a National Forest, try picking up wood along a side road. There are no restrictions about gathering downwood in National Forests, but don't cut living trees, anywhere. That makes you no better than a one-man logging company. In State Parks it's illegal to gather downwood, or anything else for that matter, but driftwood is fair game. Some kind of fuel can usually be bought at or near campgrounds. We recommend carrying a small, portable camp stove, especially when backpacking. It's easy on the environment, and you're assured of having a fire. In rain forest areas, for instance, dry wood can be hard to find.

FEES

Campground fees are too variable to list precisely. They can be affected by the number of people in the party, the kind of hookups required, length of stay, season of the year and current legislation. During the summer you can expect to pay $2 to $3.50 per night at State Parks, and $2 to $4.50 at privately owned campgrounds. In mid-summer of '73, an act of Congress stopped all fee collections at National Park and Forest campgrounds, which came as a big surprise to everyone. When the impact of this is fully realized, we expect the fee system to be reinstated. Due to the lack of maintenance funds, garbage cans seem to stay full longer and some camps have been closed. There's also pressure from private campground owners who claim they can't compete with free facilities. When the impact of this law is fully realized, we expect the fee system to be reinstated.

OFF-SEASON CAMPING

There's a lot to be said for off-season camping, which generally covers the period between Labor Day (Sep) and mid-May. Camping is just as good in September as it is in August, but you'll find a lot fewer people to hassle with, and the pick of the campsites is yours. Fees will be cheaper at some parks and campgrounds, and even non-existent at others. A lot of campgrounds are open for camping before and after the regular season, but facilities such as water, toilets and concessions, are shut down. Most National Forest and State Park camps in the snow country are available for winter use and snow camping as long as they are safely accessible. The limit of stay at National Forest campgrounds is usually extended during the off-season, since fewer people are using the campsites.

Our CAMPING CALENDAR will provide you with suggestions about where to go camping during any season of the year along with some good reasons for going.

PETS

Pets are welcome at most campgrounds, but usually with some restrictions. In National Forests, National Parks, and State Parks the general rule is that they be kept on a leash during the day and put in your vehicle at night, to keep them from disturbing other campers. At private campgrounds the rule is about the same, although a few won't allow pets at all. At State Parks, you'll be asked to show proof that your dog has been vaccinated.

You can take your pet hiking with you on National Forest trails, but not on the trails or beaches in National or State Parks. As a tip, there can be a real risk of having your dog tangle with rabid wild animals in some of the forest areas.

MOUNTAIN WEATHER

Hikers should be aware that the higher mountainous areas are subject to severe weather changes. Even in summer, a delightful day can turn into a violent storm in a matter of hours. You should carry proper gear and waterproof clothing for these extreme conditions. Winter climbing should be done only with well-equipped and experienced groups. There are special regulations (available by writing to the park) for summit climbers.

HUNTING AND FISHING LICENSES

A booklet "Game Fish and Catch Limits" states the laws for hunting wildlife, catching fish (freshwater only), the various seasons in the state and license provisions. Write to Washington State Game Dept, 600 N. Capitol Way, Olympia 98501. Also available is a map showing general public deer hunting areas.

> Resident licenses (statewide):
> Hunting and fishing — $12.
> Fishing only — $7.50.
> Hunting only — $6.50.
>
> Non-resident licenses (statewide):
> Fishing (7-day) — $6.
> Fishing only — $20.
> Hunting only — $50.

Ocean and saltwater fishing is under control of the Washington State Dept of Fisheries, General Administration Bldg, Olympia 98501. No license is needed for saltwater fish and shellfish, but a punch card for recording catches, is required for salmon. Get a copy of "Sport Fishing Regulations" and "Washington Razor Clams" (tells how to dig for and clean razor clams).

RULES OF THE ROAD

Speed Limit: 60 mph day and night, 70 mph on freeways (or, as revised by the energy crisis).
Maximum trailer towing speed: (posted truck speed).
Riders are not allowed in trailers.
Riders are permitted in camper trucks.
No overnight parking at roadside rest areas unless otherwise posted.
Tire chains are required in snow areas during the winter.

TRAILERING

Most federal and state campgrounds will accommodate up to 22-foot camp trailers, and hookups are provided in some State Parks. "Western Highway Trailer Guide" gives info about travel trailer parks (not included in this book) that provide overnight facilities in the western states. ($1.25) PO Box 699, 608 8th St, Hoquiam Wash 98550.

FOREST ROADS

Forest road numbers (such as FR N605) are used by the Forest Service to mark roads in the National Forests. Look for a small wooden sign, at intersections, with the number carved in it. These numbers are also shown on Forest Service maps. The road systems in some of the Forests are well marked with these signs, but in others you'll have to rely on road names, and sometimes even those are non-existent. Forest Roads (FR) are usually dirt roads and Forest Highways (FH) are paved. For road condition information, check with local Park or Forest Ranger Stations, especially if you're towing a trailer.

Your routes through the forests will no doubt take you over logging roads. Since a great deal of logging takes place in Washington's forests, be on the watch for trucks as they barrel down the switchbacks.

HANGING ON TO A CAMPSITE

Once you've found a campsite at a first come-first served campground, you may want to leave to check out a nearby place of interest. Unless you leave your car to indicate that the site is occupied, you will need an alternate way of staking your claim. Simple. Purchase an inexpensive tube tent, usually $1.50 to $3.50 depending on the size. The tent is a vinyl cylinder and can be erected easily by running a nylon cord through the open ends and stringing the cord between two trees. This will give the campsite the appearance of being occupied until you return. But don't leave your gear in the tent. Having a campsite ripped off is somewhat rare, but not unheard of.

WHEN CAMPGROUNDS ARE FULL

On holiday weekends it can be tough finding a campsite unless you start early. In which case, you may find that everybody else started even earlier. If you can't find a spot at a campground, then remember that National Forests are, to some extent, "camp anywhere" areas. Sometimes you can find an informal, primitive camping area long forest roads, where the only facility is a toilet. If you don't find one, then try for an appealing area. The only requirement is that you have ax, shovel and water bucket. Another suggestion is to ask a Forest Ranger for possible locations of overflow areas that you wouldn't run across otherwise.

camping calendar

spring

Put on your western garb for the **49'ER DAYS CELEBRATION** in Winthrop. (Horse show, parade, western dance and barbeque.) All the buildings in Winthrop have been permanently restored to give the appearance of an "Old West" town. The event is held in May.

- CAMPING (Map r) Several campgrounds in the area.

Spring is the best time of the year to enjoy the scenic beauty of **WATERFALLS.** They'll be running full force due to the run off from melting snows.

- CAMPING (See WATERFALLS under the CAMPING INDEX for a list of campgrounds near these spectacular sights.

During late April and early May, you can spot thousands of **BLACK BRANT** feeding and loafing in the salt marshes at Ledbetter Point on the northern-most end of Long Beach Peninsula.

- CAMPING (Map 15) at Fort Canby SP.

WILD RHODODENDRONS bloom in May in Rhododendron State Park on Whidbey Island. This is the second-largest island in the contiguous U.S.

- CAMPING (Map 2) at South Whidbey SP.

On the opening Sunday of fishing season, you can join in the **FISHERMAN'S BREAKFASTS** at Twisp and Okanogan. Write to the Chambers of Commerce for details.

- CAMPING (Map 5) at JR, Hidden and Loup Loup Campgrounds.

A weekend **DRIFTWOOD SHOW** is held around the middle of March in Grayland. Everyone is there with their natural and carved exhibits, and some get to be rather unusual. C of C, Box 306, Westport 98595.

- CAMPING (Map 15) at Twin Harbors SP.

summer

The **SPOKANE RIVER RAFT RACE** is open to anyone, but there must be a minimum of four persons per boat. It's a 15-mile race from the Idaho state line to Spokane. Usually held in late June or early July, depending on water conditions. About 3000 spectators gather to watch.

- CAMPING (Map 14) at Riverside SP.

PROSPECTOR'S DAY CELEBRATION is held at the old mining town of Republic on the 2nd or 3rd weekend in June. The activities are oriented around old-time mining operations which include "mucking" and rock drilling contests.

- CAMPING (Map 6) Nearest campgrounds are Sweat Creek and Ten Mile.

A two-day **LOGGER RODEO,** at Deming, has logging contests of every type. (Mid-June).

- CAMPING (Map 2) at Silverlake Park.

The **LUMMI STOMMISH** is an Indian celebration with war canoe races on Hales Passage, salmon bake and craft display. Held at Marietta in mid-June.

- CAMPING (Map 2) Nearest campground is Larrabee SP.

The alpine **WILDFLOWER DISPLAYS** are mind-boggling at Bird Creek Meadows, north of Trout Lake, from mid-July to late August.

- CAMPING (Map 17) at Bench Lake and Bird Lake Campgrounds.

On the 4th of July, you can enter, or watch, the **RIVER RAT RACE** on the Methow River between Winthrop and Twisp City Park. There are separate divisions for kayaks, canoes and rafts.

- CAMPING (Map 4) Several campgrounds in the area.

The **FOREST THEATER,** at Fall City, is a great place to soak up culture in a natural outdoor setting. Plays and musical programs are presented in the amphitheater during the summer, and a barbeque is served before each show. For a schedule of performances, write to Snoqualmie Falls Forest Theater, 14240 SE Allen Rd, Bellevue 98006.

- CAMPING (Map 10) Nearest campground is Green River Gorge.

Late summer is berrypicking time in the **SAWTOOTH HUCKLEBERRY FIELDS.** The west side of Forest Road 123 is available to the public, while the fields on the east side are reserved for Indians. The area is heavily used during this time and you should cooperate with the Forest Service to preserve the already reduced picking area.

- CAMPING (Map 17) See this map for location of the fields and campgrounds in the area.

The annual **MAKAH DAYS CELEBRATION** at Neah Bay, livens the Makah Indian Reservation in late August. Colorful Indian dances, contests, salmon bakes and craft displays.

- CAMPING (Map 1) at Snow Creek Resort and Pillar Point Recreation Area.

The wild and woolly **OMAK STAMPEDE** is held at Omak, the second weekend in August. Events include a rodeo, famous "suicide race" across the Okanogan River, Indian stick games and teepee village. PO Box 916, Omak 98841.

- CAMPING (Map 5) at Conconully SP.

camping calendar

fall

The self-guiding auto tour at **TURNBULL NATL WILDLIFE REFUGE** is best during the fall when ducks and geese are most plentiful. (See info about the tour on page 00.)

- CAMPING (Map 14) at Peaceful Pines and Lewis Bros Resort.

CRANBERRY PROCESSING PLANTS, near Hoquiam, are open to the public during the harvest season (Oct and Nov). Write to the Chamber of Commerce for locations.

- CAMPING (Map 15) at Lake Sylvia SP and Twin Harbors SP.

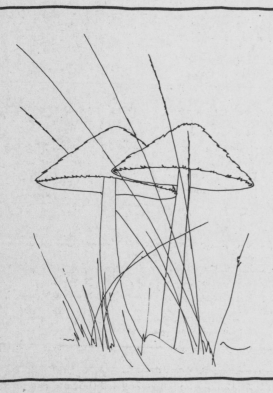

The **ELLENSBURG RODEO** is one of Washington's most popular and well-produced rodeos. It's a three-day package of events around Labor Day weekend with a western parade, RCA rodeo events, colorful night programs and an Indian village. PO Box 777, Ellensburg 98926.

- CAMPING (Map 11) Nearest campgrounds are Baker and Taneum.

Early October is a good time to take a trip across the North Cascades Hwy (State 20). The yellow larch trees stand out against the forest, prior to shedding their needles.

- CAMPING. See Maps 3 and 4 for campgrounds along the Highway.

A special day has been set aside for kids who want to participate in the Port Angeles **ANNUAL SALMON DERBY**, which takes place Friday through Monday on Labor Day weekend.

- CAMPING (Map 1) Several good campgrounds in the area.

Lumberjack skills are on display at the **LOGGER'S PLAYDAY**, during early September at Hoquiam.

- CAMPING (Map 15) at Lake Sylvia SP and Twin Harbors SP.

FISH PACKING PLANTS and CANNERIES are most active during late fall and early winter. There are several companies that offer tours to the public in Anacortes (Map 2) and Oysterville (Map 15).

- CAMPING (Map 2) Bayview and Deception Pass.
- CAMPING (Map 15) Fort Canby SP is open.

In the fall, salmon make their upstream trek to spawn. **FISH HATCHERIES** are most interesting to visit during this time. A booklet "Salmon Hatcheries," gives locations and is available from Dept of Fisheries, General Administration Bldg, Olympia 98501.

- CAMPING. See the Maps for locations of hatcheries and nearby campgrounds.

winter

SMELT FISHING is excellent at Kelso during January and February when the tiny fish battle their way up the Cowlitz River to spawn. The banks are lined with fishermen and their nets.

- CAMPING (Map 22) Paradise Point SP is open all year. Kelso is on Map 16.

MIGRATING WHALES, on their way to southern waters, are most numerous along the Washington coast in early January.

- CAMPING (Map 8) Viewpoints and winter camping at Kalaloch Campground.

Skagit Flats, south of Mount Vernon, is a major winter feeding and resting station for waterfowl on the Pacific Coast Flyway. Excellent **BIRDWATCHING** for a variety of ducks, geese, killdeer and hawks.

- CAMPING (Map 2) at Cedar Grove and Olson's.

STORM WATCHING is an exciting pastime during the winter months when the howling sea winds whip the ocean waves into an uncontrollable spectacle.

- CAMPING (Map 15) Fort Canby SP is one of the best places to watch and camp.

On weekends and holidays during the winter months, you can ski, go snowmobiling and slide on platters or inner tubes at Paradise in Mt Rainier Natl Park. The road is cleared of snow, but might be closed for short periods. Carry chains.

- CAMPING (Map 17) Sunshine Point is open all year.

Alta Lake, southwest of Brewster, freezes over during the winter and makes a good solid surface for **ICE SKATING.**

- CAMPING (Map 5) Alta Lake State Park is open all year.

At the **FOG FESTIVAL** you can watch contestants dash into the freezing surf and around a piling while braving 10-foot waves. A relay race is run using live, pinching crabs as batons. Cash prizes are given for these events at Ocean Shores in February.

- CAMPING (Map 8) at Ocean City SP. Ocean Shores is on Map 15.

the first time camper

GETTING STARTED

If you've never been camping before and you're now considering it, the best way to begin is to pack up a few essentials and "go." Let your first time out be a trial run. Maybe you'll forget something, but don't worry about that. It's all a matter of experience. If you camp in a developed recreation area, there will usually be a source of supplies nearby. Remember to keep a check list and add or subtract items that you find necessary or not. There are several books around that cover the techniques and "know-how" of camping. Find one that suits you best, or get a book about backpacking. If you're really serious about getting along in the outdoors, this type of book will lead you in the right direction. "Pleasure Packing," by Robert S. Wood, is about the easiest to use. ($3.95, Condor Books, 1736 Stockton St, San Francisco 94133.) It gives all kinds of useful info about tents, boots, cooking gear and the general essentials of camping, whether you're backpacking or not. Hopefully, his personal advice will inspire you to venture further into the wilderness.

CAMPING UGLY

This refers to how you look after several days of "roughing it." Primitive camping can be the most rewarding, if you're willing to go out and experience the great outdoors without all of the conveniences of home. What to take can vary from a little to a lot, depending on your attitude and the kind of camper you are. It isn't necessary to go out and buy a lot of expensive and elaborate equipment. Let your intuition and sense of improvisation be your guide. Only a few major items of gear will deserve some careful consideration. For example, an inadequate sleeping bag or poorly made hiking boots can make a first camping trip a real drag. Send for catalogs, rap with dealers, get suggestions from your friends about what to buy. As a basis for a check list, here are some rather essential items for any non-backpacking trip:

Sleeping bag (try renting or borrowing one for your first few trips until you find out which type is best for you)	Newspapers (for starting a fire)
	Matches
	Extra clothes
Ground pad (a foam pad or old blanket will do)	Jacket or sweater (it gets cold at night on some of those mountains)
Cooking utensils (a backpacker's mess kit is adequate for two people)	
	Camera and film
Forks, spoons, knives	Maps
Coffee pot (this should be first on the list)	Campground guide (especially this one)
Eats	Flashlight
Canteen or water bottle	First-aid kit
Wire clothes hangers (for roasting franks, shish-kabobs, marshmallows)	Toothbrush
	Litter bag (pack out what others leave behind)

WHAT TO EXPECT

If you're going camping for the first time, you'll want to know what to expect before you reach the campground. Other than being eaten by mosquitoes or driving over your canteen, you are sure to have a rewarding and matchless experience. Below is a sketch of a typical, developed campsite. On page 71, there are some comments about facilities. Read the entire section called STUFF EVERYONE SHOULD KNOW.

At several locations are showers, toilets and water supply.

Campsite number and receipt display box.

frisbee

food locker – sometimes

Typical Campsite

info directory

ADDRESSES
(Numbers refer to our Maps)

NATIONAL PARK SERVICE RECREATION AREAS

The National Park Service provides a small map-brochure for each park showing points of interest, trails, campgrounds, accommodations, what to see and things to do. Single copies are free by writing to each of the Park Headquarters below.

Coulee Dam Natl Recreation Area (6, 13)
Box 37
Coulee Dam 99116

Fort Vancouver Natl Historic Site (22)
Vancouver 98661

Mount Rainier Natl Park (17)
Longmire 98397

North Cascades Natl Park (3, 4)
Sedro Woolley 98284
(Includes Ross Lake and
Lake Chelan Natl Rec Areas)

Olympic Natl Park (1, 8)
600 East Park Ave
Port Angeles 98362

Whitman Mission Natl Historic Site (20)
Route 2
Walla Walla 99362

NATIONAL FORESTS IN WASHINGTON

See FOREST SERVICE MAPS under THE MAP TRIP for more information. Write to the following headquarters for forest maps and for information about specific forest areas and activities.

Colville Natl Forest (6, 7)
Colville 99114

Gifford Pinchot Natl Forest (16, 17, 22)
PO Box 449
Vancouver 98660

Kaniksu Natl Forest (7)
PO Box 490
Sandpoint Idaho 83864

Mount Baker Natl Forest (3)
PO Box 1198
Bellingham 98225

Okanogan Natl Forest (4, 5, 6)
Okanogan 98840

Olympic Natl Forest (1, 8, 9)
Federal Building
Olympic 98501

Snoqualmie Natl Forest (10, 16, 17)
919 Second Ave Building
Seattle 98104

Umatilla Natl Forest (21)
2517 SW Hailey
Pendleton Oregon 97801

Wenatchee Natl Forest
Wenatchee 98801

WILDERNESS AREAS IN WASHINGTON'S NATIONAL FORESTS

You can get permit applications and information for each Wilderness from the National Forest in which it is located. See the above list for addresses. (See WILDERNESS PERMIT under STUFF EVERYONE SHOULD KNOW.)

Glacier Peak Wilderness (3, 4, 10, 11)
(Mount Baker Natl Forest — west entry)
(Wenatchee Natl Forest — east entry)

Goat Rocks Wilderness (17)
(Gifford Pinchot Natl Forest — west entry)
(Snoqualmie Natl Forest — east entry)

Mount Adams Wilderness (17)
(Gifford Pinchot Natl Forest)

Pasayten Wilderness (4)
(Okanogan Natl Forest)

STATE PARKS

The State Parks Department publishes a booklet called "Washington Outdoor Recreation Guide." It shows the locations of all state parks with brief statistics about campgrounds and facilities. Single copies are free from State Parks and Recreation Commission, PO Box 1128, Olympia 98501. They also have a few individual park brochures and a booklet called "Heritage Sites."

VACATION INFORMATION

If you plan to visit Washington and need specific information about public recreation areas, scenic tours, events or an official state highway map, write to Dept of Commerce and Economic Development, General Administration Building, Olympia 98504.

BOOKS AND GUIDES

AUTO CIRCLE TOURS IN WASHINGTON STATE. Tourist Promotion Division, Dept of Commerce and Economic Development, General Administration Bldg, Olympia 98504. (Free) Nine trips to take by car in various parts of the state with mile-by-mile descriptions of features to see and explore.

CAVES OF WASHINGTON. William R. Halliday. Dept of Natural Resources, Geology and Earth Resources Div, Olympia 98504. ($1). A thoroughly descriptive guide to all of the caves, of various types, in Washington. Several individual maps are included for the most prominent caves, which point out the geological formations in each.

EXPLORING THE OLYMPIC PENINSULA. Ruth Kirk. University of Washington Press, Seattle. ($2.50) First hand information (about places, trails, campgrounds, wildlife, history, events and tours) that will make an exploration of the rugged peninsula much more meaningful.

FOSSILS OF WASHINGTON. Vaughn E. Livingston, Jr. Dept of Natural Resources, Geology and Earth Resources Div., Olympia 98504. (25¢) Describes several locations where fossils can be found, what to look for, and how to record and report interesting finds.

HERITAGE SITES. State Parks and Recreation Commission, PO Box 1128, Olympia 98501. (Free) A 22-page booklet containing descriptions of about 40 historical sites, interpretive centers, registered landmarks and old forts.

NORTH CASCADES HIGHWAY GUIDE. Written and published by Fred T. Darvill, Jr, PO Box 636, Mount Vernon Wash 98273. ($1) A compact and complete guide to one of the nations newest and most scenic highways — 88 miles of mind-blowing scenery through the North Cascades. Contains a road log of things to see and do, history of the area, plant and animal life, and an extensive trail section. It makes a handy reference guide while exploring the route.

ROOM TO ROAM. US Government Printing Office, Washington DC 20402. (75¢) This Bureau of Land Management publication lists a number of features of interest, recreation sites, rockhounding areas, caves and scenic overlooks on public domain land.

SIGNPOST. A wilderness oriented magazine published quarterly with monthly newsletters. ($7.50 annual subscription) 16812 36th Ave West, Lynnwood Wash 98036. This is the best source we've found for keeping up with trail conditions, environmental rip-offs, local folk lore, an exchange of info and ideas, and all those oddball tidbits of vital information that never seem to fit into anyone else's mag. In addition, subscribers benefit from spontaneous mailings, book discounts and a telephone service for receiving and submitting current trail information.

60 UNBEATEN PATHS. An Unusual Guide to the Unusual in the Northwest. Byron Fish. Superior Publishing Company, 708 Sixth Ave North, Seattle. ($5.95) This book is only for the curious, those who will take the time to follow backroads in search of fascinating and mysterious places to explore. It's all about shipwrecks, lighthouses, ghost towns, weird geological formations and other mind-boggling experiences in Washington, Idaho and Oregon.

WATER TRAILS OF WASHINGTON. Werner Furrer. Signpost Publications, 16812 36th Ave West, Lynnwood Wash 98036. ($2.50) A good guide to canoeing and kayaking on some of the more interesting rivers, streams and lakes in Washington. It gives safety tips, river classifications and detailed route maps.

WILDFLOWERS 1 THE CASCADES. Elizabeth Horn. Touchstone Press, PO Box 81, Beaverton Ore 97005. ($6.95) The ability to identify wildflowers is one of the things that makes a hike in the mountains much more rewarding. This book contains 180 identifications with 140 photos, vegetation zones, flower and leaf patterns, and photography tips.

The following books are published by The Mountaineers, PO Box 122, Seattle 98111. They are the most useful and comprehensive hiking guides available for beach and mountain areas in Washington. Each one is crammed with first-hand information about hiking trails, things to see along roads, the best time to be there, natural history, photographs, nearest camping facilities — anything you want to know about exploring a particular area.

TRIPS AND TRAILS, 1: Camps, Short Hikes and Viewports in the North Cascades and Olympics. ($5.95)

TRIPS AND TRAILS, 2: Family Camps, Short Hikes and View Roads in the South Cascades and Mt Rainier. ($5.95)

101 HIKES IN THE NORTH CASCADES. Harvey Manning and Ira Spring. ($5.95)

102 HIKES IN THE ALPINE LAKES, SOUTH CASCADES AND OLYMPICS. Harvey Manning and Ira Spring. ($5.95)

50 HIKES IN MT RAINIER NATIONAL PARK. Harvey Manning and Ira Spring. ($4.95)

FOOTLOOSE AROUND PUGET SOUND: 100 Walks on Beaches, Lowlands and Foothills. Janice Krenmayr. ($5.95)

There are several other books in the series, for bolder and more experienced outdoorspeople, dealing with ski touring, snowshoeing, rock and mountain climbing and mountaineering medicine. Write for a complete book list.

ENVIRONMENTAL ORGANIZATIONS

Here are some of the most active groups taking part in ecological issues around the state. They can help save our recreational and wildlife resources for us, if we give them our support. Join as many as you can. They will all provide complete details about their cause, and most publish an interesting magazine or newsletter to keep members informed of their progress.

ALPINE LAKES PROTECTION SOCIETY. PO Box 761, Ellensburg 98926. The proposal has been made to establish the Alpine Lakes Nat'l Recreation Area with an outer multiple use recreation area and an inner Wilderness core. The area lies between U.S. Hwy 2 and Int 90 in the Snoqualmie and Wenatchee Nat'l Forests and is easily accessible to large metropolitan areas. The rugged terrain contains over 600 natural mountain lakes, glaciers, climable peaks and rushing rivers, which are constantly being encroached upon by logging activities, mining interests, dams and real estate developments. The proposal is intended to be the best optimum-land-use program that would recognize and allow for all interests. If you know the area, you can't help but support the cause. Memberships: Student $4, Regular $10, Contributing $15, Sustaining $25 or more.

(A nifty map, "Alpine Lakes Recreation and Traveller's Guide," is available for $2 from the Society. It was specially produced to show the extent of the proposed Recreation Area. The backside gives a lot of good information about auto tours, tips, activities and places of interest in the region.)

AUDUBON SOCIETY. 950 Third Ave, New York 10022. A leader in conservation, they maintain wildlife sanctuaries, provide summer camp opportunities, local outings and field trips, sponsor education centers and furnish extensive educational materials to schools. (13 chapters in Washington.) Members receive the beautiful "Audubon" magazine and local monthly bulletins. Memberships: Regular $12, Family $15, Sustaining $25, Supporting $50. Tax deduct.

(The Yakima Chapter, whose most illustrious member is The Honorable William O. Douglas, has as its priority, the establishment of Cougar Lakes Wilderness. They also hold a Christmas Bird Count to study the migration and population of birds in the area.)

DEFENDERS OF WILDLIFE. 2000 "N" St NW, Suite 201, Washington DC 20036. There are a lot of innocent, lovable animals being wiped out by Man's indiscriminate and senseless destruction, usually under the guise of "predator control." DEFENDERS has an elaborate program which promotes, through education and research, the protection of all forms of wildlife, especially those species on the verge of extinction. Memberships (includes subscription to "Defenders of of Wildlife News"): Active $5, Family $7, Sustaining $10, Life $100 (no dues). Tax deduct.

FRIENDS OF THE EARTH. 529 Commercial St, San Francisco Calif 94111. One of the leaders in conservation action due to their effective lobbyists in Washington DC. They offer a number of beautiful books, posters and paperbacks dealing with environmental issues. Monthly newspaper will keep you up to date on everything that's happening. Memberships: Regular $15, Student $7.50, Supporting $25. Contributing $50 and others.

IZAAK WALTON LEAGUE OF AMERICA. 1800 N Kent St, Suite 806, Arlington Va 22209. Izaak was the "compleat angler," but the League concerns itself with all aspects of environmental preservation. It has national accomplishments in establishing game refuges, purchasing land for wilderness preserves and sponsoring protective legislation. They're working for improved recreational fishing in Puget Sound and supporting the proposed Alpine Lakes Wilderness Area. Memberships (include subscription to "Outdoor America"): Student $2, Honor $10, Supporting $25, Life $100.

NATURE CONSERVANCY. 206 Grosvenor House, Seattle 98121. They save the environment by buying it, then turning it over to an appropriate agency for continued protection. Several purchases in Washington have provided some ecologically significant land which will be preserved in its natural state and used for nature study and recreational purposes. Some areas are open to the public; others by permission. Members can get details from their local chapter. Donations of land are accepted, and what better legacy could you leave behind? Memberships: Subscribing $10, Family $15, Contributing $25 and others.

OLYMPIC PARK ASSOCIATES. 13245 — 40th N.E., Seattle 98125. The goals are to preserve the integrity and wilderness qualities of Olympic Natl Park, which is definitely one of our finest and most interesting National Parks. They're currently backing the NPS Wilderness Plan and also pressing for additional parcels that should be included to protect the Park from exploitation by outside interests. Memberships: Individual $2, Contributing $5, Life $35.

SIERRA CLUB. 1050 Mills Tower, San Francisco 94104. You all know about this one, founded by John Muir one of the oldest and most active of all conservation organizations. They feel that people who get to know the wilderness will protect the wilderness. Therefore they offer an elaborate schedule of outings — from knapsacking to mountaineering. Also, beautiful books, paperbacks on environmental subjects, films, talks and legislative support. Members receive the outing schedule and a monthly magazine and newsletter. Memberships: Junior (thru age 14) $5, Student $8, Regular $15, Senior (60 and over) $10, and others.

WILDERNESS SOCIETY. 729 15th St NW, Washington DC 20005. They fight to save the last 2½% of our land that still exists in its free, wild and natural state — the few areas that haven't been invaded by lumber companies, highways and mining interests. They sponsor wilderness trips and members receive "The Living Wilderness" quarterly along with other reports. Memberships: Regular $7.50, Contributing $12.50, Sustaining $25. Tax deduct.

several interesting tours

These tours are related to the environment and history of Washington, and there is something to be learned from each one. No prior notice or special clothing is required; just drop in. All are free unless noted.

COWLITZ STATE SALMON HATCHERY is 2¼ miles south of the town of Salkum. Self-guided tours are available from 8 AM to 4:15 PM, lasting about an hour. This is the world's largest salmon hatchery. Adult fish, as well as 3 species of juvenile salmon, can be seen all year. The city of Tacoma is providing displays in the visiting quarters. (See Map 16.)

Drive the four-mile self-guiding auto tour at **TURNBULL NATL WILDLIFE REFUGE.** It will take 15-20 minutes, or longer, if you want to fully explore the area. Pick up a guide leaflet which explains features at the numbered signposts. You'll see a collection of deer antlers, meadows, pothole lakes, beaver stick houses and more. (See Map 14.)

ROCKY REACH DAM is more than just a mass of concrete in the middle of the river. There are enough tour features to keep you busy for half a day. Films present local history and the story of the dam, and glass windows in the underwater viewing room let you "look a salmon in the eye." Outside, watch the fish ladder closely for fish making their way upstream. There is also a museum of artifacts, Indian petroglyphs, and a "Gallery of Electricity" with some interesting experiments for the kids. The tour is self-conducted from 8:15 AM until dusk. The dam is 7 miles north of Wenatchee on US 97. (See Map 11.)

When you come to the large complex of white buildings with red roofs, just NW of the town of Carnation, you've arrived at **CARNATION FARMS,** the home of "contented cows." And they should be — the lush setting of pastures and forests is enough to content anyone. You can tour the farms from 9 to 4:30, everyday except Sundays and holidays. Along the way, you'll see baby calves in the maternity ward, milk production tests for each cow, milking barns where electric machines are used, and exercise yards. Also, dog kennels, pheasant pens and a barn full of old carriages. The tours are self-conducted and take about an hour. (See Map 10.)

LIBERTY ORCHARDS COMPANY, at Cashmere, has a 15-minute tour through its fruit and nut candy plant. An explanation is given of the candy making process and everyone gets free samples of Aplets and Cotlets. The plant is located at 117 Mission St, across from the train depot. Tours are conducted from 8 to 12 and 1 to 5, Monday through Friday, except holidays. (See Map 11.)

Seattle City Light offers four **SKAGIT MINI-TOURS** at Newhalem: a boat ride on Diablo Lake to Ross Powerhouse (2 hours, $2); tour of Gorge Powerhouse (1 hour, free); Trail of the Cedars (¾ hour, free); and a ride up an Incline Lift to the top of Diablo Dam (½ hour, free). For full details about the tours write Seattle City Light, 1015 Third Ave, Seattle 98104. (Tour area on Map 3.)

MARYHILL MUSEUM OF FINE ARTS is a unique museum. It's 4 miles west of Maryhill on Hwy 14. There are strange and unexpected museum pieces donated by European Royalty, in addition to some fine artifacts and crafts of Northwest Indians, unusual chess sets from all over the world, old dolls, buttons, French mannequins and artwork by the Masters. It's open 9 to 5:30 everyday, March 15 through Nov 15. (See Map 23.)

At the **WIND RIVER TREE NURSERY,** north of Carson, you'll see pine and fir seedlings being grown for use in reforesting areas that have been harvested or burned. Individuals can check at the office for information and a booklet, then tour the grounds on your own. Groups should make advance reservations so that a guide will be on hand to explain the operations. Office hours are 7:45 AM to 4:30 PM. (See Map 22.)

When the completion of Grand Coulee Dam cut off the migration of Salmon from their spawning grounds, the **LEAVENWORTH NATL FISH HATCHERY** was placed in operation to give a helping hand. You can visit the hatchery building and production facilities. Guided tours include slide talks, fish cultural procedures and life cycles. The hatchery is open everyday, year round, from 8 AM to 4 PM. It's 3 miles south of Leavenworth via Icicle and Fish Hatchery Roads. (See Map 11.)

ICE HARBOR DAM has a self guiding tour of the powerhouse, fish ladder and counting stations, spillway and navigation lock. There is also an Indian Memorial commemorating the tribes whose family burial grounds were flooded behind the dam. The dam is 12 miles east of Pasco off Hwy 124. (See Map 20.)

If you see parachutes falling from the sky, you're near the **NORTH CASCADES SMOKEJUMPER BASE** at Winthrop. The men at this center help save our forests by flying to the site of a forest fire, making the jump, then fighting to control the fire. Visitors are welcome daily, 9 to 5, from July 1 to Sep 15 (Mon-Fri in June and after Sep 15). A smokejumper will take you on a tour of the base where you'll see fire fighting and parachuting equipment, smokejumper aircraft, helicopters, parachute packing and practice jumps. (See Map 4.)

on your own

PACIFIC CREST TRAIL

It's the greatest trail of all, extending from Mexico to Canada along the summit of the Pacific slope. Here you'll find the most scenic and peaceful environment that the mountains have to offer. The PCT overlaps the Cascade Crest Trail, and all 450 miles in Washington are complete. Only portions in California are not yet permanently established. If you want to plan a trip up or down the state, the Forest Service has information available. From Pacific Northwest Region, US Forest Service, PO Box 3623, Portland Ore 97208, you can get the following free maps and folders:

PACIFIC CREST NATIONAL SCENIC TRAIL — WASHINGTON. This folded map can be handy to you backpackers until something more complete comes along. It shows the entire Trail route across the state on some fairly detailed maps. There's a brief description of each section of the trail, noting the availability of water, horse feed, campsites, shelters and distances between points.

PCT — RESUPPLY POINTS (folder). A list of the nearest resupply points, accessible from the trail and keyed to the above map. Gives distances from the trail to post offices and facilities.

CROSSING THE INTERNATIONAL BOUNDARY (folder). Regulations for crossing into Canada and back via the PCT. Also includes an application for Grazing Permit (if you're taking horses) and Wilderness Permit.

It would be wise to write to the headquarters for each Forest that you'll be passing through. Each may have information that can be useful on the trip, notices about restrictions along the trail and Wilderness Permit applications.

Our CAMPING INDEX lists campgrounds that are on or near the trail. The route is shown on our maps.

trail blaze

PACK TRIPPING

One way to get to the wilderness backcountry is by the use of pack animals. They will ease the burden on your back and allow you to transport more gear than a backpack will allow. Get your group together, pick an appealing area — maybe a lake noted for its fishing or scenic qualities — and let the packers get you there and back. The experienced guides can show you a lot of seldom-seen country that even the avid backpacker misses. For a folder "Resorts and Packers on the National Forests," write to US Forest Service, PO Box 3623, Portland, Oregon 97208.

SKI TOURING

This ancient sport is rapidly being rediscovered among the world of ski people. With lift lines getting longer and chairlift rates going higher, ski touring becomes a very appealing way to escape the crowds and experience the real beauty of snow and the sounds of winter. About a days worth of effort is all it takes to learn the fundamentals, then you're on your way. The equipment is less expensive than for downhill, the clothing can be simple (there's no place for fashion shows in the wilderness) and anyone can participate — young, old, fat or skinny. Just find some gently rolling terrain and combine the actions of walking and gliding at a more controllable pace than downhill skiing. An alternative to ski touring is snowshoeing. It's a bit more work, but requires less experience. "The Snowshoe Book," by William Osgood and Leslie Hurley, will tell all you need to know. For those with a hardy spirit and some knowledge of winter survival and snow camping, either choice can be one of the most rewarding ways to spend some time in the white landscapes with your family and friends.

Cascade Bicycle Club
6810 Dayton Ave. N.
Seattle 98103

Portland Wheelmen Touring Club
3745 NE 64th Ave
Portland Ore 97313

Mountaineers, Bicycle Section
PO Box 133
Seattle 98111

Western Wheelmen
E. 3928 - 29th Ave
Spokane 99203

BICYCLE TOURING

It seems that bicycling may become an alternative to auto travel with the gas shortage upon us. More and more people are strapping their packs on their bikes and heading for the mountains. That's a lot of up and down country, but people do it. The push up one side of the mountain has its reward with the "zoom" down on the other side. Highway touring does have its advantages. There's access to conveniences and attractions that you wouldn't have by backpacking. You'll tend to explore and appreciate the roadside sights more fully, because your pace will allow you to stop for a real look. Campsites should be no problem. If you're traveling through a National Forest and want to avoid regular campgrounds, then pull off the road to any appealing place — beside a rushing stream, at the edge of a meadow, the top of a pass. "The Bicycle Paper" is a newsprint type magazine for enthusiasts in the Northwest. It raps about touring trails, races, bicycle repair, test data and more. ($2.25 per year.) PO Box 842, Seattle 98111.

Mission Ridge (lessons)
PO Box 542
Wenatchee 98801

Mountaineers (trips)
PO Box 122
Seattle 98111

Snowblaze (Mt. Spokane)
Rt 1, Box 416-B
Mead 99021

WATER TRAVEL

Washington has some exciting rivers for experiencing real wilderness travel. There's always an appealing stretch suitable for the amateur canoeist, the experienced river runner or the rafting enthusiast. To help choose a place to get your feet wet, see "Water Trails of Washington," page 80.

Camping along the rivers shouldn't be a problem. There are numerous developed Forest Service camps at likely put-in and take-out points. Most wild rivers wind their way through the heart of the National Forests, and the banks will provide many appealing camping places on public land. In case you should find that the area is in private ownership, have respect for "No Trespassing" signs and press on, or get the owner's permission to camp.

There are also many lakes for fine flat-water canoeing or sailing. See "Boating" in the CAMPING INDEX.

American Canoe Assn
4260 E. Evans Ave
Denver Colo 80222
(Provides info about the various kinds of boating clubs in the Pacific Northwest

Cascade Canoe Club
2333 Harris Ave
Richland 99352

Outdoor Club
Portland State Univ
Portland, Ore 97207

Univ of Wash Canoe Club
IMA Bldg
Seattle 98133

Washington Kayak Club
PO Box 24264
Seattle 98124

camping index

If you haven't found an excuse for going camping, here's help. All of the following names are campgrounds that have been indexed because of their proximity to interesting activities and features. The numbers preceding the names are our Map numbers on which the campgrounds are found. Look up the campground descriptions for more detailed information.

activities ⸺⸺⸺⸺●

BEACHCOMBING

Some parts of the coast are more conducive to beachcombing — most rewarding during late autumn and winter.

1	AGATE & CRESCENT BEACH
	SEQUIM BAY SP
	SNOW CREEK RESORT
	WHISKEY CR BEACH
8	DRIFTWOOD ACRES
15	BAY CENTER KOA
	FORT CANBY SP

BERRYPICKING

A great variety of wild berries are found in Washington, and the best time for picking them is late summer and fall. Local conditions may cause variations. Blackberries (B), chokeberries (C), huckleberries (H), strawberries (S).

3	SCHRIEBERS MDW (H)
4	CHANCELLOR (H)
	THIRTYMILE
6	DEER CR SUMMIT
	MARCUS ISLAND (C)
	SWAN LAKE
7	BROWNS LAKE
	IONE
	STAGGER INN
8	BROWN CREEK
	CAMPBELL TREE GROVE
	OCEAN CITY SP (S)
	WYNOOCHEE FALLS
10	CORRAL PASS
	CRYSTAL SPRINGS
	FISH LAKE
	HUCKLEBERRY (H)
	ROCKY RUN
	WALLACE RIVER PARK (B)
11	GRASSHOPPER MDWS
	JOHNNY CREEK
	NAPEEQUA CROSSING
	RIVERSIDE (B)
	ROCK ISLAND
16	RYAN LAKE
17	ADAMS FORK
	BLUE LAKE CR
	CULTUS CREEK (H)
	HORSESHOE LAKE
	LITTLE GOOSE (H)
	POLE PATCH (H)
	SADDLE (H)
	SOUTH (H)
	STEAMBOAT LAKE (H)
	TAKHLAKH
	TILLICUM (H)
	WOBBLY LAKE TC (H)

21	ALDER THICKET
	BIG SPRINGS
	FOREST BOUNDARY
	GOVT SPRING
	SPRUCE SPRING
	WICKIUP
22	PETERSON PRAIRIE (H)

BICYCLING

A great way to see the environment at a pace that lets you experience it. Rentals (R) and trails (T).

1	DUNGENESS REC AREA (T)
	LYRE RIVER PARK (T)
	WHISKEY CR BEACH (T)
2	WASHINGTON PARK (T)
5	CONCONULLY SP (R)
7	BLUESLIDE RESORT (T)
	LAKE THOMAS RESORT (T)
	MARSHALL LAKE RESORT (T)
8	HARLEYS RESORT (T)
	RAIN FOREST RESORT (T)
10	LAKE EASTON RESORT (R,T)
11	PINE VILLAGE KOA (R,T)
12	BIG SUN RESORT (T)
	SUN LAKES SP (R,T)
15	BAY CENTER KOA (R,T)
16	SEAQUEST SP (T)
19	C & R COLUMBIA (T)

BIRDWATCHING

Some wildlife refuges provide checklists on which you can record your observations. (See WILDLIFE REFUGES in the FEATURES section.)

1	AGATE & CRESCENT BEACH
9	PENROSE POINT SP
15	LONG ISLAND

BOAT-IN CAMPS

These camps can only be reached by boat. Facilities are usually somewhat primitive, but the seclusion is worth it.

2	JONES ISLAND
	MATIA ISLAND
	PREVOST HARBOR
	REID HARBOR
	SUCIA ISLAND

3	CAT ISLAND
	COUGAR ISLAND
	DEVILS DOME
	DRY CREEK
	GREEN POINT
	HOZOMEEN
	LIGHTNING CREEK
	LITTLE BEAVER
	MAPLE GROVE
	MAY CREEK
	RAINBOW POINT
	ROLAND POINT
	SILVER CREEK
	TEN MILE ISLAND
4	BIG CREEK
	CORRAL CREEK
	DEER POINT
	DOMKE FALLS
	ELEPHANT ROCK
	FLICK CREEK
	GRAHAM HARBOR
	HATCHERY
	PRINCE CREEK
	REFRIGERATOR HARBOR
	SAFETY HARBOR
	WEAVER POINT
6	BARNABY ISLAND
	SHERMAN CREEK
	WILMONT CREEK
9	SQUAXIN ISLAND
13	DETILLION
	JONES BAY
	PIERRE
	THREE MILE
15	LONG ISLAND

BOATING

Not your usual motorboat facilities, but a peaceful way to enjoy our lakes and streams by canoe (C) or sailboat (S). Rentals (R).

1	FAIRHOLM (C)
5	BONAPARTE LK RESORT (S,R)
7	MARSHALL LAKE RESORT (C,R)
	NOISY CREEK (S)
	SULLIVAN LAKE (S)
9	BLAKE ISLAND SP (C,S)
11	MITCHELL CREEK (S)
15	LAKE SYLVIA SP (C,S)
	WILLIAMS PARK (C)
16	BEAVER BAY (C,S)
	COUGAR (C,S)
	SWIFT CAMP (C,S)
17	HORSESHOE LAKE (C)
	PACKWOOD LK TC (R)
	TAKHLAKH
19	POTHOLES SP (C,S)
20	LYONS FERRY SP (C,S)
21	BOYER PARK (C,S,R)
22	GOOSE LAKE (C)

CAMPFIRE PROGRAMS

Usually held nightly or on weekends between Memorial Day and Labor Day. The rangers tell some interesting stories about the area.

1 ELWHA
  FAIRHOLM
  HEART OF THE HILLS
3 COLONIAL CREEK
6 KETTLE FALLS
8 HOH
  KALALOCH
  MORA
  SOLEDUCK
16 SPIRIT LAKE
17 COUGAR ROCK
  IPSUT CREEK
  OHANAPECOSH

CLAMMING

Pack your hoe and bucket, and check the tables for a low tide. There are seasonal limitations, but no license is required.

1 DUNGENESS REC AREA
  PILLAR PT REC AREA
  SEQUIM BAY SP
  WHISKEY CR BEACH
2 BIRCH BAY SP
  CAMANO ISLAND SP
  DECEPTION PASS SP
  LARRABEE SP
  SOUTH WHIDBEY SP
8 DRIFTWOOD ACRES
  KALALOCH
  OCEAN CITY SP
  POTLATCH SP
9 BELFAIR SP
  BLAKE ISLAND SP
  DASH POINT SP
  DOSEWALLIPS SP
  ILLAHEE SP
  JARREL COVE SP
  KOPACHUCK SP
  PENROSE POINT SP
  SALTWATER SP
15 BAY CENTER KOA
  BUSH PIONEER PARK
  TWIN HARBORS SP

EXCURSION BOAT TOURS

Catch the boat at a nearby landing for a day long cruise on the lake. (Also, see the introductory headings to Maps 4 and 21.)

3 COLONIAL CR (Ross Lk)
11 LAKE CHELAN SP (Lk Chelan)
  RAMONA PARK (Lk Chelan)

GLACIER CLIMBING

You should have prior experience with the hazards of climbing on ice before tackling a glacier. Avalanches and sudden storms aren't to be sneezed at.

4 LONE FIR
17 IPSUT CREEK
  PARADISE
  WHITE RIVER

GOLDPANNING

A gold pan only costs about two dollars and there just may be some nuggets that the old-timers overlooked.

3 GOLD BASIN
  SUNNYWIDE
11 BAKER
  MINERAL SPRINGS

GROUP CAMPING

There are several campgrounds in National Forests and State Parks that have areas set aside solely for use by organized groups. Usually there is a special rate for the group. Make reservations in advance.

2 MORAN SP
3 GOODELL CREEK
7 SULLIVAN LAKE GC
9 ILLAHEE SP
16 COUGAR PARK GC

GUIDED NATURE WALKS

Some interesting things can be gained from the Ranger's explanations as he guides you on a nature tour.

3 COLONIAL CREEK
8 HOH
  KALALOCH
  MORA
  SOLEDUCK
17 OHANAPECOSH

HAYRIDES

A country style activity for the whole family.

11 PINE VILLAGE KOA
12 SUN LAKES SP

HORSEBACK RIDING

Let a horse do your walking for you. Rentals (R) and trails (T).

3 BRIDGE (R,T)
  DOUGLAS FIR (R,T)
  NOOKSACK (R,T)
5 ALTA LAKE SP (R,T)
10 CLE ELUM RIVER (R,T)
  RED MOUNTAIN (R,T)
  SALMON LA SAC (R,T)
  WISH POOSH (R,T)
11 ATKINSON FLAT (T)
  CHATTER CREEK (T)
  EIGHTMILE (R)
  GLACIER VIEW (R)
  LAKE WENATCHEE SP (R,T)
  LION ROCK SPRING (T)
  NASON RIDGE (R,T)
  WHITEPINE (R,T)
12 SUN LAKES SP (R,T)
15 TWIN HARBORS SP (R,T)
16 MILLERSYLVANIA SP (R,T)
17 BUMPING BOAT LDG (R)
  BUMPING CROSSING (R)
  BUMPING LAKE (R)
  CLEAR LAKE (R,T)
  COUGAR FLAT (R)
  INDIAN CREEK (R)
  SILVER SPRINGS (R,T)
21 CABIN SADDLE (T)
  GODMAN (T)
  TUCANNON (T)

HORSEMEN'S CAMPS

These campgrounds can be used by anyone camping with horses. Basic facilities for boarding stock, such as tie rails, watering troughs and loading ramps, are usually provided.

3 OWL CREEK
  RIVER BAR
4 ANDREWS CREEK
  COTTONWOOD
  LAKE CREEK
  LAKE CREEK CORRAL
  PHELPS CREEK
  ROBINSON CREEK
  THIRTYMILE
7 CIRCLE MOON
10 LAKE JANUS TC
11 CHIWAUKUM CREEK
  EIGHTMILE
  LAKE CREEK
  LION ROCK SPRING
  TAMARACK SPRING
17 DEEP CREEK
  LITTLE GOOSE
  MIRROR LAKE
  WALUPT LAKE
22 CREST

MOUNTAIN CLIMBING

See how many summits you can add to your record. Be well conditioned, carry proper equipment and always let someone know where you're going.

3 BIG FOUR
  GRINERS
  HANNEGAN PASS TC
  KULSHAN CABIN
  LAKE ANN TC
  MARBLE CREEK
  MINERAL PARK
  MONTE CRISTO
  MOWITCH
  SLOAN CREEK
4 HOLDEN
  LONE FIR
8 ELKHORN
  HAMMA HAMMA
  LENA CREEK
10 ANNETTE LAKE TC
  DINGFORD JUNCTION
  FISH LAKE
  TAYLOR RIVER
  TUCQUALA MDWS
11 BEVERLY
  BRIDGE CREEK
  ROCK CREEK
16 SPIRIT LAKE
  TIMBERLINE
17 BENCH LAKE
  BIRD LAKE
  CHAMBERS LAKE
  COLD SPRINGS
  CORA LAKE TC
  HORSESHOE LAKE
  KILLEN CREEK
  MIRROR LAKE
  MORRISON CREEK
  TAKHLAKH
  TIMBERLINE

MOUNTAIN TOP CAMPING

Camping near the clouds.

4 SOUTH NAVARRE
11 BIG HILL
14 MOUNT SPOKANE SP

MUSHROOM GATHERING

Check at Ranger Stations for information about mushroom seasons. Be sure the ones you pick are edible — some are very poisonous.

1	SNOW CREEK RESORT
3	MOWITCH
10	KACHESS
11	STAFFORD
22	BEAVER

PACIFIC CREST TRAIL (Access)

These campgrounds are on, or near, the Trail.

4	BRIDGE CREEK
	HIGH BRIDGE
	MEADOWS
10	COUGAR VALLEY
	FISH LAKE
	GOVT MDW TC
	TUCQUALA MDWS
17	CULTUS CREEK
	DEEP CREEK
	DOG LAKE
	MIDWAY MDWS
	UPPER BUMPING
	WALUPT LAKE
	WHITE PASS LAKE
22	CREST

PACK TRIPS

Let a horse or burro do you backpacking for you on your next trip into the wilderness.

4	EARLY WINTERS
11	LAKE WENATCHEE SP

RIVER FLOATING

An inner tube or air mattress is all you need.

8	WYNOOCHEE RIVER PARK
11	PINE VILLAGE KOA

RIVER RUNNING

A little fast water adds a thrill to being on the river.

3	BACON CREEK (Skagit R)
	VERLOT (Sauk R)
	WHITE CHUCK (Sauk R)
8	HOH (Hoh R)
10	MONEY CR (Skykomish R)

ROCKCLIMBING

Man against the mountain.

17	TOWER ROCK
22	BEACON ROCK SP

ROCKHOUNDING

Makes your camping trip a treasure hunt and maybe you'll find something of value to take back home. You can get rockhounding maps from Tourist Promotion Division, General Administration Bldg, Olympia 98501.

1	AGATE & CRESCENT BEACH
	DUNGENESS REC AREA (agates)
	LYRE RIVER PARK (jasper)
	WHISKEY CREEK BEACH

4	MEADOWS
7	BLUESLIDE RESORT
8	DRIFTWOOD ACRES
11	LION ROCK SPRING
15	LONG ISLAND (agates)
17	MILK POND

SKINDIVING

Explore the underwater environment that few people see.

1	AGATE & CRESCENT BEACH
	PILLAR POINT

STORM WATCHING

An interesting pastime in the middle of winter.

1	AGATE & CRESCENT BEACH
15	FORT CANBY SP

SURF FISHING

Check the "Sport Fishing Regulations," available from the Dept of Fisheries, for license, season, size and limit information.

1	PILLAR POINT REC AREA
	WHISKEY CR BEACH
8	DRIFTWOOD ACRES
	KALALOCH
	MORA
	OCEAN CITY SP
15	FORT CANBY SP

SURFING

There are only a few points along the coast where the underwater topography produces the right kind of waves, sometimes.

8	OCEAN CITY SP

SWIMMING

These are not the only places to swim — just some of the more interesting ones.

1	FAIRHOLM (scenic lake)
2	SEQUIM BAY SP (pier)
6	SNAG COVE (shallow cove)
9	BELFAIR SP (warm saltwater)
10	DENNY CR (swimming holes)
11	LAKE WENATCHEE SP
12	SUN LAKES SP
15	FORT CANBY (mild surf)
17	GRANITE LAKE (alpine)
19	POTHOLES SP
22	GOOSE LAKE (blue water)
23	MARYHILL SP (river beach)

WHALE-WATCHING

Keep your eyes peeled from late November to mid-February when gray whales migrate from the Bering Sea to the Gulf of California. A high cliff will offer the best vantage point.

8	KALALOCH

WILDERNESS TRAILHEADS

These campgrounds are near Wilderness Areas. You can spend the night, become acclimated to the altitude, then head for the high country the next morning along a trail that starts at the campground. There is usually a place to leave your car outside the camp. To hike into one of these areas, you will need a permit. (See WILDERNESS PERMIT, page 00.) Glacier Peak (GL), Goat Rocks (GR), Mt Adams (MA) and Pasayten (P).

3	DOWNEY CR (GP)
	LIGHTNING CR (P)
	OAK CREEK (GP)
	SLOAN CREEK (GP)
4	ANDREWS CR (P)
	CHANCELLOR (P)
	COMPANY CR (GP)
	HIGH BRIDGE (GP)
	HOLDEN (GP)
	PHELPS CR (GP)
	ROBINSON CR (P)
	THIRTYMILE (P)
5	FOURTEEN MILE (P)
	LONG SWAMP (P)
11	GRASSHOPPER MDWS (GP)
	NAPEEQUA CROSSING (GP)
17	CHAMBERS LAKE (GR)
	COLD SPRINGS (MA)
	KILLEN CR (MA)
	PACKWOOD LK TC (GR)
	SPRING CR (MA)
	TIMBERLINE (MA)
	WALUPT LAKE (GR)

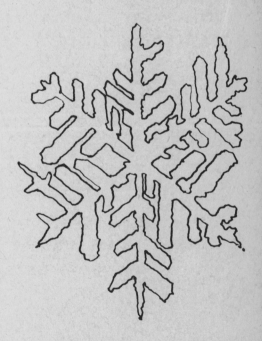

WINTER SPORTS

(See the CAMPING CALENDAR for other winter activities.)

3	MT PILCHUCK (skiing)
5	ALTA LAKE SP (ice skating)
	LK OSOYOOS SP (ice skating)
7	CARNEYS BLACK LAKE RESORT (snowmobile trails)
	CIRCLE MOON (skiing)
	SKOOKUM CHINOOK (snowmobiling)
11	SQUILLCHUCK SP (skiing, sledding)
21	FIELDS SPR SP (sledding, ski touring)

YEAR-ROUND CAMPING

You'll find the following camps open and available for camping at any time of the year.

1 AGATE AND CRESCENT BEACH
DUNGENESS REC AREA
ELWHA
ELWHA RESORT
LYRE RIVER PARK
SALT CREEK REC AREA
2 CEDAR GROVE RESORT
FORT CASEY SP
LARRABEE SP
OAKS
OLD FORT TOWNSEND SP
OLSEN'S
SILVERLAKE PARK
3 GOODELL CREEK
SKAGIT COUNTY PARK
5 ALTA LAKE SP
6 BRADBURY BEACH
CLOVER LEAF
GIFFORD
HAAG COVE
KAMLOOPS ISLAND
KETTLE FALLS
KETTLE RIVER
MARCUS ISLAND
NORTH GORGE
SANPOIL BAY
SNAG COVE

7 BLUESLIDE RESORT
CIRCLE MOON
LAKE THOMAS RESORT
8 GRAVES CREEK
HOH
JULY CREEK
KALALOCH
MORA
QUEETS RIVER
RAIN FOREST RESORT
9 BLAKE ISLAND SP
DOSEWALLIPS SP
FAY-BAINBRIDGE SP
ILLAHEE SP
KOPACHUCK SP
PENROSE POINT SP
SALTWATER SP
SCENIC BEACH SP
TWANOH SP
10 GREENWATER PARK
WALLACE RIVER PARK
11 DICKEY CREEK
SQUILLCHUCK SP
TEANAWAY
TWENTYNINE PINES
12 SUNLAKES SP
13 FORT SPOKANE
HAWK CREEK
KELLER FERRY
SPRING CANYON
14 LITTLE FALLS
PEACEFUL PINES
RIVERSIDE SP

15 BAY CENTER KOA
BRUCEPORT
BUSH PIONEER PARK
LAKE SYLVIA SP
RAINBOW FALLS SP
TWIN HARBORS SP
16 BEAVER BAY
MILLERSYLVANIA SP
17 LA WIS WIS
MAPLE LEAF
SUNSHINE POINT
18 HANGING TREE
NACHES
WENAS
19 MAR-DON RESORT
POTHOLES SP
20 LEWIS AND CLARK SP
LYONS FERRY SP
PALOUSE FALLS SP
21 FIELDS SPRING SP
22 HORSETHIEF LAKE SP
PARADISE POINT SP
23 THREE CREEKS
UPPER BOWMAN CREEK

features

ARCHEOLOGICAL SITES

Some facts about the early history of man has been uncovered here.

20 LYONS FERRY SP (Marmes Man)
21 BOYER PARK (Indian site)
22 HORSETHIEF LK SP (Indian village)

AUTUMN FOLIAGE

Late September and early October are the best times to observe the changing colors.

9 VASA PARK RESORT
10 CORRAL PASS
LAKE EASTON SP
WALLACE RIVER PARK

BEAVER PONDS

Interesting animals to watch as they occupy themselves with various building projects.

3 BIG FOUR

BOTANICAL AREAS

(Also, see the introductory headings to Maps 7, 8 and 11.)

3 EXCELSIOR (natural area)
5 LOST LAKE (big trees)
7 STAGGER INN (ancient cedars)
8 FALLS CR (big tree grove)
10 KACHESS (big tree trail)
THE DALLES (Douglas fir)
16 SPIRIT LAKE (trail)
17 BIRD LAKE (wildflowers)
18 WENAS (nature camp)

CAVES

Spelunking for amateurs, professionals or just sight-seers. (See the introductory headings to Maps 7, 11, 16, 17 and 22.)

8 DRIFTWOOD ACRES
HARLEYS RESORT
12 COULEE LODGE
SUN LAKES SP
15 FORT CANBY SP
17 BOULDER CAVE
18 WINDY POINT
22 PETERSON PRAIRIE

DRIFTWOOD

You may find some beautifully grotesque shapes that have washed ashore.

1 DUNGENESS REC AREA
10 WISH POOSH
15 FORT CANBY SP
20 LYONS FERRY SP

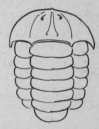

FOSSILS

Some types can provide valuable information about the evolution of life on earth. Preserve any that you find. (Also, see the introductory heading to Map 4.)

1 WHISKEY CREEK BEACH
4 HARTS PASS

GEOLOGICAL FORMATIONS

Interesting results in the evolution of the landscapes. (Also, see the introductory headings to Maps 1, 8, 15 and 22.)

1	DUNGENESS (sand cliff)
2	WASHINGTON PARK (glacial polish)
3	SUNNYSIDE (earthslide)
4	GATE CR (Goat Wall)
5	CRAWFISH LK (balanced rock)
10	TAYLOR RIVER
17	LITTLE NACHES (basalt)
	MCDANIEL LK
	TAKHLAKH (rocks)
	TOWER ROCK
20	PALOUSE FALLS (rocks)
21	BOYER PARK (cliffs)
22	BEACON ROCK SP
	CREST (lava beds)
	HORSETHIEF LK (bluffs)

GHOST TOWNS and MINING CAMPS

The remains of old communities whose reason for being has faded into the past. (See the introductory headings to Maps 3, 5 and 6.)

3	BIG FOUR (resort & dam)
	MONTE CRISTO (townsite)
4	PHELPS CR (Trinity)
	ROADS END (Gilbert)
6	CURLEW LAKE SP
11	SCOTTY
17	DEEP CR (Copper City)

HISTORICAL SITES

Good places to acquire some knowledge of Washington's local history. (See the introductory headings to Maps 6, 9, 10, 13, 14, 15, 18 and 20.)

1	AGATE & CRESCENT BEACH (Port Crescent, pioneer cemetery)
2	FORT CASEY SP (fort)
	FORT FLAGLER SP (fort)
	OLD FORT TOWNSEND
3	ROCKPORT SP (marker)
	SKAGIT COUNTY (cabin)
4	LONE FIR (cabin)
6	SHERMAN CR (lumber mill)
9	FAY-BAINBRIDGE (fort)
	SCENIC BEACH SP (town)
10	DENNY CR (wagon trail)
	GOVT MDW TC (trail)
11	SCOTTY (mining site)
	TAMARACK SPR (grave)
13	FORT SPOKANE (museum)
	HAWK CR (railroad)
15	FORT CANBY SP (lighthouse)
17	KANER FLAT (wagon train campsite)
18	AHTANUM MISSION
20	FORT WALLA WALLA PK (village)
	LEWIS & CLARK TRAIL SP
22	CREST (Indian racetrack)
	GOOSE LK (footprints)

LOOKOUTS

From these vantage points, near campgrounds, you'll see a large chunk of the countryside.

1	ELWHA
2	MORAN SP
7	CRESCENT LAKE
	SKOOKUM CHINOOK
10	HUCKLEBERRY
11	HANDY SPRING
	JUNIOR POINT
	LAKE WENATCHEE RS
	LION ROCK SPR

17	CLOVER SPRS
	GRANITE LK
	SADDLE
22	BEACON ROCK SP
	GOVT MINERAL SPRS

MEADOWS

Peaceful places to relax.

4	ALPINE MEADOW
8	DEER PARK
11	GRASSHOPPER MDWS
	TRONSEN
17	INDIAN CREEK
	PLEASANT VALLEY

MINERAL SPRINGS

Many are now on private property and some are being tested for geothermal power. Several wild, bubbling springs can still be enjoyed by the public near these campgrounds. (Also, see the introductory headings to Maps 8 and 22.)

3	MOROVITZ
	SLOAN CREEK
	SULPHUR CREEK
8	BOULDER CREEK
11	MINERAL SPRINGS
	SODA SPRING
16	KALAMA SPRING
17	OHANAPECOSH
	SILVER SPRINGS
	SODA SPRINGS
22	GOVT MINERAL SPRINGS
	LITTLE SODA SPRINGS

MINING SITES

Also see the introductory headings to Maps 4 and 11.

3	RED BRIDGE
4	CHANCELLOR
7	MARSHALL LK RESORT
11	SCOTTY

NATURE/INTERPRETIVE TRAILS

Self-guiding trails with identification and explanation of plant life and other features. (Also, see the introductory headings to Maps 10 and 16.)

1	KLAHOWYA (Pioneers Path)
2	DECEPTION PASS SP
8	FALLS CR (Big Tree Grove)
	HOH (Hall of Mosses)
10	KACHESS (Big Tree)
	THE DALLES (John Muir)
11	SWAUK (Sculpture Rocks)
16	SPIRIT LK (Ancient Forest)

OYSTER BEDS

No license is required and the limit is 18 oysters per day. If you replace the shells in the oyster beds it will help the reseeding process.

9	DOSEWALLIPS SP
	SEAL ROCK
	SQUAXIN ISLAND
15	BRUCEPORT

RAIN FORESTS

Explore the strange environments created by an abundance of rain.

8	BOGACHIEL SP
	FALLS CREEK
	HOH
	OLALLIE
	QUEETS RIVER
	WILLABY

SAND DUNES

These ever-changing sand piles provide sheer delight for bare feet.

8	OCEAN CITY SP
15	FORT CANBY SP
	TWIN HARBORS SP
19	MAR-DON RESORT
	POTHOLES SP

SCENIC VIEWS

(Also, see the introductory headings to Maps 4 and 17.)

1	DUNGENESS REC AREA
2	BAY VIEW SP
4	SOUTH NAVARRE
10	FISH LAKE
11	BIG HILL
14	MOUNT SPOKANE SP
17	COLD SPRINGS
	HORSESHOE LAKE
	OLALLIE LAKE
	POLE PATCH
	TAKHLAKH
21	FIELDS SPRING SP
	KAMIAK BUTTE
	MISERY SPRING

SPAWNING FISH

This marks the end of the road for the fish that have fought their way upstream to lay eggs.

4	CAMP 4 (Aug)
	CHEWACK (Salmon)
6	NORTH GORGE (summer)
8	SOLEDUCK (salmon)
	FALLS CR (fish ladder)
9	TWANOH SP (salmon)
13	PORCUPINE BAY (summer)

TIDEPOOLS

Exploring these rocky, water-filled pockets is a fascinating experience while the tide is out. But, please don't disturb the fragile marine life, which is already in danger of disappearing.

2	DECEPTION PASS SP
8	KALALOCH

VOLCANIC ACTIVITY

Explore the landforms created by underground eruptions thousands of years ago. (Also, see the introductory headings to Maps 16, 17 and 22.)

14 RIVERSIDE SP (lava)
17 SAWMILL FLAT (basalt cliffs)
22 GOOSE LAKE (lava beds)
    PETERSON PRAIRIE (cave)

WATERFALLS

Most enjoyable during the spring when the streams run full from the melting snows. (Also, see the introductory headings to Maps 5, 7, 10 and 12.)

2 MORAN SP
4 FALLS CREEK
6 WILMONT CREEK
8 SOLEDUCK
   STAIRCASE
   WYNOOCHEE FALLS

9   FALLS VIEW
10 DENNY CREEK
11 DE ROUX
    SILVER FALLS
    WHITE RIVER FALLS
12 SUN LAKES SP
14 RIVERSIDE SP
17 LA WIS WIS
    OHANAPECOSH
    TWIN FALLS
22 BEACON ROCK SP
    SUNSET

WILDFLOWERS

An interesting subject for close-up photography.

1   AGATE & CRESCENT BEACH
8   DEER PARK
    HOH
11 JUNIOR POINT
17 BENCH LAKE
    BIRD LAKE
    PARADISE
    SUNRISE
18 WENAS

WILDLIFE REFUGES

Good places for nature study and wildlife watching. Ask at the Refuge headquarters for particularly interesting places to observe and explore. (Also, see the introductory headings to Maps 2, 14 and 15.)

1   DUNGENESS REC AREA
7   PEND OREILLE SP
8   LONG ISLAND
10 CORRAL PASS
14 PEACEFUL PINES

north to alaska

An expedition to the 49th state isn't quite what it was in the days of '98, but it still requires considerable advance planning. Here you find a true wilderness with long distances between civilized points. The best place to get planning information for your trip is from the Alaska Division of Tourism, Pouch E, Juneau 99801. An official state map is free from the State Dept of Highways, Box 1467, Juneau 99801.

ROUTES

BUS & TRAIN. Alaskan Coachways offers direct bus connections from the other states to Fairbanks and Anchorage via the Alaska Highway. The Alaska Railroad serves Seward, Anchorage, Mt. McKinley and Fairbanks. The White Pass & Yukon Route connects Skagway with Whitehorse, but there is no rail connection to the lower 48 states.

FERRIES. A scenic route north is via the Alaska State Ferry System to the Panhandle. Lots of backpackers use it to get to the mountains, which are practically at wharfside when you disembark, or you can put your camper aboard and drive away into the wilds of the interior. Early reservations are a must for this trip from Seattle to Juneau or Skagway. Offices are located in Seattle, or get information directly from Alaska State Ferry System, Pouch R, Juneau 99801.

ALASKA HIGHWAY. Connections can be made using various Canadian highways to Dawson Creek, British Columbia, which is Mile Zero of the Alaska Highway. From there, it's more than 1200 miles to the Alaska border. The Alaska State Marine Highway System allows a combination trip, part by ferry and part by highway. Offering the traveler almost everything that he wants to know about going to Alaska, "The Milepost" is the complete guidebook. Available from Alaska Northwest Publishing, Box 4-EEE, Anchorage 99509 (600 pages, maps, highway log, $3.95 + airmail $1).

CAMPING AND EXPLORING

Camping and campgrounds in Alaska have a special character. Find out about them in "Camping and Trailering in Alaska" ($2), or find an idea for a special adventure in "Off the Beaten Path in Alaska" ($1.50). Both books from Alaskabooks, Box 1494, Juneau 99801 (add 50¢ each, airmail). Other places with specialized information: State Division of Parks, 323 East 4th Ave, Anchorage 99501 (State Parks and the Chilkoot Trail); and the Bureau of Land Management, 555 Cordova St, Anchorage 99501 (canoeing, highway logs, hiking trails); and the Bureau of Sport Fisheries and Wildlife, 813 "D" St, Anchorage 99501 (canoeing, wildlife refuges, waterfowl). If you have a particular trip in mind: Regional Forester, USFS, Box 1628, Juneau 99801 (Chugach and Tongass NF's maps, wilderness cabins); or Glacier Bay Natl Mon, Box 1089, Juneau 99801 (hiking, tours); or Mt. McKinley Natl Park, Box 9, McKinley Park Alaska 99755 (travel, hiking, mountaineering).

visiting canada

CROSSING THE BORDER

• There's no big hassle in crossing unless the border guards think you're a suspicious character. All you need is a valid driver's license and a piece of identification that shows you are a U.S. citizen. A birth certificate or voter's registration will do. A passport can be used if you have nothing else, but it's not required unless you're from outside the U.S.

• From your insurance company, get a Non-Resident Interprovince Motor Vehicle Liability Insurance Card. You don't need this to enter Canada, but some provinces require proof of financial responsibility in case of an accident. (Not required in Alberta, British Columbia, Manitoba and Ontario.) Also carry your Motor Vehicle Registration Forms for car and trailer.

• If you're taking your dog along, you'll need a certificate, signed by a licensed veterinarian, showing that Fido had a rabies vaccination during the past twelve months. (Not required for other pets.)

• Only rifles and shotguns are allowed across the border (no hand guns or fully automatic weapons). You'll have to get the applicable non-resident licenses for hunting and fishing and observe closed seasons.

These are the basic things you'll need to know for getting into Canada. If you want all of the minute details about firearms, boats, weather, bringing back merchandise, maps and sources of free tourist information, write for a copy of "So You're Going to Canada." It's a 45-page booklet that will tell you everything you need to know. British Columbia Dept of Travel Industry, Parliament Bldgs, Victoria, British Columbia, Canada.

GETTING THERE

FERRIES. Ferries travel from Anacortes, Port Angeles and Seattle Washington, to Victoria and Sidney, British Columbia. Schedules, fares and reservation information are available from Washington State Ferries, Seattle Ferry Terminal (Pier 52), Seattle 98104.

AMTRAK. Operates between Portland, Oregon and Vancouver, B.C. There is also a Spokane-Everett-Vancouver route. Contact your nearest AMTRAK Station for schedules. (See AMTRAK, under HOW TO BEAT THE GAS SHORTAGE.)

BUS. The only direct Greyhound bus route to Vancouver is along Interstate 5 (Portland-Tacoma-Seattle-Bellingham). You can also get there from Spokane via Wenatchee and Everett.

FEET. Probably, the most rewarding way to get to Canada is by way of the Pacific Crest Trail. The Trail ends at Monument #78 on the Canadian border, but connecting trails in E.C. Manning Park, in British Columbia, will lead you to civilization on the other side. (See Pacific Crest Trail under ON YOUR OWN.)

CAMPING INFORMATION

• "Beautiful British Columbia Road Map" is a colored, semi-topographical map that pinpoints the 117 Provincial campgrounds described on the reverse side. Also info about hunting and fishing licenses, and a "when and where" fishing guide. (Free).

• "British Columbia Tourist Directory" contains 127 pages of statistics about commercial campgrounds, trailer parks, resorts as well as motels and hotels. Tells where to find tourist information, gives descriptions of attractions and parks, and points out miscellaneous things you should know. (Free).

Both publications are available from British Columbia Dept of Travel Industry, Parliament Bldgs, Victoria, British Columbia, Canada.

NATIONAL PARKS

• A handy folder "Canada's National and Historic Parks," gives a brief description of the 57 National Parks, and their attractions, in all of the provinces. Write to Canadian Government Travel Bureau, Suite 1117, Plaza 600, 600 Stewart St, Seattle 98101.

EVENTS

• A 30-page booklet, "British Columbia Calendar of Events," lists just about everything that's happening of interest to visitors, plus square dancing, major attractions in the province and industrial tours. (Free).

• "Canada Events" lists the main holiday celebrations across Canada. (Free).

Both calendars are available from British Columbia Dept of Travel Industry, Parliament Bldgs, Victoria, British Columbia, Canada.

how to beat the gas shortage

Well, the fuel crisis is here. The environmentalists warned us about it for years, but no one listened. Now we'll have to rearrange our attitudes about the conservation of vital resources and find new ways of carrying out old routines. Getting to the mountains is one of those routines. We don't believe that all those wilderness-addicts will suddenly give up the greatest pastime of all just because they can't drive their vehicles to the trailhead. They'll simply find an alternate way of getting there. Consider the possibilities:

BICYCLING. Don't be afraid to use your bicycle for more than just a trip around the neighborhood. If there's time on your hands, strap on your pack and head for the nearest beach or mountains. It adds to the quality of life to know that you can get places under your own power. Books, like "Bicycling the Backroads Around Puget Sound," by Erin and Bill Woods, should convince you. (Published by The Mountaineers.) The route descriptions tell about some fascinating trips and give good info on where to camp. (Also, see BICYCLE TOURING, page 84.)

TRAIN. AMTRAK heads eastward from Everett on a scenic route across the Cascades to Spokane. Stopping points are Wenatchee and Ephrata. One-way fare to Wenatchee from Everett is only about $5.50 (a little more from Spokane). You can carry a backpack or skiis onto the train, or, for a couple of dollars, you can check a bicycle as baggage. Wenatchee (see Map 11) is within bicycling distance of several campgrounds in the area and some fine mountain scenery. This is only one application of the AMTRAK system. Get their route and schedule brochure to determine others. "Riding the rails" is, and always has been, a groovy way to travel. If you're bold enough to try it once, you'll see what we mean.

BUSSES. Greyhound and Continental cover a lot of territory, but there are the restrictions of scheduled stopping points and not having your bicycle along. Backpacks can be stashed in the baggage compartment. Metro Transit, operating in King County, makes it easy to get from the Seattle area to the Cascades via North Bend, Skykomish, etc. They're also more informal about picking up the letting off passengers. Look up the article "Metro-Mountaineering," in the Summer '73 issue of Signpost (see page 80) for some good suggestions about using this system. Check the routes of other bus lines in your area to see if they offer possibilities.

HITCH-HIKING. Washington is not the greatest state for thumbing because of its overly restrictive laws. However, it has been done without a hassle, and it is a cheap and efficient way of getting around. If you've never considered this method of travel before, maybe now is the time. If you have a little patience and don't look too weird then you can get just about any place you want to go. We suggest you make a sign giving your destination. It helps the motorist size you up, and who could turn down someone whose sign says "Mount Rainier."

POOL YOUR RESOURCES. Give more serious thought to car pools and group camping. One gas eating vehicle on the road is better than three, and two or three couples in a van can make for a fairly efficient weekend in the mountains. Outing clubs tend to promote car pooling on their trips to the wilderness. Consider Inter-Mountain Alpine Club, PO Box 505, Richland 99352, and Washington Alpine Club, PO Box 352, Seattle 98111.

"CAMPING WITHOUT GASOLINE." This is the name of our new book. It's all about how to continue your enjoyment of the outdoors in spite of the fuel crisis. Included are tips and suggestions about how to go anywhere anytime, for recreation away from the city — mostly without your car. Available from Random House Inc, 201 East 50th St, New York 10022. ($1.65).

We hope these suggestions will help you become bolder and more receptive to the use of alternate forms of transportation. The wild places are a real source of inspiration to those who take the time to explore them. To give them up because of an empty gas tank would be totally unfair. Perhaps one consolation is that all those people who were never really in tune with the mountains, yet added to their overuse, may now seek activities closer to home. It will be refreshing to stay at a forest campground, for a change, and not find a gigantic motor coach blocking the view, or hiking a trail that's not littered with pop cans and candy wrappers.

The mountains need a rest. Maybe this is their chance.

notes

WHY WE MADE THIS BOOK.

Anyone who does a lot of camping needs a good campground guide — the kind of guide that shows you exactly how to reach campgrounds. This was the basis for our two-volume series about California. The series is being expanded to cover all areas of the country (beginning with those we know best). Hopefully, these books will become the standard reference for as many campers as possible. This is your map book to Washington.

HANDMADE MAPS

Next to exploring campgrounds, the best part of putting this book together was drawing the maps. Although some really long hours were spent in this backbreaking, painstaking effort, it was fun. As a result, we learned a lot about a very great part of the country. Our basic object of having easy-to-read and visually handsome maps led to an elaborate and expensive system for making the maps that almost freaked Don, our publisher. After several trial maps were printed, to check for size and looks and to assess the best way to symbolize different information, we all agreed that going halfway wasn't good enough. We went to work.

For the base maps, we used 1:250,000 scale USGS maps. For accuracy of roads, forests and trails, we checked with every other map that we could find. Information came from our camping experience, from helpful people in the National Park Service and Forest Service, questionnaires, telephone calls, as well as special trips to particular areas. Spotting all the campgrounds accurately had its frustrating moments. (If we mis-located any, let us know about it.) For drawings we made overlays of three acetates for each map, with each acetate showing a different kind of information. In the hands of the lithographer, magic things happened to create a negative, producing maps with white, black and various shades in between. The end result, when printed, was much satisfaction.

If you'll let us know about things we haven't covered, it will help us keep this book unique. Maybe you know of a way to make the book more useful, or have additional information about the camps we've listed (better routes to them, their good and bad aspects, even new campgrounds). We'll explore your suggestions and discoveries for use in our future editions.

Write to us.

Jim Crain & Terry Milne / Box 1884 / San Francisco 94101

Share your knowledge about camping around Washington.

What did we leave out?

We dig maps — turn us on to some new ones.

This volume is one of a series of guides to camping in interesting sections of the country.

Books in the series

CAMPING AROUND CALIFORNIA — The North
CAMPING AROUND CALIFORNIA — The South
CAMPING AROUND NEW ENGLAND
CAMPING AROUND WASHINGTON
CAMPING AROUND THE APPALACHIAN MOUNTAINS